Ancient Mystery Cults

Carl Newell Jackson Lectures

Ancient Mystery Cults

Walter Burkert

Harvard University Press
Cambridge, Massachusetts,
and London, England

To Zeph Stewart
ΜΑΙΕΥΤΙΚΩΙ ΚΑΙ ΕΛΕΓΚΤΙΚΩΙ

Library of Congress Cataloging-in-Publication Data
Burkert, Walter, 1931–
  Ancient mystery cults.

  "Carl Newell Jackson lectures"—Half t.p.
  Bibliography: p.
  Includes indexes.
  1. Mysteries, Religious. 2. Greece—Religion.
3. Rome—Religion. I. Title. II. Title: Carl Newell
Jackson lectures.
BL610.B87   1987   291'.093   87-8379

ISBN 0-674-03387-6 (paper)

Preface

This book is based on four Carl Newell Jackson Lectures presented at Harvard University in April 1982. In preparing the text for publication I tried to preserve the distinct articulations of the lecture format and to resist adding an amorphous mass of bibliographical references and reports of controversies. This is meant to remain a readable account, not a thesaurus; the aim is to give a perceptive view of ancient mystery cults with some graphic details and adequate documentation, and thus to provoke thoughts rather than bury them in an avalanche of material.

My thanks go first of all to the Department of the Classics at Harvard University and its former chairman, Zeph Stewart, for the invitation that brought about these lectures and for the generous hospitality that made them develop in a most stimulating atmosphere. I wish to thank Zeph Stewart as well for his unceasing help in producing the final version of this book. Albert Henrichs also deserves thanks for his help in reviewing the manuscript. Thanks are due as well to Nancy Evans, Brown University, for correcting the English, and to Eveline Krummen, University of Zurich, for expert help with documentation and preparation of the manuscript.

Walter Burkert
Zurich, June 1986

Contents

ꙩꙩꙩꙩꙩꙩꙩꙩꙩꙩꙩꙩꙩꙩꙩꙩꙩꙩꙩꙩꙩꙩꙩꙩꙩꙩꙩꙩꙩꙩꙩꙩꙩꙩꙩꙩꙩꙩ

Illustrations

Introduction

ꙮꙮꙮꙮꙮꙮꙮꙮꙮꙮꙮꙮꙮꙮꙮꙮꙮꙮꙮꙮꙮꙮꙮꙮꙮꙮꙮꙮꙮꙮꙮꙮꙮ

THE WORD *mysteries* conveys the fascination of secrecy and the promise of thrilling revelations. Even those not well acquainted with mysteries may associate them with the concept of orgies. This book contains no revelations of this kind; instead it aims at the methodical interpretation of scattered and often frustrating evidence about forms of religion that have long been extinct.

The term "mystery religions of late antiquity" has become well known. It is commonly used with reference to the worship of Isis, of Mater Magna, and of Mithras in particular. These phenomena have drawn special attention from classicists, historians of religion, and theologians since the beginning of this century, with two great scholars, Richard Reitzenstein and Franz Cumont, setting the pace.[1] Interest is bound to continue as long as the emergence of Christianity remains a central problem in the study of antiquity and in the history of mankind. The postwar decades have been marked by vast collections of documents, mainly archaeological, still reflecting Cumont's work; most prominent is the prodigious series *Etudes préliminaires aux religions orientales dans l'empire romain,* founded by Maarten J. Vermaseren.[2] Mithraic studies were patronized for a while by the Shah of Iran.[3] Vast surveys have been provided recently in the series *Aufstieg und Niedergang der Römischen Welt.*[4] The sheer mass of evidence has sometimes threatened to obscure the basic issues. In recent years, however, the critical discussion of principles and concepts has been advanced, especially by Italian scholars. As a result, a gradual erosion of Cumont's and Reitzenstein's positions is taking place.[5] Nevertheless, there remain some stereotypes or preconceptions in the study of the so-called mystery religions that must be challenged, since they lead to half-truths at best, if not to downright misunderstandings.

The first stereotype is that the mystery religions are "late," that they are typical of late antiquity, that is, the Imperial or possibly the later Hellenistic period,[6] when the brilliance of the Hellenic mind was giving way to the irrational, heading as it were for the dark Middle Ages. However, although it is correct to state that the cult of Isis was definitively installed in Rome under Caligula and that the monuments for Mater Magna–Taurobolium and the Mithraic caves are concentrated in the second to fourth centuries A.D., still what represented the mysteries proper for pagan antiquity, the cult of Eleusis, is known to have flourished without interruption from the sixth century B.C. onward, and the most widely spread type of mysteries, those of Dionysus-Bacchus, appear just slightly later in the documentation. Even the Mother Goddess is established in Greek cult, from Asia Minor to southern Italy, by the archaic period.[7]

The second stereotype is that the mystery religions are Oriental in origin, style, and spirit. The standard work of Franz Cumont has the title *The Oriental Religions in Roman Paganism,* and the no less influential book of Richard Reitzenstein, *Hellenistic Mystery Religions,* defines "Hellenistic" in just this sense: it means Oriental spirituality in a Hellenized form.[8] But even though it is evident that Mater Magna is the Phrygian Goddess for both Greeks and Romans, and that Isis is Egyptian and Mithras is Iranian, the institution of mysteries cannot be traced to either Anatolia, Egypt, or Iran; rather, they seem to reflect the older model of Eleusis or Dionysus, or both.[9] Yet these cults have received less attention than those of Meter, Isis, and Mithras, probably because they lack the "mysterious" Oriental touch. The term "Oriental" betrays the perspective of Westerners; ancient Anatolia, Egypt, and Iran were separate worlds, each in its own right, even if all of them are situated more or less east of Western Europe.

The third stereotype is that the mystery religions are spiritual, that they are indicative of a basic change in religious attitude, one that transcends the realistic and practical outlook of the pagan in a search for higher spirituality.[10] In this view, the mystery religions are considered religions of salvation, *Erlösungsreligionen,* and thus preparatory or parallel to the rise of Christianity. In a way this would make Christianity just another—indeed, the most successful—of the Oriental mystery religions. Now it is true that some ancient Christian writers were struck by certain similarities between Christian worship and mysteries, and they denounced the latter as devilish counterfeits of the one true religion.[11] Certain Gnostic sects seem to have practiced mystery initiations, imitating or rather outdoing the pagans,[12] and even orthodox Christianity adopted the mystery metaphor that had long been used in Platonic philosophy: to speak of the "mysteries" of baptism and the Eucharist has remained common usage.[13] Yet this does not imply that Greek mysteries by themselves should be seen as predestined to move toward Christianity. The constant use of Christianity as a reference system when dealing with the so-called mystery religions leads to distortions as well as partial clarification, obscuring the often radical differences between the two. Ernest Renan once said, "If the growth of Christianity had been halted by some mortal illness, the world would have become Mithraic."[14] Most scholars today agree there never was a chance for that, since Mithraism was not even a religion in the full sense of the word.

In this book a decidedly pagan approach to the ancient mysteries is followed, which abandons the concept of mystery *religions* from the start. Initiation at Eleusis or worship of Isis or Mithras does not constitute adherence to a religion in the sense we are familiar with, being confronted with mutually exclusive religions such as Judaism, Christianity, and Islam. Whereas in these religions there has been much conscious emphasis on self-definition and on demarcating one religion as against the other,[15] in the pre-Christian epoch the various forms of worship, including new and foreign gods in general and the institution of mysteries in particular, are never exclusive; they appear as varying forms, trends, or options within the one disparate yet continuous conglomerate of ancient religion.

What is attempted with this approach could be called a comparative phenomenology of ancient mysteries. For reasons of economy the following inquiries will be restricted to five of these: the mysteries of Eleusis, the Dionysiac or Bacchic mysteries, the mysteries of Meter, those of Isis, and those of Mithras. There were others as well, some of them quite prominent,[16] but these five variations will suffice to indicate the range of differences as well as the constants in diversity. This approach may be criticized as ahistorical. What is covered is a period of about a thousand years, and shifts, changes, and revolutions were constantly occurring at the social, political, and intellectual levels. Yet there were traits of identity maintained through continuous tradition, and it is important to keep sight of these in studying the ancient mystery cults.

For orientation, a few basic facts about these five variants should be recalled. The mysteries of Eleusis[17] were devoted to the "Two Goddesses," Demeter the grain goddess and her daughter Persephone, locally called Pherephatta or just "the Maiden," Kore. These mysteries were organized by the *polis* of Athens and supervised by the *archon basileus,* the "king." For the Athenians these were the Mysteries *tout court,* and it was largely the literary prestige of Athens that ensured their lasting fame. Inscriptions and excavations in addition to literature and iconography provide abundant documentation. The well-known myth depicts Demeter searching for Kore, who has been carried off by Hades, the god of the netherworld. Kore finally comes back, if only for a limited period, to Eleusis itself. There the Athenians celebrated the great autumn festival, the Mysteria; the procession went from Athens to Eleusis and culminated in a nocturnal celebration in the Hall of Initiations, the Telesterion, capable of holding thousands of initiates, where the hierophant revealed "the holy things." There were two gifts that Demeter bestowed on Eleusis, so people said: grain as the basis of civilized life, and the mysteries that held the promise of "better hopes" for a happy afterlife. These mysteries took place exclusively at Eleusis and nowhere else.

Dionysus, the god of wine and ecstasy, was worshiped everywhere; every drinker in fact could claim to be a servant of this god. The existence of mysteries proper, of personal and secret initiations with the promise of eternal bliss in the beyond, has recently been confirmed by the gold tablet of Hipponion, mentioning the *mystai* and *bakchoi* on their "sacred way" in the netherworld.[18] Yet there is no local center for Bacchic mysteries, in contrast to Eleusis; they seem to have appeared everywhere from the Black Sea to Egypt and from Asia Minor to southern Italy. Most famous or rather infamous became the Bacchanalia in Rome and Italy, brutally suppressed by the Roman senate in 186 B.C.[19] The most fascinating artistic document of Bacchic mysteries is the frescoes of the Villa of the Mysteries at Pompeii, dating from the time of Caesar. Evidently there was great variety in Bacchic mysteries. The myth of the dismemberment of Dionysus is sometimes connected with these mysteries, but we cannot be sure that it was applied to all of them. A special problem is the interrelation of Bacchic mysteries with books and groups of people called "Orphic," as if originating from Orpheus, the mythical singer.[20]

The Mother Goddess from Asia Minor is commonly called Magna Mater today, although in proper Latin the name is Mater Magna, or, with the full title, Mater Deum Magna Idaea.[21] Perhaps it is best to call her just Meter, as did the Greeks. The cult of a Mother Goddess in Anatolia can be traced to long before the invention of writing, back to the Neolithic epoch; for the Greeks her Phrygian name, Matar Kubileya, became most influential. She was called Kybeleia or Kybele in Greek, but mostly just "Mother of the Mountain," sometimes with the addition of a special mountain's name: Meter Idaia, Meter Dindymene.[22] What provoked the most attention and awe in this cult was the institution of eunuch priests, the self-castrating *galloi* who had their home especially at Pessinus; their representative in myth is Attis, the *paredros* and lover of the Mother, who is castrated and dies under a pine tree. This cult was brought to Rome in 204 B.C. during the Hannibalic war, by the command of oracles, and later spread from there. Different forms of personal and secret rites, of *teletai* and *mysteria*, existed in cults of Meter.[23] The most spectacular form was the *taurobolium*, known to have existed from the second century A.D., where the initiand, crouching in a pit covered with wooded beams on which a bull was slaughtered, was drenched by the bull's gushing blood.[24]

Among the many Egyptian gods, the Greeks had given special prominence to Isis and Osiris from the archaic age onward.[25] The identification of these two with Demeter and Dionysus seems to be established from the start.[26] The Ptolemaic epoch added Sarapis, that is, Osiris-Apis,[27] though he gradually had to give way again to Isis. Sanctuaries of the Egyptian gods with Egyptian or Egyptianizing priests were established in many places. The big temple of Isis at Rome was founded under the rule of Caligula. The myth of Osiris, killed and dismembered by Seth, mourned, searched for, found and reassembled by Isis, who then conceives and gives birth to Horos, is well known, especially through Plutarch's book *On Isis and Osiris*. The mysteries of Isis are described in the most extensive mystery text we have from pagan antiquity, the last book of the *Golden Ass* of Apuleius.[28]

Mithras is a very old Indo-Iranian deity, attested from the Bronze Age onward and worshiped wherever Iranian tradition came to dominate. His name means "the middle one" in the sense of "treaty," "promise of allegiance." Yet the characteristic mysteries of Mithras are not in evidence before 100 A.D.; how they were founded and what their exact relation is to Iranian tradition are both problems that remain unsolved.[29] The cult was held in subterranean "caves" where small groups of men met for the initiations and for sacrificial meals in front of the depiction of Mithras slaying the bull, which always occupies the apse of the "cave." There were seven grades of initiation. Mithraic iconography is surprisingly uniform, with many symbols, but the concomitant myth is not transmitted in literature. The cult of Mithras is closely associated with the Roman legions, the worshipers having been recruited mainly among soldiers, merchants, and officials of the Roman empire.

Sound methodology requires that clear definitions stand at the beginning of research; in the study of religions, however, a satisfactory definition may rather be the final outcome. Nonetheless, it is useful to discuss the ancient and modern terms to be applied in this book, and the characteristic phenomena designated by these terms. In modern languages the word *mystery* is mainly used in the sense of "secret," a usage that goes back to the New Testament.[30] In fact, secrecy was a necessary attribute of ancient mysteries, manifesting itself in the form of the *cista mystica*, a wooden basket closed by a lid.[31] But this definition is not specific enough. Not all secret cults are mysteries; the term does not apply to private magic or to elaborate priestly hierarchies with restricted access to the sacred places or objects. It is also quite misleading to associate mysteries with mysticism in its true sense, that is, the transformation of consciousness through meditation, yoga, or related means. It is only through a complicated development of Platonic and Christian metaphors that the word *mystikos* finally acquired this meaning, apparently not before the writings of Dionysius the Areopagite.[32] More revealing is the established Latin translation of *mysteria, myein, myesis* as *initia, initiare, initiatio*,[33] which brought the word and the concept of "initiation" into our language. Following this line, we find

that mysteries are initiation ceremonies, cults in which admission and participation depend upon some personal ritual
to be performed on the initiand. Secrecy and in most cases a
nocturnal setting are concomitants of this exclusiveness.

Initiations are a well-known phenomenon often discussed
by anthropologists. They are found in a wide range of settings, from the most primitive Australian tribes to American
universities. There are many different forms of initiations,
including puberty rites, consecration of priests or kings, and
admission to secret societies. From a sociological point of
view, initiation in general has been defined as "status dramatization" or ritual change of status.[34] Seen against this background, ancient mysteries still seem to form a special category: they are not puberty rites on a tribal level; they do not
constitute secret societies with strong mutual ties (except in
the case of Mithras); admission is largely independent of
either sex or age; and there is no visible change of outward
status for those who undergo these initiations. From the perspective of the participant, the change of status affects his
relation to a god or a goddess; the agnostic, in his view from
outside, has to acknowledge not so much a social as a personal change, a new state of mind through experience of the
sacred. Experience remains fluid; in contrast to typical initiations that bring about an irrevocable change, ancient mysteries, or at least parts of their ritual, could be repeated.[35]

Etymology does not contribute toward the understanding
of the Greek terms. The verbal root *my(s)-* seems to be attested in Mycenaean Greek, possibly for the initiation of an
official, but the context and interpretation are far from
clear.[36] It is more important to note that the word *mysteria*
conforms to a well-established type of word formation to
designate festivals in Mycenaean as well as in later Greek.[37]
For Athenians, *Mysteria* was, and remained, one of the great
festivals of the year. There is slight archaeological evidence,
and great enthusiasm among scholars, for Mycenaean antecedents of the Eleusinian cult.[38] The word *mystes* used to
designate the initiate is of a type that is seen to evolve in

Mycenean Greek.[39] The verb *myeo*, "to initiate" (in the passive, "to receive initiation") is secondary and indeed much less used than *mystes* and *Mysteria*. The seminal role of Eleusis in the institution and designation of mysteries is thus confirmed even from the linguistic point of view.

A word family that largely overlaps with *mysteria* is *telein*, "to accomplish," "to celebrate," "to initiate"; *telete*, "festival," "ritual," "initiation"; *telestes*, "initiation priest"; *telesterion*, "initiation hall," and so forth. Its etymology, which seemed to be clear, has been lost again on account of the Mycenaean evidence.[40] It is evident that this word family is much more general in meaning; usually it does not suffice to identify mysteries proper, but can be used for any kind of cult or ritual.[41] Such a term becomes specific, however, when used with a personal object and with a god's name in the dative: to perform a ritual on a person for a specific god is the same as to "initiate" this person; *Dionysoi telesthenai* means to be initiated into the mysteries of Dionysus.[42]

Another general word for "ritual" that enjoyed wide currency in the context of mysteries is *orgia*.[43] Both *teletai* and *orgia* become more specific in this connection by the added stipulation of secrecy. Two adjectives, *aporrheta* ("forbidden") and *arrheta* ("unspeakable"), seem to be nearly interchangeable in this usage,[44] hinting at a basic problem inherent in the "secret" of mysteries: a mystery must not be betrayed, but it cannot really be betrayed because told in public it would appear insignificant; thus violations of the secrecy that did occur did no harm to the institutions,[45] but protection of the secrecy greatly added to the prestige of the most sacred cults. This terminology was indeed in constant use to refer to and characterize the mysteries that are the subject of this book. The festival of Eleusis is *ta Mysteria* as such, but it is equally well called an *arrhetos telete*, and the main building in the sanctuary is the Telesterion.[46] *Teletai* is used with a certain preference with regard to Dionysus, but *mystai*, *mysteria*, and *myeo* also occur as early as Heraclitus; *mystai* and *bakchoi* are found in the Hipponion tablet.[47] Similarly, there are various *teletai* in the worship of Meter, but *mysteria* are also attested at an early date; the taurobolium is a *telete* for a *mystipolos*.[48] In his Isis-book Apuleius generally speaks of *mysteria* but also uses the term *teletae*.[49] As for Mithras, "the mysteries of Mithras" seems to have been the normal designation, but these were *teletai* as well.[50]

It should be noted that in most cases there exist forms of a "normal" cult alongside the mysteries, that is, worship for the noninitiated, independent of possible candidacy for *myesis* or *telete*. There were yearly festivals at fixed dates; private offerings were invited and accepted without restriction—only Mithras constitutes a special case. The interrelations between private initiations and official festivals are complicated and far from uniform. At Eleusis, initiation (*myesis*) normally culminated in the autumn festival called Mysteria; the initiation of Apuleius, on the other hand, was not linked to a fixed festival date but determined by divine command through dreams; still, the *initiati* as a body took part in the yearly procession of Ploiaphesia at Corinth.[51] In sanctuaries of Isis the resident clergy would execute a painstaking daily service for the Egyptian gods from morning to night. In Rome, Mater Magna had her great festival in the spring, but the reported dates of taurobolia are unrelated to calendrical events. In any case, mysteries are seen to be a special form of worship offered in the larger context of religious practice. Thus the use of the term "mystery religions," as a pervasive and exclusive name for a closed system, is inappropriate.

Mystery initiations were an optional activity within polytheistic religion, comparable to, say, a pilgrimage to Santiago di Compostela within the Christian system.

In the ancient world, then, mysteries were anything but obligatory and unavoidable; there was an element of personal choice, an individual decision in each case. Initiation was not inescapably prescribed by tribal or family adherence. Although there was, of course, some pressure of family tradition, youths could resist their parents, as the novelistic account about the Roman Bacchanalia illustrates.[52] Herodotus writes with regard to Eleusis: "Whoever of the Athenians

and the other Greeks wishes, is initiated," and with regard to
the Scythian king Skyles at Olbia: "He conceived the wish to
be initiated to Dionysos Bakcheios."[53] It was his private desire to be initiated; there were signs to warn him, and he
could have stopped. Of course there was direct invitation,
there was propaganda from the initiation priests as well: "It
is worthwhile to acquire this knowledge."[54] But many would
hesitate. Hence the picture of Oknos, Hesitation personified,
plaiting a rope which his donkey eats away;[55] the uninitiated
never reach consummation, *telos*. Some would take this seriously while others would remain indifferent; there was no
unquestionable authority as to *teletai*. "Those who wish to be
initiated have the custom, I believe, to turn first to the
'father' of the sacred rites, to map out what preparations
have to be made"—this is the description of the procedure in
Tertullian.[56] Of course, there were means to refuse unprom-
ising candidates as well. Priests of Isis could have recourse to
dream oracles, as the case of Lucius-Apuleius shows.

This role of private initiative is obviously linked to the state
of society that had evolved by the sixth century B.C., with
emphasis on the discovery of the individual;[57] it is hardly a
coincidence that the first clear evidence of mysteries proper
comes from this epoch—whatever the festival Mysteria may
have been in the Mycenaean period. It is also characteristic
that the advocates of rigorous state or tribal control were
generally suspicious of private mysteries. Whereas Plato in
his *Laws* was willing to allow some tolerance, Cicero the Roman and Philo the Jew advocated repression of private
cults.[58] But for those who took part in the chances and risks
of individual freedom that had come into existence in the
Hellenic world, the mysteries may have been a decisive "invention": cults which were not prescribed or restricted by
family, clan, or class, but which could be chosen at will, still
promising some personal security through integration into
a festival and through the corresponding personal closeness
to some great divinity. Mysteries were initiation rituals of
a voluntary, personal, and secret character that aimed at a
change of mind through experience of the sacred.[59]

I

Personal Needs in This Life and after Death

MYSTERIES ARE A FORM of personal religion,[1] depending on a private decision and aiming at some form of salvation through closeness to the divine. This finding has often prompted scholars to look for a deeper, "truly religious," spiritual dimension, and they cannot be said to be totally mistaken. Yet there is a danger that searching for the beyond means overlooking what is nearest and most obvious. There is another form of personal religion—elementary, widespread, and quite down-to-earth—that constitutes the background for the practice of mysteries: it is the practice of making vows, "votive religion," as it has been called. "Those who are ill, or in danger, or in need of any kind, and conversely when people attain some kind of affluence"[2]—such individuals make promises to the gods and usually fulfill them by offering more or less precious donations. This phenomenon is so common that it is seldom discussed in any depth. The practice has far outlived the ancient world; indeed, it has survived to the present day even in Christianity, where Protestant or rationalistic expurgations have failed to suppress it.

In the study of pre-Christian antiquity, every archaeologist and historian of religion is familiar with the mass of votive objects that usually identify a sanctuary, whether it is oriental, Minoan-Mycenaean, Greek, Etruscan, Roman, or belong-

[margin note:] Asclepius will

[margin note:] objects

ing to outlying "barbarians." Thousands of objects may be found in such a setting, though unknown numbers made of perishable material must have vanished. These objects represent a humble aspect of religion; we know they had to be disposed of from time to time in order to clear the sacred precinct of rubbish. Yet each of these objects, great or small, bears witness to a personal story, a story of anxiety, hope, prayer, and fulfillment, to an act of personal religion. For the ruling class, the major risk was war; spectacular vows were therefore made to try to control it—as evidenced by some of the most celebrated art monuments in Greek sanctuaries, or nearly all the temples of Rome.[3] For the average man or woman there were the uncertainties of craft or trade, especially the dangers of a sea voyage, the incalculable risks of birth and child rearing, and the recurrent sufferings of individual illness. Both seafaring[4] and healing from illness were prominent occasions for setting up private votive gifts in nearly every sanctuary of the ancient world.

The practice of vows can be seen as a major human strategy for coping with the future. It makes time manageable by contract. From crippling depression, man can rise to impress the structure of "if-then" upon the uncertainties of the future. If salvation from present anxiety and distress occurs, if the success or profit hoped for is attained, then a special and circumscribed renunciation will be made, a finite loss in the interest of larger gain. There is a natural tendency toward perpetuation; when setting up the votive gift the worshiper prays for further help: "Be pleased and give occasion to set up another one":[5] *da ut dem.*

The intensity of religious feeling involved in this practice must not be underrated. There is the agonizing experience of distress, the search for some escape or help, the decision of faith; not rarely, votive inscriptions refer to supernatural intervention in decision making, to dreams, visions, or divine command;[6] and after all there is the experience of success. Skeptics may point to statistics; as Diagoras the atheist said at Samothrace regarding all the votive offerings of seafaring people saved by the Great Gods, these would have been much more numerous if all who had been drowned at sea had had an opportunity to make offerings as well.[7] But the world belongs to those who have survived, and in each individual case there is a feeling of overwhelming certainty: the gods have given help. In fact, votive religion did provide help by raising hopes, by socializing anxieties and sufferings: the individual is encouraged to try once more, and he encounters the interest and reinforcement offered by priests and fellow worshipers. The vow is made in public, and the fulfillment is demonstratively public, with many others profiting from the investment—craftsmen, shopkeepers, and all those sharing in the sacrificial banquets.

What is implied in the decision is an act of faith, *pistis;*[8] this is especially true in the case of illness. Faith healing is taken much more seriously today than it used to be some decades ago.[9] Votive objects, however humble, are documents of a personal faith in one specific god, who in return gives some form of salvation, *soteria.*

This should sound familiar even to a Christian ear—if only to bring out the differences. "Faith" and "salvation" in votive religion do not imply "conversion," even if they presuppose a change in orientation when an individual turns to the god. In Arthur Darby Nock's terms, these acts of worship stay within the category of "useful supplements," not "substitutes" that imply conscious rejection of what was before.[10] Votive religion is, rather, of an experimental character: one may well try several possibilities to find the really effective expedient. Uncommonly bad cases, most of all, will prompt people to adopt new and untested means. An individual struggling for a new chance in the midst of sufferings has to make a fresh start: perhaps a new god will do better. Thus votive religion, although its general structure is clearly quite old and very widespread, presents an incentive for religious change. It is well known how state religion developed in this way, with even Rome adopting new temples and new gods.[11] Countless similar cases must have occurred on a private level, sometimes short-lived and without consequences, sometimes adding up to what we may call a religious trend, a fashion of the time, or a religious movement.

The relevance of all this for mystery cults is threefold. First, the practice of personal initiation, in motivation and function, was largely parallel to votive practice and should be seen against this background as a new form in a similar quest for salvation. Second, the appearance of new forms of mystery cults with new gods is just what one would expect as a result of these practical functions. Third, the spreading of the so-called Oriental mystery religions occurred primarily in the form of votive religion, with mysteries sometimes forming just an appendix to the general movement.

The votive character of most monuments to Meter, Isis, and Mithras needs little comment. Anyone who studies the corpora is familiar with the recurring votive formulas, and even in the absence of inscriptions there is seldom doubt as to the interpretation of the monuments. All these gods are worshiped in a search for "salvation,"[12] which takes many forms. Not surprisingly, the themes of seafaring[13] and of illness stand out. More altruistic aspects come to the foreground with vows for relatives and friends—father, brother, and very often the children[14] because of the high mortality rate. On an official level there are the vows *pro salute imperatoris*, figuring prominently in sanctuaries of Meter, Isis, and Mithras.[15] The Egyptian gods, Sarapis and Isis in particular, specialize in healing, with considerable success, as the evidence shows: "All the world is eager to bestow honors on Isis because she clearly reveals herself in the cures of disease."[16] The *iatreia*, healing fees, must have been a sizable source of income for the sanctuaries. Isis has close ties to Asclepius. At Athens she has a temple within the sanctuary of Asclepius, and incubation is practiced in the sanctuaries of Isis as well as those of Asclepius. Isis herself is Hygieia, Health deified, among other identities. The poet Tibullus, troubled by illness, hopes that Isis will aid him through his beloved Delia, a devoted worshiper of Isis; he refers to the numerous painted tablets in the Isis temple that testify to the healing power of the goddess. If he recovers, then Delia will sit in linen clothes, with loose hair, at the temple entrance amidst the Egyptian clergy and will speak aloud the praise of Isis twice a day.[17] This practice is called *votivas reddere voces*, returning thanks for fulfillment of the vow by loud and public praise of the divinity's effective powers (*aretai*): aretalogy as temple propaganda. Another practice connected with worship of Isis is a confession of sins as a prerequisite for healing, as in certain Anatolian cults.[18] This may well have therapeutic effects, as a form of psychoanalysis; it is not necessarily linked to mysteries, however.

The favor of Isis and her companion gods pertains to other spheres of life as well, including wealth and money making. "Even the acquisition of wealth is given by Sarapis," Aelius Aristides proclaims, and votive inscriptions address Sarapis as the "savior who gives riches," Soter Ploutodotes.[19] He may even be given credit for a tax reduction. If the motive for dealing with such gods is salvation (*soteria, salus*), it is a quite practical, here-and-now salvation that is hoped for.

Mithras does not stand apart in this context; most of the Mithraic inscriptions gathered in the corpus of Vermaseren are votive in character. The offerings may include the installation of a whole Mithraeum, that is, the cave, the altars and statues, and the cult relief.[20] In fact, the cave is the place to make vows in a "pure" way (*euchesthai hagnos*), as one Greek inscription puts it.[21] Even more explicit is a Latin dedication claiming that the cave has been adorned by the donor "in order that the participants, united by joining hands, may joyously celebrate their vows for all time" (*ut possint syndexi hilares celebrare vota per aevom*)[22]—a miserable hexameter, yet clear as to its contents. Taking the right hand is the old Iranian form of a promise of allegiance, whence Mithraic *mystai* are *syndexioi*. As such they "celebrate the vows"; the essence of Mithraic worship in the cave is the experience of success and the act of faith renewed in the common feast. Vows of this kind clearly carry the expectation of fulfillment within the near future: success is to be seen in this life. Mithras is the *deus invictus,* and soldiers, who know what victory means, were prominent among his followers. Mithraism thus appears as a complete fusion of votive religion and mystery cult.

It is true that such a close interdependence of vows and initiations is not the rule. We are not quite sure whether Tibullus' Delia was an initiate of Isis mysteries in a formal sense (see n. 17). There is, rather, a parallelism; but this is evident and pervasive. It is not even absent from the famous text of Apuleius on the Isis initiations of Lucius—the only extant account of a mystery initiation in a first-person style. This has been called a conversion in the full sense.[23] Yet in spite of the religious rhetoric, the picture is not dominated by spiritual preoccupations; it remains realistic and is fused with normal psychology in an interesting way. The so-called conversion to Isis does not result in withdrawal from the world and worldly interests; on the contrary, the runaway student who had been roaming wildly through the Greco-Roman world now finally becomes integrated into respectable society. He starts his career as a lawyer in Rome and proves to be quite successful. This is felt to be a result of the favor of Isis and Osiris: they are givers of riches, *ploutodotai,* quite deservedly in this case because the repeated initiations had literally cost a fortune and deprived the man from Madaura of all his father's inheritance.[24] Indeed, the man's success is so remarkable that it arouses envy; this brings on a new nervous crisis with anxiety, sleep disturbances, and nocturnal visions. The initiation therefore must be repeated once again; the god then personally assures the ambitious man that he should pursue his glorious career without qualms, and himself elects him to a respected and unassailable position in the collegium of the *pastophori* of the Egyptian gods.[25] Professional stress is alleviated by a religious hobby, with the mystery god taking the position of psychiatrist. Whatever the autobiographical content of this story may be, the therapy is seen to make sense.

On a general and more basic level, Isis is credited with power even over destiny, *fatum:* she has the authority to forestall impending death and to grant a new life, *novae salutis curricula.*[26] This most precious gift of Isis, the gift of life, is described in authentic Egyptian sources as well as in the Greek versions of the cult. But it evidently means life in this world of ours. It must be a "new life," since the old one has worn down and is about to break, and yet it is not of a different order but rather a replacement to keep things going, prolongation instead of a "substitute" in Arthur Darby Nock's terms (see n. 10). Salvation of this kind, as guaranteed by the mysteries of Isis, is more radical and, it is hoped, more permanent than other experiences of *soteria,* but it still stays on the same level as the hopes expressed in votive religion.

The same is true of the most spectacular mystery rite, the taurobolium. One fact established definitively about this ritual is that it was to be repeated after twenty years, as if the bull's blood were a magical coating that wore away and must be renewed after a certain time. Thus once again the perspective of votive religion can be seen: through the taurobolium the initiate "takes up his vows for the circle of twenty years", *bis deni vota suscipit orbis,*[27] "in order that he may sacrifice sheep with golden horns on the occasion of the repetition." A cycle of repetitions will perpetuate prosperous life in this world of ours. The taurobolium is a "token of good luck," *symbolon eutychies,*[28] an insurance against all evil that may befall a person.

The same orientation is apparent in the Dionysiac mysteries, to which the extant collection of Orphic hymns belongs. Constantly referring to the *mystai* who have experienced the sacred *teletai,* the texts pray for health and wealth, for a good year, for good luck at sea, and in general for a pleasant life, with death as late as possible.[29] A relief from the time of Hadrian presents allegorical figures of Telete together with Prosperity (Eythenia) and Additional Gain of Wealth (Epiktesis);[30] a down-to-earth interpretation seems to make sense.

The practical orientation of *teletai* is no less obvious in the earlier evidence about Dionysus and Meter, who are seen to concentrate on psychosomatic therapy. Plato, in the *Phaedrus,* has Dionysus presiding over "telestic madness," and he specifies that these are rituals performed as a cure for "diseases and the greatest sufferings which manifest themselves in certain families, on account of some ancient cause of wrath." The supernatural etiology should not distract our view from the reality of the sufferings, or psychosomatic disturbances in modern terms, which are explained with reference to traumata of the past and treated by ritually induced "divine madness," which leads to an outburst of repressed emotional forces. "*Teletai* and purifications" are performed by people masking as Nymphs, Panes, Silens, and Satyrs, as Plato has it in the *Laws.*[31] A similar function of ritual involving Meter is indicated by Aristotle's much-discussed remarks about "purification," *katharsis,* which brings relief through violent emotion.[32] In the *Wasps* of Aristophanes, Bdelykleon tells of the various cathartic or telestic cures he has tried out on the madness of his father, the trial addict. In his case neither the Corybantic *teletai* nor Hecate of Aigina nor incubation at Asclepius' shrine proved of any use; with Meter's tympanon in hand, the father ran off again to court.[33] Some decades later Aeschines' mother performed initiations of Dionysus Sabazius, assisted by her son, as Demosthenes acidly describes. The initiate finally proclaimed: "I escaped from evil, I found the better." This, then, must have been the immediate experience of successful mysteries: "feeling better now." "All who use these rites," Aristotle writes with regard to the cathartic cures, "experience relief mixed with joy."[34] The long struggle of enlightenment against all forms of superstition tried to eliminate all aspects of charlatanism from the concept of "true" religion, but nevertheless they remained. All those everyday needs and hopes were met by practitioners with rituals evidently well attuned to psychic receptivity.

Mysteries that must be mentioned in this context are those

of Samothrace: their avowed object was to save people from drowning at sea, as Odysseus had been saved by Leukothea.[35] The practical aspect is not absent even from Eleusis; there are rich collections of votive objects from the site. The favor of the Two Goddesses was not restricted to the mystery nights. Demeter was the giver of grain, of riches, *Ploutos,* in the most basic sense; the maintenance of the Mysteries had the practical effect of guaranteeing the grain supply. The hierophant therefore played a leading role in the general festival held just before sowing in the fall, the *Proerosia;* the sanctuary invited gifts of grain, *aparchai,* from Athens as well as from the rest of the world in return for Demeter's gift.[36] Even healing miracles are not absent from Eleusis: a man who had been blind suddenly could behold the sacred exhibition;[37] mysteries are to be "seen" at Eleusis.

There is a further strange link of the Eleusinian proceedings with therapeutic *teletai,* demonstrating a close connection with Egyptian healing magic in etiological mythology. Demeter, the story goes, when received at Eleusis took the little child of the queen and put it into the fire of the hearth at night in order to make it immortal. Interrupted by the frightened mother, she revealed herself and installed the mysteries instead.[38] In an Egyptian text, Isis, wandering about, is not well received by the lady of a house; in consequence a scorpion who is accompanying Isis bites the woman's little son, and the house is set afire. But rain comes to quench the fire, and Isis takes pity and cures the little boy.[39] This is a charm against scorpion bite and fever; in the magical formula the child is identified with Horos, son of Isis, himself; texts about "burning Horos" and his salvation are extant in various Egyptian and Greek documents.[40] This diffusion of the Egyptian charm and its integration in Egyptian ideology make quite unlikely that an origin in Greek literature should be assumed,[41] even if the main Egyptian document, the "Metternich Stele," is later than the *Homeric Hymn to Demeter.* If there is any connection, the influence must have come from Egypt to Greece.[42] The reception of the wandering goddess, her power that can be used either for good or for evil, the child in the fire, danger and salvation: these form an impressive and characteristic complex and not just a superficial parallel. This would suggest some Egyptian influence on the Eleusinian cult or at least on Eleusinian mythology right at the beginning of the sixth century, in a context of practical "healing magic."[43]

Nevertheless, radical differences remain between the Egyptian healing rituals and the Eleusinian cult. The mysteries of Eleusis, when we get clear information about them, are not at all a collection of practical charms. The catchword is not "rescue" or "salvation" but "blessedness," and it is taken to refer to the afterlife more than to anything else: the "other gift" of Demeter, besides the bringing of grain, is the promise of a privileged life beyond the grave for those who have "seen" the mysteries. The evidence ranges from the earliest text, the *Hymn to Demeter,* down to the last rhetorical exercises of the Imperial period,[44] including the epitaphs of some hierophants about 200 A.D., one of which states with impressive simplicity that what the hierophant has "shown" in the sacred nights "is that death is not only not an evil, but good."[45] In Cicero's phrasing, at Eleusis it is shown "how to live in joy, and how to die with better hopes."[46] There is no attack on the joys of living, but the accent is indeed on the other side. The content of the promise is anything but explicit, but it is made to sound serious.

The same is true for the Dionysiac mysteries from at least the fifth century B.C. onward. Scholars have been reluctant to acknowledge this dimension of Dionysiac worship, on the assumption that concern about the afterlife should be seen to have developed in later epochs; but the clearest evidence is concentrated right in the classical period, whatever we make of the indication at the end of the *Odyssey* that a vase of Dionysus is to hold the bones of Achilles and Patroclus.[47] The itinerant practitioners of *teletai* in Plato's caricature state that their cures are good and bring relief during this life as well as after death; for those who decline the rites, however, terrible things are waiting.[48] The Hipponion gold leaf, published in 1974, depicts the *mystai* and *bakchoi* in the netherworld proceeding on the sacred way toward eternal bliss,[49] just as the Eleusinian *mystai* are still celebrating their joyous festival in Hades, according to Aristophanes' *Frogs*. A well-known inscription from Cumae reserves a special burial ground for those who have participated in the bacchic rites (*bebakcheumenoi*).[50] Herodotus refers to special funerary customs of Orphika and Bakchika.[51] Even earlier is an inscription on a late sixth century mirror from a tomb at Olbia: a woman and her son are acclaimed with the Dionysiac cry of ecstasy, *euhai;* both evidently had taken part in the *orgia,* and this is to be recorded even in their tomb.[52] "Happy they all on account of the *teletai* that free from suffering," Pindar says in one of his *Dirges*.[53] In contrast, there are those labors in vain, *mataioponia,* of the uninitiated in Hades who have missed the *teletai* in their lifetime, as seen in the underworld picture of Polygnotus: they are carrying water in a sieve to a leaking *pithos*. Indeed, even before Polygnotus this motif appears in vase painting.[54]

Dionysiac mysteries are seen to develop especially in Italy as a kind of analogue to the Eleusinian rites.[55] An elaborate funerary symbolism of Bacchic character is seen to flourish on southern Italian vases of the fourth century, and it also spread to the Etruscan and the Italiote world.[56] Later on, Bacchic imagery continues to adorn various kinds of funerary monuments, aediculae, stelae, and altars, down to its last flowering in the art of the sarcophagi.[57] However, one must note that it cannot be proved, and it is even far from probable, that each Apulian tomb with Bacchic vases or each Dionysiac sarcophagus of the second or third century A.D. was designed to hold a Dionysiac initiate. Imagery takes its own ways. But it is still remarkable that it was the cult of Dionysus that provided a form of artistic expression, *a façon de parler,* if it was no more, in response to the blatant senselessness of death. There are constant references to Bacchic ecstasy in this kind of funerary art, above all through the recurrent appearance of the tympanon and the cymbala of the maenads. There are not infrequent indications of mysteries proper: the *cista mystica* with the snake, the *liknon* with phallus. A few sarcophagi have explicit initiation scenes.[58] The combination of *kiste* and *kalathos* on funerary stelae from Lilybaeum is especially suggestive, even if we have no directly related text.[59] But there are at least literary testimonies concerning Bacchic rites performed right at the tombs of the deceased members of Bacchic associations;[60] mourning and ecstasy somehow seem to fuse. There is only one text, however—a clumsy Latin epigram from Philippi that seems to describe a special Bacchic paradise, where Bacchants invite the deceased child to join their dances as a little satyr, and even this is just an imaginative possibility.[61] The promise remains vague even here.

Fear of death is a fact of life. "As one gets closer to the expectation of death," Plato wrote, "fear and concern about things not thought of before appear"; many people therefore, in Plutarch's words, "think that some sort of initiations and purifications will help: once purified, they believe, they will go on playing and dancing in Hades in places full of brightness, pure air and light."[62] Thus mysteries were meeting practical needs even in their promises for an afterlife. It remains for us to wonder what really constituted the intrinsic unity of these two dimensions of mysteries—realistic cures and immunizations, on the one hand, and imaginary guarantees of bliss after death, on the other. It is not enough to appeal to multiple levels of meaning in one kind of symbolism, such as the natural cycle of sowing, growing, and reaping, or the change of grapes into wine; faith makes use of symbolism, but hardly arises from there.[63] It is tempting to assume that the central idea of all initiations should be death and resurrection, so that extinction and salvation are anticipated in the ritual, and real death becomes a repetition of secondary importance; but the pagan evidence for resurrection symbolism is uncompelling at best.[64] In a more general way initiation is a change of status, and it might seem natural that this should be reflected in a better status after death. Yet such a change of status is not at all visible in ancient mysteries, and thus it is difficult to see how the privileges of an afterlife could be its projection.[65]

There may be another answer inherent in the practical cures. "Manifest sufferings," to use Plato's words, are traced to some "ancient cause of wrath," *menima:* some terrible deed of the past has aroused still-active powers of destruction; spirits of ancestors, victims of murder, or someone deprived of proper burial is harassing the living. To explain illness or depression in this way is quite common in various civilizations, including the Near East and archaic Greece.[66] The cure, in consequence, is to assuage the anger and the envy of the dead: as they are made to feel cheerful and happy, *hileoi,* the real patient will feel better too. These, then, are the "purifications through joyous festivals" that are good "both for the living and for those who have died," as described, and denounced, by Plato.[67] The two belong together because disturbances in the beyond are felt so grievously in this life; hence ritual that has the effect of eliminating grief and sorrow and establishing a "blessed" status immediately has its repercussions on the other side. This is why the deceased are imagined to join in the mystery festival, to continue blissful *teletai* even in the netherworld;[68] conversely, "terrible things are waiting" for those who decline to sacrifice. This threat is already found in the *Hymn to Demeter,* with the assurance that Persephone will release those who honor her through ritual.[69]

This concept seems to make "magic" one of the main roots of mysteries. But even magic has its place, its functions and meanings within an elaborate social cosmos. It may have psychotherapeutic effects that are not negligible; it makes sense for those who use it. Perhaps it would be more attractive, from a modern theorist's point of view, to regard mysteries as derived from tribal initiations. Even the latter, however, may well have had to do with the dead, and with corresponding "magic" in their presumed prehistoric settings.

In the documents of the so-called Oriental cults, the dimension of an afterlife is much less obvious. The Hellenized form of worship of Meter became partly fused with Dionysus at an early date, and thus the tympanon of Meter was introduced into all forms of Bacchic worship and imagery. But the Pessinuntian-Roman form of the cult, with *galloi* and the elaborate yearly festival that we know about from the late sources, seems to have been much less concerned with individual survival after death than with avoiding catastrophes in this life. There is just one remark in Augustine that the castration of the *galloi* aims at future bliss, *ut post mortem vivat beate;*[70] but what about the other, more normal worshipers? There are some instances of common burial for the worshipers of Magna Mater, but this is by no means the rule; private burials even of *archigalloi* are found as well.[71] Some altars and sarcophagi are adorned with a figure called "mourning Attis,"[72] but whether this carries any hope for the believer or whether it is just to be understood as an expression of waning strength, death, and mourning is far from clear. The change from lament to joy, "descent" (*katabasis*) to Hilaria, in the Meter festival may signify rescue from death, as Damascius has it; but Damascius, in this often quoted text, is referring to a real adventure, a dangerous visit to the volcanic chasm at Hierapolis made by some Athenian Neoplatonists, and their ensuing dream. It is improper to reverse the situation, to make the sign—the dream of the festival—the subject and the real event its meaning, as Cumont has done.[73] One famous and often quoted taurobolium inscription, the dedication of Aedesius, claims that he is *in aeternum renatus.*[74] This inscription was set up in 376 A.D., two generations after the victory of Christianity and half a generation after Julian, in the midst of a pagan reaction. It obviously contradicts the multiple and earlier evidence that the *taurobolium* is effective for twenty years and no more; the most likely explanation is that it has drawn on the well-known Christian proclamations and is trying to beat the adversary by imitation.

The cult of Osiris is intimately connected with the cult of the dead in Egypt. The formula "May Osiris give you the

cool water" was developed in Egypt but occurs in other
places as well, notably in Rome.[75] We hear of "Osiris-burials"
even in the Greco-Roman world.[76] Mummification, however,
was scarcely practiced outside Egypt. Funerary monuments
of worshipers of the Egyptian gods exist in great numbers;
there are the *insignia* of the cult, sistrum, patera, water vessel,
and inscriptions mentioning the rank of priestesses and
priests,[77] although these seem to fulfill a commemorative
function rather than point toward the future or toward a
special message about an afterlife. One sarcophagus at
Ravenna, with unusual pictures and inscriptions, has been
interpreted as referring to special "mystic" hopes, but the
fragmentary text leaves much room for speculation, as does
the imagery.[78] More explicit is a recently found epitaph from
Bithynia; a priest of Isis proclaims that, because of the secret
rites he performed during his life, he has traveled not to
dark Acheron but to the "harbor of the blessed," and he invokes the testimony of the Isiakoi for his reputation.[79] This is
still in keeping with the style of Greek funerary epigrams.
Boys who had died prematurely were iconographically
identified with Horos through the characteristic lock of
hair.[80] There is nothing to indicate that this symbolism was
dependent on ritual; figurative deification of this kind occurred with other gods too, including Dionysus.

Isis herself, in her revelation to Lucius-Apuleius, is less
explicit than some paraphrases would have it. "And when
you have completed your lifetime and go down to the underworld," she is made to say, "you will find me in the subterranean vault, shining in the darkness of Acheron and reigning
in the innermost quarters of Styx, while you yourself inhabit
the Elysian fields, and you will adore me frequently, as I am
well-disposed toward you." Compare the following curse
against a grave robber: "He will have the sacred rites of Isis,
which mean peace for the deceased, turned in rage against
himself."[81] This harks back to the practical charms for the
quiet of the dead. With Acheron and Elysium, Isis is made
to adopt normal Greek mythology; this is on a footing with

the hopes of Eleusinian and Dionysiac *mystai* as seen from the fifth century onward. The identification of Isis with the moon and with Persephone—and with Demeter as well—makes her shine as well as reign in the netherworld. The main emphasis, at any rate, is on the power of Isis ruling in this cosmos, changing the fates here and now for her protégé. But one must not forget the truth that holds even for the worshiper of Isis: "From nature, man has received death as a common allotment."[82]

If we turn finally to Mithras, we are left with a surprising dearth of relevant evidence. It has generally been assumed, as a result of our ideas of what a "mystery religion" should be like, that Mithras should guarantee his followers some kind of transcendent salvation—immortality, ascent to heaven from the "cave" which is the cosmos. Clear evidence, however, is lacking. This is all the more surprising because spiritual life, the immortality of the soul, and the ascent of the righteous to heaven are such well-established ideas in Iranian, Zoroastrian tradition. But this is not so with Mithras. Although Cumont wrote that Mithraists practiced common burial as a closed group of "believers," this is flatly contradicted by the evidence.[83] In Mithraic iconography, the scene of Mithras mounting the chariot of Helios often recurs; the combination with the Mithraic grade of Heliodromus is unexceptionable. Interpreters think of an ascent toward and beyond the zodiac, right into transcendence.[84] Yet Helios is not known to leave the cosmos; he continues to circle around the globe. There is no evidence for a breakthrough to some genuine beyond apart from some Platonizing hints in Origen and Porphyry.[85] Mithraism may in fact have been anti-Gnostic, heroically facing and maintaining this cosmos built on violence and sacrifice.[86]

There remains the testimony of Julian, who was an initiate of Mithras and eager to promote his cult. Julian introduces Hermes, who is made to tell him that because of his acquaintance with Mithras, the "father," he has found "a safe anchor in life," and that "when it will be necessary to depart from here, you may do this with good hope, because you have taken as your leader a god well-disposed towards you." This is surprisingly close to what Isis told Lucius, and clearer still is the common background in the work and thought of Plato: "good hope" echoes the *Phaedo,* and divine leadership echoes an even more celebrated passage of the *Phaedrus.*[87] Mithras stands on a level with the speculations of philosophy and the promises of other mysteries, but there is neither a special content nor a special foundation of faith, just the general intimation of "hope." The emphasis is, once again, on a "safe anchor" in this life. A redirection of religion toward otherworldly concerns, contrary to what is often assumed, is not to be found with the "Oriental" gods and their mysteries. At best they continue what was already there. In the eyes of a pagan, Christianity was a religion of tombs, excessively concerned about death and decay.[88] None of the pagan mysteries made such an impression. There never was mortification; *laetitia vivendi* was left unimpeached.[89]

Seen in contrast to Christianity, mysteries appear both more fragile and more human. A funerary inscription from Rome, dating from the third or fourth century A.D., provides a fine example. It is for a boy who died at the age of seven.[90] Through the pious care of his parents, he had already been made a priest of "all the gods: first of Bona Dea, then of the Mother of the Gods and of Dionysus Kathegemon. For them I performed the mysteries always in august fashion. Now I have left the august sweet light of Helios. Therefore you, *mystai* or friends of whatever kind of life, forget all the august mysteries of life, one after the other; for nobody can dissolve the thread spun by the Fates. For I, Antonios the august, (only) lived seven years and twelve days." Some interpreters evidently did not dare to understand the plain text of this epigram. Instead of "forget . . . the mysteries," Kaibel paraphrased: "if you keep yourself from undergoing the mysteries, remember, nobody can escape death"; this yields pious sense but spoils the syntax. Moretti curiously translates *celamini de . . . mysteriis* as "keep yourself secret as to the mysteries," which is unclear. The simple translation "forget" is fully justified for later Greek,[91] and the order of thought is made clear by the twofold "for" (*gar*). We should accept the disillusionment of the bereft parents: mysteries do not help against death—forget about them; *exemplum docet.*

Of course one cannot attach too much importance to a single document of lost faith, but in fact it is not even an isolated one.[92] There was no dogmatic faith in overcoming death in mysteries, as there was no devaluation of life. There was neither gospel nor revelation to immunize believers against the disasters of this life. Mysteries, like votive religion, remained to some extent an experimental form of religion. As such, they could at times disappoint the hopes of believers.

II

Organizations and Identities

RELIGION MEANT KNOWLEDGE about ultimate reality to more dogmatic ages; it meant history of ideas to the nineteenth century; for moderns, poised between nihilism and linguistics, it has become "constructing worlds of meaning."[1] Religious ideas and meanings nevertheless exist for living men and women who keep struggling through the ups and downs of their individual lives with multiple needs and interests. There are considerable investments and corresponding emoluments in religion, and this holds true for pagan mysteries as well. It is worthwhile to investigate who the individuals were who executed, propagated, and perpetuated religious practices, the crew managing the vehicle, so to speak, and how they were recruited. These questions have to do with the social background of a cult—its organization and its active nucleus. It is clear that those who are professionals, who make a living out of a religious life, will be the most energetic torchbearers of their respective traditions.

In this respect ancient mysteries turn out to be anything but uniform. The main finding is negative: despite a vocabulary often applied to ancient mysteries without much circumspection, the existence of mystery communities, *Mysteriengemeinden*,[2] cannot be taken for granted. There are important differences among the various mysteries in regard to social organization and coherence, but none of them approaches the Christian model of a church, *ekklesia*. Still less should we speak of separate and self-sufficient "religions."

To begin with a typological survey, there seem to be at least three major forms of organization in the practice of ancient mysteries: the itinerant practitioner or charismatic, the clergy attached to a sanctuary, and the association of worshipers in a form of club, *thiasos*. The first type, the itinerant practitioner or charismatic, has been studied mainly in the context of late antiquity—individuals such as Apollonius of Tyana or Alexander of Abonuteichos—but the "mantic and telestic" way of life[3] is quite an ancient one. The wandering seer and priest, dealing with purifications and initiations, appears in the archaic period (for example, Epimenides) and is also seen in Empedocles, author of *Katharmoi*. He has made his way into Greek mythology in tales about Melampus, Calchas, Mopsus, and similar characters. A good characterization of the charismatic is given by the Derveni papyrus as "he who makes the sacred a craft"—the craftsman of religion.[4] This means, as for other craftsmen, that there is an invoking of tradition, of a craft handed down by a master, of a real or spiritual "father"; at the same time, transmission takes the form of *telete*.[5] The Hippocratic corpus offers well-known parallels with the famous *Oath* and the *Nomos*.[6] Continuity and coherence of tradition are thus guaranteed by a kind of family model. Yet, like other craftsmen, the charismatic works by himself at his own risk and profit. The profits could be staggering, especially for a seer in wartime, but the normal situation for an itinerant practitioner would be a marginal existence threatened by poverty and exposed to hostility, contempt, and ridicule by the establishment.[7] There was no backing by a corporation or community.

The second type, the clergy at a sanctuary, is more common in the Near East and Egypt than in Greece.[8] Greek sanctuaries were not normally independent economic units, but part of the administration of the *polis* or else family property. Yet private worship could bring considerable income to a priest through offerings and sacrifices, and with some gift and luck or through the grace of a particular god, a flourishing enterprise could come into being. The oracles in the archaic period and the sanctuaries of Asclepius in the classical period became quite successful organizations of their kind. Other establishments, especially in Asia Minor, some of them very old, kept pace, and still others followed suit in Hellenistic times. The priestly figures officiating at such sanctuaries can be clearly distinguished from the itinerant type by local stability and relative security, but at the same time they had to accept some form of hierarchy to avoid interference. The number of beneficiaries was always restricted but still could become considerable.

The third type, which may be termed a "club," is called *thiasos* or just *koinon*, the "common" association. It is as characteristic of Greek society as the various *collegia* or *sodalitates* were for the Roman world—"countless flocks, countless *teletai*," in the words of Marcus Aurelius.[9] Details differ, but the essential feature is the coming together of equals in a common interest. The individuals remain independent, especially on the economic level, fully integrated into the complex structures of family and *polis;* but they contribute interest, time, influence, and part of their private property to the common cause. Such contributions are expected from the wealthy citizens, who receive remuneration in the form of honors bestowed on them, often documented in inscriptions. This type of association has a legal status and a place to meet; there is often common property; but there is no stable hierarchy or charismatic leadership.

These three types of religious organization are compatible with one another, but each is essentially independent. A charismatic may bring together his own devoted *thiasos;* a member of a clergy may turn out to be a successful charismatic; a practitioner as well as a *thiasos* may have special ties to some local sanctuary; but these relations are not vital for any of these forms of organization. Each may well become detached again and continue to function in its own way.

In regard to the ancient mysteries, the itinerant practitioners and charismatics are most characteristic of the *teletai* of
Dionysus and Meter in the earlier period. A key document is
the edict of Ptolemy IV Philopator, dating from about 210
B.C., which gives orders that "those who perform initiations
for Dionysus in the country" should travel to Alexandria and
register there, declaring "from whom they have received the
sacred things, up to three generations, and to hand in the
hieros logos in a sealed exemplar."[10] This testifies to the family
model of transmission: each must know not only his spiritual
"father," but also his grandfather and great-grandfather,
"up to three generations." Part of the tradition is a "sacred
tale" in written form. The Roman Bacchanalia, in Livy's account, are traced to some *sacrificulus et vates* or "petty
sacrificer and seer," a Greek probably from Magna Graecia
who migrated to Etruria, whence the practice spread to
Rome. One priestess from Campania gained special influence, claiming direct inspiration from the god and alter-
ing the traditions accordingly; Roman citizens from the
lower class became the heads of the "conspiracy."[11] As early
as in Euripides' *Bacchae,* the itinerant charismatic (alias
Dionysus) appears on stage, a stranger from Lydia in the
eyes of Pentheus; this man is offering his *teletai* and performing miracles. He claims to have received his *orgia* in direct
revelation from his god.[12] Women who "perform initiations
for Dionysus in the city or in the country" are described at
Miletus in the early third century B.C.; they were required to
report to the official priestess of Dionysus in the city and to
pay a regular fee.[13] In the Milesian colony of Olbia, the *teletai*
of Dionysus were already flourishing in the fifth century.[14]
Glaukothea, the mother of Aeschines the orator, was offering initiations to Dionysus Sabazius by about 380 B.C.[15] It is
interesting to note that she belonged to a family of seers;
evidently she was trying to make a living in difficult postwar
times by having recourse to spiritual family traditions. Plato
and Theophrastus refer to the *Orpheotelestai* of their times.[16]
The diffusion of the famous gold plates which are usually

called "Orphic," but which have been identified as "Bacchic"
by the Hipponion *lamella,* can be explained by the existence
of these "families" of migrating craftsmen. The texts have
come to light, in different recensions, in southern Italy, in
Thessaly, and in Crete, stretching over a period of nearly
200 years.[17]

It is a striking fact that after the catastrophe of the Roman
Bacchanalia in 186 B.C. the itinerant initiation priest seems to
have totally disappeared from Bacchic mysteries, although
the mysteries make their appearance again in Italy by the
time of Caesar. They left many inscriptions throughout the
empire, as well as splendid monuments such as the frescoes
of the Villa of the Mysteries at Pompeii or the stucco room of
the Villa Farnesina in Rome. Of course the itinerant practitioners did not disappear altogether after the event of 186
B.C., but they followed other traditions; witness Apollonius
of Tyana or Alexander of Abonuteichos, not to mention
Jesus and Saint Paul. With Dionysus, we find well-developed
forms of *thiasoi* instead, usually dependent on a wealthy
founder or president, sometimes closely attached to an official cult of the city or a rich private house. There must have
been some form of esoteric tradition regarding the practice
of Bacchic initiation and its interpretation, but we have no
clue thus far to discover how the organization worked. We
are left only with a fascinating and enigmatic iconography,
notably the picture of the phallus in the *liknon* revealed to the
initiand.[18] A special form of the spreading of Dionysiac *orgia*
is seen in an inscription from Magnesia: with the approval of
the Delphic oracle, the Magnesians are made to import three
"genuine" maenads from Thebes, descendants of Ino, the
nurse of Dionysus and the archetypal maenad.[19] This is once
again a form of charismatic family tradition, involving however not the lonely specialist but a nuclear group of worshipers in whom the power of the god is manifest: "Many are the
narthex-bearers, but few are *bakchoi*"[20]—but here they were,
radiating their energies into a new *thiasos.* In the large *thiasos*
of Agripinilla at Rome, known from the New York inscrip-

tion,[21] the *boukoloi,* "cowherds," form the largest group and are apparently the normal *mystai.* Some are designated as *hieroi boukoloi,* "sacred," belonging to the god in a special way. Are they the real *bakchoi* among the thyrsus-bearers, with a mediumistic gift for ecstasy, or are they professionals maintained by the club? The answer, like the diachronic and synchronic interrelations among Dionysiac groups of the later period in general, remains unclear. Bacchic mysteries seem to be ubiquitous, but the living reality is difficult to grasp behind the lasting conventions of iconography and the literary impact of Euripides' play. Nevertheless, Bacchic mysteries were still performed in the fourth century A.D.[22]

Worship of Meter in Greece evidently began in a similar way with itinerant specialists. From Semonides onward there are testimonies about *homines religiosi* of this type, the "beggars of Mother" (*metragyrtai*) who unabashedly made their living from their craft.[23] They must have been responsible for the spreading of votive monuments for Meter through the Greek world as early as the archaic period, from Cyzicus in Asia Minor to Locri in southern Italy.[24] They were often treated with contempt. As an insult, Cratinus in one of his comedies called Lampon, the famous seer of Athens and specialist for various mysteries, a "beggar of Cybele," *agersikybelis,* and the Athenian general Iphicrates called Callias, the worthy *daduchos* of Eleusis, a *metragyrtes.*[25] *Metragyrtai* performed with cymbals and tambourines, being "possessed by the divinity," *theophorumenoi*; the most graphic illustration is the Naples mosaic of Dioscurides, featuring Menander's *Theophorumene.*[26] We have very little knowledge of how these people received their own initiation, their "tradition of the holy things." The tyrant Dionysius II, finally overthrown and expelled from Sicily, is said to have become a *metragyrtes* in a last desperate attempt to make a living; could he claim any tradition of either Syracuse or Locri?[27]

The organization that was to win respectability and success in the worship of Meter was the local sanctuary with a permanent clergy attached to it. The sanctuary of Pessinus in

Anatolia—with a tradition that goes back to the Bronze Age, distinguished by the gruesome institution of eunuch priests, the *galloi*—developed diplomatic skill in making arrangements with the prevailing political powers and even with the barbarian invaders, providentially called Galli themselves.[28] When the Roman request for the Mother Goddess, transmitted through Pergamene mediation, arrived in 205/204 B.C., the Pessinuntians were quick to respond, and thus the most influential center of Mater Magna was founded right on the Palatine in Rome; a later offshoot was the Phrygianum in the *ager Vaticanus,* where the taurobolium sacrifices took place.[29] The sanctuaries had their own special clergy. The charismatic nucleus consisted of the *galli,* castrated by the order of their goddess "in order to spread awe among men," as an Akkadian text puts it,[30] with horrifying performances of ecstatic self-wounding on the "day of blood," *dies sanguinis.* The term *fanatici* did apply to them.[31] We may wonder at the fact that there were apparently no difficulties in recruiting *galli.* It was a recognized and even a profitable way of life, and at the same time these individuals were attached to their goddess and their sanctuary in a way that made apostasy impossible for the rest of their lives; witness Catullus' Attis poem. State control added a superstructure of Roman officials who were not eunuchs, of course. Elections had to be approved by the Quindecimviri.[32] Priests appointed outside Rome needed the endorsement of the central sanctuary.[33] Parallel to the professionals there developed respectable collegia paying homage to the cult;[34] there were *cannophori* and *dendrophori,* playing their role mainly in the context of the great yearly festival in March. Similar organizations of *galli,* official priests, and collegia appear at Ostia, where a large precinct of Meter and Attis has been fully excavated.[35] There is not much more evidence about the interrelations of local groups, but probably it was essential to import at least some of those strange mediators with the divine, the *galli,* as Rome did in 204 B.C.

Eleusis stands out in contrast by having renounced any

expansion beyond the local sanctuary. It is true that a general form of worshiping Demeter Eleusinia had spread throughout Greece at an early date, especially to Ionia;[36] yet it was agreed that the mysteries could only be held at the one place selected by the goddess herself, as the myth stressed. Two local aristocratic families, the Eumolpidai and the Kerykes, cooperated in a sophisticated system of rank: the Eumolpids provided the main priest, the hierophant, while the Kerykes provided the two ranking next in dignity, the *daduchos*, "torchbearer," and the *hierokeryx*, "herald of the sacred." Members of both families retained the privilege of performing initiation, *myein*.[37] It was the "knowledge coming out of the priesthood that has been in the family for so many generations," to quote a Hellenistic inscription,[38] on which their authority was based. From the earliest documentation there was in addition a state-controlled superstructure: the annually elected "king," *basileus*, was charged with the general supervision of the mysteries, while a board of *epistatai* dealt with the finances.[39] Far-reaching Eleusinian propaganda is found in literature and especially in iconography, extending to southern Russia, to Italy, and to Egypt by the fourth century B.C.[40] It even penetrated into royal and imperial iconography; the splendid silver bowl of Aquileia, preserved at Vienna, depicts a dynast—Marc Antony, according to Andreas Alföldi—posing as Triptolemus.[41] In the fifth century a charismatic seer, Lampon, is found working for the benefit of Eleusis.[42] In about 300 B.C. a Eumolpid, Timotheus, apparently became an itinerant charismatic: he organized the cult of Sarapis at Alexandria and also gave an elaborate account of the Pessinuntian Attis myth.[43] Whether there was also a mystery cult of the Eleusinian type installed at Alexandria, which had a suburb by the name of Eleusis, is a question that has been hotly debated; the evidence is inconclusive.[44] Women initiates of Demeter are featured in the sixth hymn of Callimachus; the restriction to the female sex is contrary to Eleusinian practice, but has its parallels elsewhere.[45] Eduard Norden's *Die Geburt des Kindes* has made

famous a remarkable festival that took place on January 6 in
a sanctuary of Kore where "Kore gives birth to Aion," the
god of eternity.[46] Some parallel to the Eleusinian *dromena,*
where "Brimo gives birth to Brimos," has to be acknowledged. However, it seems that the Alexandrian festival took
place in a temple, without previous initiation; it was not a
mystery celebration but rather belonged to an Egyptian setting. Eleusis wished to remain unique, and largely succeeded
in doing so.[47] It seems that in a way Dionysiac mysteries
could be viewed as a substitute for the Eleusinian ones in
other places. A choral ode in Sophocles' *Antigone,* performed
about the time of the founding of Thurii in Italy, appeals to
Dionysus as the Lord of Italy who at the same time rules in
the recess of Eleusis.[48]

Most complex is the picture presented by the cult of Isis.
One basic fact seems to be that, by virtue of a tradition of
millennia, Egyptian cults had to deal with statues in which
the divinity was considered to reside. Thus a house, that is, a
temple, was needed, with constant tending by the priests.
This meant that clergy members had to be permanently attached to the temple, as had always been the case in Egypt,
with higher ranks, lower ranks, and simple servants. The
most detailed account of the installation of an Egyptian cult
in Greece is given in an inscription from Delos termed the
"Sarapis aretalogy" in modern scholarship.[49] Apollonios the
Egyptian, from a priestly family, emigrated to Delos "carrying the god," that is, carrying a sacred statue. He had to keep
his god in rented apartments, until finally his grandson de-
cided to build a Sarapieion on neglected premises close to the
marketplace. This involved him in a lawsuit with the local
building authorities, but he was victorious through the help
of his god, and "Sarapieion A" was thus installed. Later state
control took over, and the bigger "Sarapieion B" run by the
polis became predominant. The accretion of riches took place
through votive offerings. In other cases too the initiative for
founding Egyptian cults abroad came from emigrant Egyptians,[50] but *thiasoi* in Greek style, that is, associations of

Sarapiastai, Isiastai, and *Anubiastai,* developed around the nucleus.[51] In Rome, the collegium of *pastophori* is said to go back to the time of Sulla.[52] During that period the Iseum of Pompeii was actually founded.[53] The Roman senate was strongly opposed to the cult of Isis for some generations, and as a result the altar of Isis was destroyed repeatedly by the magistrates; but finally under Caligula the great temple in the *Campus Martius* was built and the triumph of Isis was assured.[54]

Because the clergy always stressed the relationship with Egypt and the necessity "to worship the gods of the fathers with the rites from home,"[55] "the Egyptian" had to be present to perform the sacrifice "with expertise";[56] therefore at least some of the priests would normally have been Egyptians. They used, and possibly even read, hieroglyphic books and handled sacred water from the Nile. As in Egypt, they performed a daily service from morning to night, solemnly awakening the gods, clothing them, feeding them, and putting them to bed. In addition, there were the great yearly festivals with pompous processions. The self-interest of the clergy found its expression in a well-organized propaganda, extolling every miracle wrought by the gods, as in the previously mentioned case of Delia praying for Tibullus in the temple.[57] The collegia of those participating in the cult in one way or another were multiplied: in addition to the *pastophori* we find *hieraphoroi, melanophoroi,* and *sindonophoroi.*[58] The wearing of linen instead of wool seems to have been the most general form of demonstrating attachment to the worship of Isis, and the "crowd with linen clothes and shaved heads" is a standard formula for describing an Egyptianized sanctuary in literature.[59] There were further groups of worshipers (*therapeutai, cultores*) without rank or function,[60] some of whom would rent an apartment within the sanctuary to live close to the divinity as long as they could afford to. A vivid picture of such activities in both Corinth and Rome is given in the romance of Apuleius.

The main problem regarding the mysteries of Isis is how

and where initiation (*telete*, *myesis*) actually occurred. Testimonies for *mystai* of Isis are deplorably scanty, at least outside Apuleius' book. Among about 800 inscriptions brought together in the *Sylloge* of Vidman, only three refer to *mystai*, which come from Rome, Tralles, and Prusa.[61] The oldest literary witness for mysteries of Isis is in fact Tibullus. We find the *cista mystica* appearing in Isiac iconography in the first century A.D.[62] In addition, there are about a dozen attestations of "sacred" persons, *hieroi*, *sacri*, *sacrae*, among the worshipers of the Egyptian gods in Rome and some other places.[63] It is tempting to assume that they were *mystai*, "belonging to the god" in a special way, as the term *sacred* indicates, but we cannot be sure; perhaps one should think of some form of *katoche*.[64] In Apuleius, Lucius, once unmasked as the "man from Madaura," first becomes a *cultor* living within the sanctuary and waiting for his initiation. He is then made to undergo several mystery initiations, to Isis as well as to Osiris, and finally becomes a member of the *pastophori* in Rome.[65] Initiation would thus mark a step between the state of worshiper in general and election to the governing body. Yet there is no indication that such a neat *cursus honorum* was prescribed.

There seems in fact to be a double misunderstanding in cross-cultural relations lurking in the background of the mysteries of Isis. To the Greeks, as early as the sixth century B.C., celebrations of Osiris with nocturnal ritual and lamentation suggested "mysteries," and the hierarchical esotericism of Egyptian priests reinforced this impression. Modern scholars agree that there were initiation rites for priests at various levels in Egypt, and there were secret rites in which only the higher priests were allowed to participate, but there were no *mysteria* of the Greek style, open to the public upon application.[66] Yet in the eyes of the Greeks, who admired the aboriginal age of Egyptian civilization, Egypt appeared to be the very homeland and origin of mysteries as such; this is the teaching of both Herodotus and Hecataeus of Abdera.[67] The statuettes of youthful Harpocrates putting his finger to his lips were interpreted as the epitome of "mystical" silence. The Greek perspective was then adopted in turn by propaganda for Isis, as evidenced by the so-called Isis aretalogies in which Isis, among her other civilizing activities, is seen as the founder of mysteries throughout the world. The oldest extant text of this type, the "Isis aretalogy" from Maroneia, makes it clear that it is the mysteries of Eleusis for which Isis is finally made responsible, and much later still Mesomedes hints at Eleusis in his hymn to Isis.[68] But the later versions of the aretalogies are vaguer and thus seem to promise more; through this intentional ambiguity people surmised that there must be authentic Egyptian mysteries behind offshoots such as Eleusis, mysteries that were more original, more difficult to gain access to, and much more effective. Curiosity and demand could well be met. Sanctuaries of Isis began to offer forms of personal initiation upon request, modeled after those of Eleusis and Dionysus, though in a style perfectly adapted to Egyptian forms of ritual and mythology. Apuleius clearly indicates that initiations to Isis and Osiris were extremely expensive and time-consuming. They must have been a rather rare event, reserved to the fortunate few who could afford them, with the numerous other worshipers gladly joining in the festival. Mysteries of this kind are not the root and center of Isis worship, but only one element in the much more complex canvas of cults of the Egyptian gods, meeting the various needs of those in search of salvation and success. The *mysteria* were a special service delivered to those who had the desire and the means for it, bringing, like other mysteries, a more personal experience of close attachment to the gods.

The picture presented by the mysteries of Mithras is totally different: one finds neither itinerant charismatics nor public *thiasoi* nor the display of temple and clergy. All seems to center on the initiations performed by secret clubs. The best parallel, which is often invoked, may be the Masons, whose clubs began to flourish rather rapidly on both sides of the Atlantic in the eighteenth century and persist to the present day. In some respects the mysteries of Mithras are closer to the general type of secret societies with initiation rituals, as known in social anthropology, than the other, "normal" Greek mysteries. With Mithras, secrecy seems to have been nearly absolute. The Mithraea must have been much less accessible in their time than in modern excavations, museums, and publications. The scarcity of literary references to mysteries of Mithras is strange when compared to the richness of the archaeological evidence. By comparison, the literary documentation about Eleusis is abundant. Mithraea usually were quite small, holding about twenty persons on average. This makes a good team, but not a mass religion. With enlarging membership a new "cave" would be established by some wealthy donor, instead of the existing constructions being enlarged.[69]

In the body of participants in mysteries of Mithras we find not the dichotomy of clergy versus general adherents, as with Isis, but a strict hierarchy of initiation grades. There are seven of these grades, named in Greek originally but normally referred to in Latin, since Rome was the center from which the cult spread to the provinces: Corax, Nymphus, Miles, Leo, Persa, Heliodromus, and Pater.[70] There is even the title *pater patrum* for a central authority.[71] Evidently it was the responsibility of the *patres* to watch over the correct form of these mysteries. Inscriptions indicate that in order to inaugurate a new Mithraeum and thus to found a new group, a *pater* had to be present.[72] Thus Mithraism was guided by a *sanctissimus ordo*. A *pater* would also supervise the transmission of initiation grades, *tradere leontica, persica, heliaca, patrica*. This organization explains the surprising uniformity of sanctuaries and iconography of Mithras from the Rhine to the Danube and hence to Dura Europos as well as Africa. Soldiers and merchants were the main reservoir for the recruitment of Mithras *mystai*. Indeed, the mobility of the Roman legions was essential for the spreading of the cult. Much depended upon the initiative of individual rich and devoted members. It is remarkable that slaves were admitted—with a strict selection process, no doubt—while women remained excluded.[73] This again is quite unique among ancient mysteries, but corresponds to more general practices of secret men's societies.

With this incomplete but realistic picture of the organization and functioning of mysteries as a social phenomenon, with nuclear groups of participants who also guarantee some form of diachronic stability, we can now turn to the question of whether mysteries presupposed or created communities, *Mysteriengemeinden.* The answer will differ according to the types involved. One point is already evident, although it has often been overlooked: we find forms of mysteries that do not result in any kind of organized and stable community. The itinerant charismatic who provides cures for various needs will go on traveling after a time, just as the people who sought initiation as a help against manifest sufferings may joyously pursue their own ways, feeling better than before. These individuals will have gained some precepts about their future life, some rules for a "diet" in a moral or spiritual sense, but they are not irrevocably integrated into a permanent group.

It is important to have met fellow-patients, of course. As a rule, mysteries lead to integration into a "blessed chorus" for celebrations, the therapeutic effect of which is obvious. Skyles at Olbia is seen moving through the city in a frenzied Bacchic *thiasos;* Aeschines is seen to lead similar *thiasoi* at Athens; Philocleon is supposed to beat the tympanon together with the Corybants;[74] thousands of *mystai* and *epoptai* meet for blessed visions in the mystery night at Eleusis. Yet festive togetherness of this kind does not outlast the festival; the chorus dances for a day or a night and is disbanded thereafter. There remains the memory of a sacred experience that can be resuscitated. The Eleusinian initiate is invited to come back for another celebration the following year as an *epoptes;* but in the meantime his civil life does not change. The unity of the group has been in action and in experience, not in faith. There is no Credo.

Some charismatics will easily develop a personal clientele. This is not encouraged within the society of a *polis*, however, and it may even become dangerous if some form of conspiracy is suspected. The clergy at a sanctuary, on the other hand, is a recognized form of community, but this is a closed society, integrated by common orientation, ritual, and interest. These clergy members, being professionals who live on their benefice, must be careful not to increase their number beyond their means. They remain dependent on the worshipers outside the group to bring their gifts; a corporation of this kind cannot develop into a self-sufficient, alternative religious community in the full sense.

There remains the *thiasos* form of organization. This is a type of "community"; *koinon* is one of its most common designations. It may persist through several generations. There are "devoted" members who spend considerable time, energy, and money for the god and for their fellow-initiates. The term *symmystai* denotes the mutual attachment. One dedication is "to Dionysus and the *symmystai*," expressing the twofold ties a member would experience.[75] Participants engage in common activities, especially in sacrifices with the ensuing ceremonial meal, and also in demonstrations, *pompai*, which move through the city and make clear to everyone who belongs to the group. Obligations similar to those of private *amicitia* include helping in lawsuits and attending funerals.[76] Further attempts at social welfare seem to be lacking; the clubs are not for have-nots. In fact, in accordance with the prevailing social system, competition is valued more highly than cooperation. It is honor, *time*, that is sought amidst the *symmystai* of a *thiasos*, honor gained especially by generous financial contributions. Honorary inscriptions loom large in the evidence, especially with regard to Bacchic mysteries. In any case the members of a club are and remain autonomous, detached individuals with private interests, occupations, and property. Since joining the group is a matter of individual decision, there is hardly a problem in leaving it again; there is no loss of identity or fear of trauma and curse.

The term "brother," *adelphos,* is used even at Eleusis for those who receive initiation together.[77] This is remarkable, even if it is to be understood more in terms of a clan system than of emotional affection. Plato's Seventh Letter refers to the uncommonly close ties of friendship that develop through hospitality and common participation in the mysteries—those of Eleusis, no doubt—although for the philosopher this kind of friendship lacks the stable basis provided only by philosophy.[78] A metaphorical passage in Philo indicates that *mystai* were encouraged to seek contacts: "If you meet another initiate, don't let him go but stick to him and ask him if he happens to know still a newer form of *telete.*"[79] There are *symbola* to enable the *mystai* to recognize each other; this may lead to some kind of familiarity even between strangers.

These tendencies are checked, however, by the exclusiveness that is characteristic of closed societies. These associations tended to restrict membership; the *thiasos* of Agripinilla, comprised of about 500 persons, is surely exceptional.[80] The rank of *adlector collegii* in Isis cult is significant.[81] There is very little evidence that groups worshiping the same god in different places were interested in mutual contacts, despite the apparent interest of migrating individuals in such contacts. When Lucius-Apuleius comes from Corinth to Rome and immediately seeks the company of worshipers of Isis, to which he has become accustomed, they require a second initiation of him; the one performed at Corinth is found to be insufficient. There is a special initiation to Osiris, they point out, and furthermore his sacred clothes have been left behind at Corinth.[82] Groups of clergy as well as *thiasoi* conformed to the departmental and local character of Greco-Roman society. It is impossible to imagine correspondence of the Pauline type among various groups of this kind. Above all, there was the obligation of secrecy, deemed essential for all true mysteries; those who were "in" wished to be kept distinct from those who were "out." The main concern was not propagating a faith, but withholding the central revelation. This made mysteries attractive, but kept them in seclusion; they could not coalesce into a "church."

These characteristics become clearer if we ask to what extent mysteries conferred a religious identity, in the sense in which a Christian knows that "I am a Christian," *Christianus sum,* and not a pagan or a Jew. It is true that *mystai* were urged to "remember" their initiation;[83] they learned those *symbola* or *synthemata* that bore cryptic testimony to their full initiation and even kept material tokens of these at home.[84] Christians adopted the term *symbolon* for their own Credo, but this only serves to emphasize the enormous difference. In Christianity there are articles of faith, to be believed and to be confessed, whereas in the mysteries there is reference to a sequence of rituals that have taken place.[85] If there is some kind of identity in both cases, then it lies in the actual experience in mysteries but is dependent on constructions of metaphysical meaning alone in Christianity. It has been assumed that there should be some esoteric theology behind even a formula like the Eleusinian *synthema.* But ritual does not need explicit theology to be effective. There is not the slightest evidence to support Reitzenstein's assertion that mystery communities were held together by fixed forms of a Credo.[86]

Some cults prescribed a certain life-style, such as the "Orphic life" described by various authors from Plato to Plutarch.[87] A graffito from Olbia now seems to refer to *Orphikoi,* most probably in the sense of a "community," in the fifth century B.C.[88] Orphism is a special case within the complex of ancient mysteries; even so, the scarcity of references to "Orphics" in the sense expected by modern scholars remains a fact. For the other mysteries the problem of terminology is even more strange, at least from our perspective. There is no general designation for the followers or adherents of Eleusinian, Bacchic, Metroac, or Mithraic mysteries; one has to use clumsy circumlocutions in Greek, such as "those who have been initiated to Dionysus."[89] It is true that the term *bakchoi* is used for the followers of the god as well as for the god himself, but these *bakchoi* are a special group, not identical with *mystai* in general but standing out among them. The impact of particularism is even stronger: it is not essential to be initiated to Dionysus as such, but rather one would belong to a group such as "those around Dionysus Briseus" or some other specialization, that is, to a unique and exclusive club.[90] The lack of vocabulary is most surprising in the case of Mithras. Modern scholars cannot do without a name for the followers of Mithras, and modern languages have artificially coined their own terms: "Mithraists" or "Mithracists" (*les mithriaques, die Mithraisten*).[91] This cannot be said in either Greek or Latin. The small groups of men in the caves must have experienced an intimate feeling of togetherness, but in the texts the language is circumstantial and individualistic: "You who have got Mithras as a guide . . ." Hermes says to Julian.[92] We know from Tertullian that a Mithraist (our term) at the grade of *miles* was told never again to wear a crown, but to say "Mithras is my crown."[93] This is a conscious expression of permanent identity, but it is not made explicit by a linguistic term or by any form of Credo. Rather, it manifests itself in behavior, as in the case of the Orphic who would not eat eggs or the Eleusinian who avoided red mullets. This is the ancient usage of *symbolon*.

The case of Isis is different; there we find the common designation *Isiakoi, Isiaci*.[94] It may have come from outside observers, referring to the *grex liniger et calvus* so prominent at all sanctuaries of Isis; but insiders used it as well. The true *Isiakos*, Plutarch writes, is made not by his linen clothes and a shaved head but by his pious and philosophical orientation. This is a rare instance of spiritual self-definition versus ritual identity, and it is not a coincidence that it comes from a philosopher: the obvious model for the distinction is in reflections on the "true" philosopher, the "true" Cynic, and so on, in contrast to outward appearance.[95] But the term *Isiakoi* is presupposed. In a recently published funerary epigram from Prusa, a priest of Isis invokes the testimony of the *Isiakoi* for his pious performance of the secret ceremonies

that will earn him eternal life among the blessed.[96] A more
secular use appears in graffiti at Pompeii: "all the followers
of Isis" are summoned to vote "Helvius Sabinus for Aedil!"
(*Cn. Helvium Sabinum aedilem Isiaci universi rogant*).[97] Here we
have a religious organization engaging in political action, or
perhaps a politician trying to mobilize a religious group for
the sake of his career. The term *Isiaci universi* is evidently
meant to make the group seem as large as possible, including
all the various "flocks" who have taken interest in the Egyptian gods—priests, collegia, *cultores, sacri,* and, if present,
mystae. According to modern estimates, this could amount to
about 10 percent of the population. But we have to keep in
mind that we are dealing with a political construct rather
than with an actual religious "movement."

The testimony of funeral inscriptions deserves brief comment.[98] There are references to Eleusis, Dionysus, Meter,
and Isis in both texts and iconography of funerary monuments. They are not too frequent, however, apart from the
ubiquitous and conventional use of Dionysiac symbolism.
References are made mostly to priests of the respective cults,
to hierophants and other dignitaries, and not to simple
initiates. More often we encounter honorary titles, insignia
of the deceased, a form of personal *time* bestowed by relatives
and friends. This does not mean that the decreased were
included in a community of believers with collective claims
and hopes; individual distinction prevailed over group identity.

The general lack of organization, solidarity, and coherence in ancient mysteries, which may appear as a deficiency
from a Jewish or Christian point of view, is outweighed by
some positive aspects with which we may easily sympathize.
The absence of religious demarcation and conscious group
identity means the absence of any rigid frontiers against
competing cults as well as the absence of any concept of
heresy, not to mention excommunication. The pagan gods,
even the gods of mysteries, are not jealous of one another;
they form, as it were, an open society. If Mithras is somehow

a stranger, he still keeps good company with familiar divinities such as Helios, Kronos, and Zeus. The findings in the sanctuaries and the texts of the inscriptions are eloquent, though confusing to scholars who look for neat systematization. It is quite common in sanctuaries of Sarapis and Isis, as well as those of Meter and Mithras, to dedicate statues of other gods or to make vows to them.[99] Mithraea in particular have yielded a rich harvest of divine statues of all kinds. Cumont's attempts to find Avestan avatars in each case obviously cannot be upheld.[100] A *mystes* initiated to a particular god is not in any way prevented from turning to another god in addition. Apuleius introduces a priest of Isis with the name of Mithras.[101] A *tauroboliatus* is found to set up a statue of Dionysus, a Mithraic *pater* to make dedications to the Syrian gods, and even a *pater patrum* to set up an altar to Meter and Attis. Even Apollo gives advice on how to deal with Sarapis or Mithras, and Osiris orders sacrifices to Zeus the Almighty and to the Great Mother.[102] The interrelations between Isis-Osiris and Demeter-Dionysus are well known and very old. It is not surprising that a priest of Isis is at the same time *Iakchagogos* of the Eleusinian cult at Athens; the daughter of a priest of Sarapis at Delos becomes "basketbearer" of Dionysus; and a priestess of Isis institutes a festival of Dionysus.[103] It is quite common for one person to accumulate different priesthoods; combinations of Egyptian gods and Meter are especially in evidence. The final stage is the almost tedious multiplication of priesthoods and initiations in the circle of Praetextatus, in the time of the pagan opposition between 360 and 390 A.D.[104] The theoretical justification for all this was not only that the gods are free of envy—"envy stands outside the divine chorus," as a famous saying of Plato's put it[105]—but in particular that the main gods most probably are identical. This does not mean that the many individual gods and their names are unimportant or that they ought to be dropped, but that there are degrees of authenticity and proximity. In this sense Isis would claim that she has "infinitely many names" around the world; she is *myrionymos.* The document included in Oxyrynchus papyrus 1380 contains an almost endless list of these equivalences;[106] but he who turns to Isis, who knows her name and the special forms of Egyptian ritual, has the most direct access to the divine.[107]

Another document from Egypt, extant in two exemplars, is an oath of secrecy exacted from *mystai* at the initiation ceremony, termed *Eid der Isismysten* by Merkelbach.[108] The formula of the oath makes an impressive appeal to the creator god "who separated earth from sky, darkness from light," and so forth, and surprisingly adds: "I also swear by the gods I revere." Interpreters have tried to identify these gods, suggesting other Egyptian gods such as Harpocrates, Anubis, or Thoth. This approach overlooks the tradition of oath formulas that have similar provisions from ancient times: each partner has to swear "the greatest local oath" because only such an oath, by one's own gods "whom I revere," will be a serious obligation. The "mystery oath" complies with this practice; it is built on the foundations of a previous and lasting religious attachment to the "gods I actually worship." This, of course, is the absolute opposite of "conversion," of the injunction to "burn what you have adored." There is no unsettling or destroying of personality in mystery initiations of this kind, but rather a deepening or extending of preexisting piety through a new intimacy with the divine in both familiar and novel shapes.

In one case, Mithras appears in a different light. Eunapius tells how Nestorius, the hierophant of Eleusis from about 355 to 380 A.D., made the prophecy that his successor would not be qualified "to touch the hierophantic throne, since he would have been consecrated to other gods and would have sworn secret oaths not to supervise other shrines"; it turned out that his successor—in fact the last hierophant of Eleusis—was a Mithraic *pater*.[109] This makes Mithraism incompatible with the highest rank in the Eleusinian cult. Still, we should remember that there are incompatibilities even between much more ancient cults, requirements that certain priests or priestesses should not see or talk to each other; an inscription from Sardis, going back to the fourth century B.C., forbids the worshipers of "Zeus" to take part in the mysteries of Sabazius and Ma.[110] It remains puzzling that Nestorius is made to refer to an obligation of which the succeeding Mithraist himself seems to be happily ignorant. One might speculate that Nestorius—whom Eunapius knew and admired—had made a cryptic utterance referring to the probable takeover by the Christians, and when the end of Eleusis was forestalled and another hierophant could be appointed, the prediction was reinterpreted to fit the actual successor, who was a Mithraist. At any rate, the stance taken against Mithraism by Nestorius-Eunapius is a stance of "caution" on archaic lines; it does not have to do with battling false gods. There is acknowledgment as well as demarcation.

In summary, ancient mystery cults did not form religious communities in the sense of Judaism or Christianity. Even Richard Reitzenstein had to acknowledge that the concept of church, *ekklesia,* has no equivalent in pagan religion; it goes back to the Septuagint.[111] It is remarkable that a term borrowed from the Greek *polis* system came to designate an organization that was to overthrow and eliminate this very system. *Ekklesia* indicates quite a different level of involvement, and a claim about the organization of life different from that inherent in a private club or a limited and local clergy. A new and contrasting form of *politeia* was emerging; we find Philo applying this very term of "political activity," *politeia,* to the Jewish way of life, and Christians following suit in their own terminology.[112] The Jews had refused total integration into ancient society, and with Christianity there appeared an alternative society in the full sense of potentially independent, self-sufficient, and self-reproducing communities. Here we find from the beginning a concern for the poor, economic cooperation at a level quite uncommon in pagan religion, and the inclusion of the family as the basic unit of piety in the religious system. To educate the children in the fear of God suddenly became the supreme duty of

parents, as the Apostolic Fathers already taught.[113] And
since the believers were at the same time encouraged to mul-
tiply, with a new morality ousting all the well-established
forms of population control such as the exposure of children, homosexuality, and prostitution, the *ekklesia* became
a self-reproducing type of community that could not be
stopped.

No religious organization outside Judaism had developed
such a system,[114] least of all the mysteries with their exclusiveness, their individualism, and their dependence on private wealth. It is true that there were initiations of children;
they frequently appear in Bacchic mysteries, and even at
Eleusis there was a "child from the hearth" initiated at each
festival.[115] But this was a special honor or provision of concerned parents, not a religious or moral duty. It was unthink-
able that the entire life of the family should be subject to a
special religious orientation, and that every child should find
himself inescapably merged in a religious system where apostasy was considered to be worse than death.[116] The very idea
of Bacchic, Metroac, or even Isiac "education of children"
would approach the ridiculous. Mithras, for one, did not
even admit women; he stood for men's clubs in opposition to
family life.

There is only one slight indication of a possible movement
of mysteries in a similar direction: in the case of the Bacchanalia in 186 B.C., the accusation was that there had been a
huge conspiracy (*coniuratio*) that was to overthrow the existing *res publica;* "another people is about to arise," *alterum iam
populum esse.*[117] This vision of "another people" that is to oust
the *populus Romanus Quiritium* is a frightening one which in a
strange way foretells the proclamation of a new *politeia,* a new
civitas by later Christians. This may also explain why repression was so cruel and radical, with some 6,000 executions at a
time. There is nothing comparable in religious history before
the persecutions of Christians. One might also mention the
movement started in Sicily by Eunous, the inspired prophet
and miracle worker of the Syrian Goddess, who became the

charismatic leader of the slave revolt that lasted from 136 to 132 B.C.[118] Again, the repression was absolutely relentless. But here the social issues were much more prominent than the religious overtones. Much later, it was for Augustine to proclaim triumphantly that Christianity had swept like a blazing fire through the Oikumene (*incendia concitarunt*).[119] Earlier pagan charismatics were well advised to beware of arson, and most of them circumspectly avoided launching a "movement."

The basic difference between ancient mysteries, on the one hand, and religious communities, sects, and churches of the Judeo-Christian type, on the other, is borne out by the verdict of history. Jewish, Christian, and Islamic sects have demonstrated astounding capacities for survival, even as minorities in a hostile environment. The Samaritans, split from Jewish orthodoxy, have survived in the world for about 2,400 years; the Mandaeans are about as old as Christianity; the Albingensian movement survived even the European Inquisition; countless sects have been active ever since the Reformation. Christian outposts in Ethiopia, Armenia, and Georgia are no less remarkable for this tenacious vitality. It was quite different with the ancient mysteries, whether those of Eleusis, Bacchus, Meter, Isis, or even Mithras, the "invincible god." With the imperial decrees of 391/92 A.D. prohibiting all pagan cults and with the forceful destruction of the sanctuaries, the mysteries simply and suddenly disappeared. There is not much to be said for either the Masons' or modern witches' claim that they are perpetuating ancient mysteries through continuous tradition.[120] Mysteries could not go underground because they lacked any lasting organization. They were not self-sufficient sects; they were intimately bound to the social system of antiquity that was to pass away. Nothing remained but curiosity, which has tried in vain to resuscitate them.

Figure 1. Daduchos Vase, Eleusis. Priest with two torches (*daduchos* or hierophant), in rich dress, leading an initiand, with bundle of twigs, toward initiation. Female figure representing Eleusis (?).

Figure 2. Eleusinian initiation. Heracles, in lion skin, advancing toward a low altar with a pig for sacrifice; priest with offering tray, pouring a libation. (See p. 94.)

Figure 3. Eleusinian initiation. Veiled initiand sitting on a stool covered with a fleece, with a ram's horn under his foot; priestess holding a *liknon* over his head. (See p. 94.)

Figure 4. Eleusinian initiation. Demeter, ears of grain in her hair, sitting on a big *kiste,* holding a torch; snake coiling around the *kiste;* initiate with a bundle of twigs, advancing to touch the snake's head. Behind Demeter, Kore approaching with a torch. (See p. 94.)

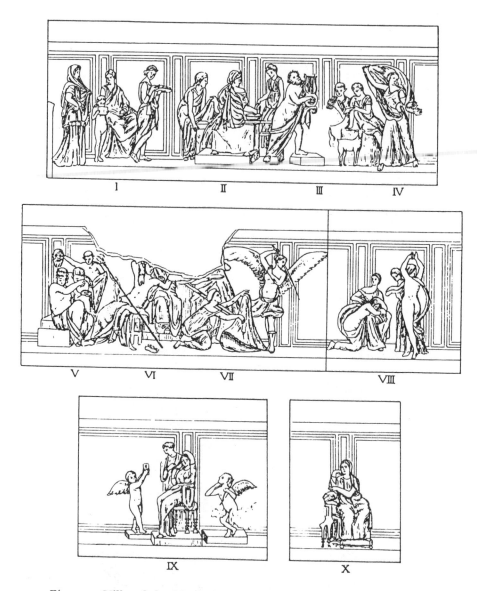

Figure 5. Villa of the Mysteries: survey. I: Woman advancing; boy reading from a scroll; matron; attendant with tray. II: Seated woman revealing a tray and washing her hand. III: Silenus; two satyresses nursing animals. IV: Woman in alarm. V: drinking/lecanomancy? VI: Dionysus and Ariadne. VII: Kneeling female revealing a phallus in the *liknon;* winged demon, wielding a rod, with a gesture of aversion. VIII: Kneeling female exposed; dancing maenad with cymbals. IX: Woman being adorned; two amoretti. X: Seated matron. (See pp. 95–96, 104.)

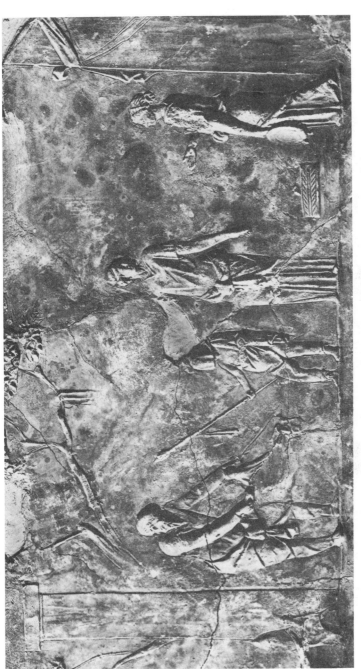

Figure 6. Bacchic initiation. Sanctuary with columns and tree; silenus-like priest revealing a phallus in a *liknon*; boy, carrying a thyrsus, with veiled head, led by a female toward initiation; mystic *kiste*; female attendant with tympanon. (See p. 95.)

Figure 7. Bacchic initiation. Kneeling female revealing a phallus in a *liknon*; female (demon? allegory?) fleeing with a gesture of aversion; seated matron. (See p. 95.)

Figure 8. Festival of Isis. Foreground: sacrifice with priest; two choruses singing under the direction of an Egyptian; flute player to the right; background: temple door flanked by two sphinxes and palm trees; priest exiting with the Nile water vessel ("Osiris") between a black priest ("Anubis") and a priestess ("Isis").

Figure 9. Meter and Attis. Meter enthroned, with tympanon and lion; in the front, portable altar with fire, torch, Phrygian cap, jug and plate; ram and ewe; in the center, pine tree with a shepherd's crook, flute, cymbals; two Corybants with helmets and shields, one grasping Attis, with Phrygian cap and syrinx, collapsing on a rock; behind Meter, a female attendant with cymbals, with aureole (Hecate/Selene?).

Figure 10. Procession for Meter. Four men in Phrygian caps carrying a bier, on which, between the statues of two Phrygian attendants, is the throne of Meter, represented by a *kiste* with pointed lid.

Figure 11. Mithras relief from Neuenheim. Main scene: Mithras killing the bull, tail turning into ears of grain; on Mithras' cloak, raven (destroyed); below, Kautopates and Kautes; snake, scorpion, krater, lion. Frame, starting at bottom left: Persian wielding the globe (?); Kronos asleep; Kronos yielding the scepter to Zeus; Mithras' birth from the rock; bust of wind god.   Mithras making fire with a drill; Mithras shooting at the rock to procure rain; Mithras mounting the chariot of Helios; Moon goddess setting; Mithras shooting at the rock; birth from a fig tree (?).   Bust of wind god; the bull grazing; Mithras carrying the bull; Mithras riding the bull; Mithras dragging the bull to the cave. (See pp. 73–74.)

Figure 12. Mithraic initiation. Naked initiand, kneeling and blind-folded, arms bound behind his back; behind him, mystagogue (wearing a white *tunica* with red lining); advancing dignitary with Persian cap (red cloak; pater?), wielding a spear or staff. (See p. 103.)

III

𝕽𝕽

Theologia and Mysteries
Myth, Allegory, and Platonism

THE TERM "mystery theology" has been widely used ever since Reitzenstein. Yet in comparison to the libraries of theological literature that survive from ancient Judaism and Christianity, the dearth of relevant texts from pagan mysteries is depressing. Cumont called the loss of the liturgical books of paganism the most regrettable one in the great shipwreck of ancient literature.[1] Hopes have been raised and attempts have been made to make good the loss through the study of indirect sources presumed to derive from the sphere of ancient mysteries. Three kinds of texts have been invoked as evidence: the Gnostic/Hermetic literature, the magical papyri, and the Greek romances. These three types are quite different, involving speculative revelation, ritual technique, and seemingly naive narrative. Each group presents its own specific problems, and none of these approaches has proved immune to the attacks of skeptics.

The interpretation of romances as mystery texts was inaugurated by Karl Kerényi and ingeniously pursued by Reinhold Merkelbach.[2] The romance of the "Golden Ass," in the version of Apuleius, ends with initiations into the mysteries of Isis and Osiris, providing the basis for more daring theses. Yet further symbolic interpretations of narrative plots and graphic details have found few adherents. It will be granted, I think, that there is an initiation structure in the plot of most ancient romances,[3] but the same is true of many common Greek myths, as it is of fairy tales. Romances not infrequently introduce elaborate scenes of religious ritual, presenting some of the most vivid depictions of ancient religion, but it is difficult to decide whether these are just for literary effect or indicate some deeper involvement, and whether we are confronted with an isolated motif or with symbols pervading the structure of the whole. The romance that most diligently exploits a religious dimension, Heliodorus' *Aethiopica,* is one of the latest compositions in the series of ancient romances, and it centers not on mysteries proper but on the Helios cult. Thus the romances are notable for their illustrative details but cannot be used independently as a key to mysteries.

The study of the Gnostic and Hermetic literature has been provided with a new foundation by the publication of the Nag Hammadi library.[4] Work is proceeding in many directions, and it is not yet possible to judge the comprehensive picture that will finally emerge. As far as I can see, the new evidence has made it more difficult to maintain the thesis of a pagan origin of Gnosticism, a thesis that had fascinated Reitzenstein and the *religionswissenschaftliche Schule.* If some of the texts are found to be pre-Christian, they still are not pre-Jewish but are attached to the speculations of Hellenistic Judaism. The *Poimandres* treatise in particular, which opens our *Corpus Hermeticum,* has a Jewish-Christian background overlooked by Reitzenstein.[5] Thus whatever elements of pagan mysteries show up are modified by the filter of a religious system that differs radically from the environment in which pagan mysteries were known to thrive. There is, in fact, a downright inflation of terms such as *mysteria* and *mystikos* in Gnostic and Hermetic texts, which causes a corresponding devaluation of meaning. Much of the language is metaphor on the lines established from Plato to Philo;[6] in certain cases, as in the "mystery of the bridal chamber," there is a degree of directness in describing sexual encounters that is hardly paralleled even in the Roman Bacchanalia.[7] The delicate balance of traditional mysteries has broken down. Much work remains to be done for a balanced assessment of Gnostic versus Hellenic religion, but the immediate value of these texts as a source for knowledge of pagan mysteries remains limited.

The interest in magical papyri for the history of religion was initiated by Albrecht Dieterich in his books *Abraxas* and *Eine Mithrasliturgie,* the success of which was lasting and well-deserved.[8] Yet the thesis implied in the title *Mithrasliturgie,* that the fantastic voyage to heaven, as contained in this magical book, was enacted in the mysteries of Mithras, was criticized immediately and can hardly be maintained. The text describes a private trip in a quest for oracular revelations, not a communal mystery rite, with special elaborations on a syncretistic background. There remain puzzling problems in explaining this and similar texts. The tradition of magic and that of mysteries have coexisted for a long time, with multiple contacts and mutual interrelations, especially at the level of charismatic craftmanship. The advent of Demeter at Eleusis has its curious parallel in Egyptian magical texts,[9] and one of the last Eleusinian hierophants was an active, and successful, theurgist.[10] Yet in the magical books recovered from Egypt there is hardly anything directly related to Eleusis or Samothrace, to Bacchus or even Mater Magna. More prominent is Apollo of Delphi in the quest for private oracles, but the Egyptian and the Jewish elements are the most outstanding, sometimes side by side with Christian ones; some Syro-Mesopotamian traits are in evidence as well. This is not the place to inquire more deeply into the distinctions and interrelations of magic and religion. Contrasting tendencies can be seen in the fact that mysteries usually tend to integrate the initiate into a group celebrating a communal festival, a "blessed chorus" or *thiasos,* while the magician remains solitary among his dreams of omnipotence, aiming at the same time at narrowly circumscribed, practical ends: knowledge of the future, possession of riches and concubines. Healing, curiously enough, has receded to the back-

ground in the strata represented by the magical papyri; it is
mainly left to either Asclepius or scientific medicine. On the
whole, the overlap between mysteries and magical papyri is
not extensive enough to extract "mystery liturgies" from the
latter.

It could be held that the quest for mystery texts is essentially futile for more basic reasons: no Nag Hammadi library
of mysteries will ever be discovered because it never existed,
and there was not even a shipwreck as imagined by Cumont.
Is it not true that the mysteries were "unspeakable," *arrheta*,[11]
not just in the sense of artificial secrecy utilized to arouse
curiosity, but in the sense that what was central and decisive
was not accessible to verbalization? There is an "unspeakable
sympatheia" of the souls with the rituals, Proclus states,[12] and
much older is the well-known pronouncement of Aristotle
that those undergoing mysteries (*teloumenoi*) should not
"learn" (*mathein*) but should "be affected," "suffer," or "experience" (*pathein*).[13] This statement, however, calls for qualification; the quotation from Aristotle must be read in its context. Synesius uses it in an effort to distinguish between the
primitive mysticism of Egyptian monks, on the one hand,
who in one jump get from here to highest exaltation and
back to their miserable surroundings, and philosophical mysticism, on the other hand, which leads step by step to higher
levels. At the highest grade of philosophical mysticism,
learning comes to an end, and the pure vision, analogous to
epopteia, is granted to the *teloumenoi*, but only "after they have
become fit for the purpose, of course," as Synesius is anxious
to add. Learning is not denied in the mysteries but rather is
presupposed.

In fact, there are quite a few testimonies about the preparatory "learning" and "transmission" (*paradosis*) that took
place in mysteries, as well as about the "complete" or exact
"knowledge" that was to be acquired.[14] Speech, *logos*, had an
important role to play, and the injunction "not to tell" the
uninitiated was taken so seriously because verbalization was
central to the proceedings. Mysteries were presumed to pos-

sess a "sacred tale," *hieros logos*,[15] and this could well have been contained in a book. Evidently *mystai* were to learn more about gods and their previously unknown details, aspects, or identities. Chrysippus the Stoic considered "transmission" of a "*logos* about gods," that is, "theology," to be the essence of *teletai*.[16] Echoes of such a *logos* are already present in Empedocles and Parmenides,[17] as in the mystagogic speech of Diotima in Plato's *Symposium*.[18]

Books were used in mysteries from an early date. Aeschines, as a boy, had to "read the books while his mother performed the initiations"; such a scene is neatly illustrated at the beginning of the great frieze in the Villa of the Mysteries, and in some other instances.[19] The decree of Ptolemy Philopator requires the initiation priests of Dionysus to hand over their *hieros logos* in a sealed exemplar to a royal official at Alexandria,[20] so that in case of suspicion the secret teachings could be exposed and prosecution by the state could begin. There is no question that those priests all had their books. When the local mysteries of Andania in Messenia were reinstalled in the time of Epameinondas, a tin scroll containing "the" *telete* was appropriately retrieved from the earth at Mount Ithome, and kept from then on among the treasures of the sanctuary.[21] In the cult of Isis, Egyptian books were commonly exhibited.[22] As for Mithras, it is only at Dura-Europus that Magi with books are represented in a wall painting;[23] books of this kind evidently did not penetrate to Pannonia, Germania, or Africa. Considering the fact that most Mithraic epigrams, including the precious inscriptions from Santa Prisca in Rome, are deplorable from a literary point of view, one is led to the conclusion that the worshipers of Mithras were not in close contact with the literary elite. We hear nothing about books in the cult of Meter, or even in relation to the festival at Eleusis; there was family tradition, there was some sort of archive, but there was no library of theology.[24]

The most intriguing fragment of a Hellenistic mystery book is the "Gurob papyrus" in Dublin, which might even

have come from Philopator's collection. The text is very fragmentary, but it is clear that there are invocations to gods and
prayers interspersed with short ritual prescriptions and for-
mulae. Such a structure is more reminiscent of Mesopotamian magical texts than of known Greek types. The reference to a Bacchic-Orphic cult is evident from the gods'
names, including Erikepaios, and ritual details such as the
playthings of Dionysus.[25] Comparable to some degree are
the texts from later Egypt which Merkelbach calls the "oath
of the Isis *mystai*"; unfortunately the remains of the texts
beyond the oath formula are extremely enigmatic.[26] For the
rest, we must try to form an idea of such books from the
secondary testimonies about *hieroi logoi* and the like. There is
an interesting account in Livy of how a praetor at Rome,
trying to eliminate the new forms of religious superstition
that were encroaching on the people under the pressure of
the Hannibalic war, had all relevant books confiscated.[27]
These consisted of books of prophecy (*libri vaticinii*), prayer
books (*precationes*), and prescriptions for sacrifice (*ars sacrifi-
candi conscripta*); nothing resembling "theology" in our sense
is mentioned. We may add the *hieros logos* as a fourth genus.
Plato, however, speaks in a well-known passage about private
mysteries performed by charlatans with many "books of
Musaios and Orpheus" in hand, "according to which they
perform their sacrifices,"[28] thus indicating that a *hieros logos*
in the style of Orpheus and "prescriptions for sacrifice"
might even be identical.

There were *logoi and even written texts in mysteries*, as in
other pagan cults. This fact, however, should not create the
illusion that these texts were the very basis of religion, in the
way in which the Torah, the Bible, and the Koran are credited to be the divine foundation of Judaism, Christianity, and
Islam, respectively. A significant passage about the status of
logoi in the context of religious cults is found in Plato's *Meno*:
Socrates, introducing the doctrine of metempsychosis, pre-
tends to have learned it from "men and women who are wise
about things divine," from "priests and priestesses who care

about being able to give an account of what they are do-ing."[29] This implies that there were other priests and priest-esses who did not care and who just performed their manip-ulations without any "account" (*logos*); they would have learned what to do from traditional practice. In fact, the magical or even religious effect is possible without anteced-ent conceptual clarification, even if Plato evidently prefers those priests and priestesses who are not content with manip-ulating things but endeavor to find a plausible explanation, an "account" that can be communicated to others. This ac-count, however, is not fixed by tradition, nor does it ever become dogma; there was no organization to control a *logos*.[30]

Further illustration comes from the polemical passage by the author of the Derveni papyrus, who complains that the "craftsmen" of private mysteries just take the money but do not lead their clients to "knowledge." The clients, too shy and baffled even to ask questions, thus lose both their money and their hope of attaining knowledge.[31] The author himself is of course anxious to supply such higher knowledge, even if his explanations will strike modern readers as more bizarre than crude mythology. In any event, we learn that although there were *logoi* within practical mysteries, there were additional *logoi* adduced from outside, both from "priests and priest-esses" in need of plausible explanations and from inquisitive intellectuals writing "on mysteries." It was tempting "to take a *logos* from philosophy as mystagogue" in order to penetrate to the core of mysteries[32]—and to discover one's own pre-suppositions. Both sorts of *logoi*, the esoteric and the exo-teric, would of course interact in consequence, as has always happened in theology.

These *logoi* both in the mysteries and about the mysteries, as far as can be seen, developed on three different levels: those of myth, nature allegory, and metaphysics.[33] These levels emerged in a historical sequence, without the later stages destroying the earlier ones; they may be seen as an evolution from the Homeric through the Presocratic to the

Platonic stage. If this sequence is seen as one of increasing intellectual elaboration, the contact with the practice of mysteries declines simultaneously, until in later Platonism one could find just *logos* without any corresponding ritual.

Myth, a form of traditional tale structured by a sequence of actions performed by anthropomorphic "actants," is the oldest and most widespread form of "speaking about gods" in the ancient world, rooted in oral tradition. It especially holds sway over the mysteries. Nilsson, who tended to play down the importance of myth for religion, still had to acknowledge in regard to Eleusis that "myth had an unusually pervasive effect on the religion of Demeter."[34] But the same is true for the mysteries of Meter, Dionysus, and Isis. In general, each divinity of a mystery cult has a specific myth to which he or she is intimately bound. Usually the general outlines are well known; some details, though, are said to be "sacred" and are allegedly kept secret. Thus the myths about Demeter-Persephone[35] and Isis-Osiris[36] are extant in several detailed elaborations. For Attis, by contrast, we have basically one source, the *hieros logos* of Pessinus as published by Timotheus the Eumolpid about 300 B.C., on which Pausanias and Arnobius are dependent.[37] As for Dionysus, there is a rich variety of Bacchic mythology, but with regard to mysteries one tale has commanded attention, perhaps too exclusively: the story of Chthonian Dionysus born from Persephone and slaughtered by the Titans, the ancestors of man. This myth is explicitly connected with the mysteries by several authors,[38] and it seems that Herodotus considered it a secret although he has several allusions to it. Later texts treat it as just part of normal mythology.

More frustrating is the case of Mithras. Clearly there was a Mithras myth; a sequence of stories is documented by the series of scenes that usually surround the central panel of the Mithras reliefs in the caves (see Fig. 11). The center refers to what must have been the fundamental event in this complex, Mithras slaying the bull. But no text has been preserved to tell the story; only the catchword "cattle-thief," *bouklopos*, survives.[39] In the series of representations we may recognize a theogonic sequence depicting Oceanus; Kronos voluntarily yielding the scepter to Zeus; Zeus fighting the giants; and the birth of Mithras from the rock. This last incident is well known in literature as well as in inscriptions—but who was his father?[40] There is also the quest sequence of Mithras finding, pursuing, fighting, subduing, and riding the bull, which is finally dragged into the cave for sacrifice.[41] We see Mithras and Helios feasting on the bull, and Mithras climbing into Helios' chariot. But there are also scenes that remain enigmatic, for example, Helios bowing to Mithras who is threatening him with an object that has been variously identified as a thigh-piece of the bull or a Phrygian cap.[42] Theogony and quest are well-known mythological types, and for the taming of the bull and the institution of sacrifice, Heracles and especially Hermes the cattle-thief provide the closest parallels.[43] The combination of a theogonic succession myth with a quest and combat myth has venerable models from the Babylonian theogony to Hesiod. But considerations of this kind cannot make up for the loss of all the texts that may have told the Mithras myth.

There are indications that even in the other mysteries there were certain parts or aspects of the myths that were only told to the initiates, sealed by horrible oaths of secrecy. Allusions point to particularly bizarre, cruel, or obscene incidents. There are hints of Demeter's sexual relations in an Eleusinian setting and the birth of a child,[44] or of various castration stories;[45] apparently the dismemberment myth of Dionysus was felt by some to belong to this forbidden category. Still it is clear that motifs or tales of this kind, however horrifying, could not constitute the actual secret of the mysteries—nor destroy them when told in public—but would be understandable and impressive only in the whole context of mythological paradigms, ritual signs, preparations, and explanations that led to the "soul's *sympatheia*."

It has long been held that mystery myths are of a particular type, that of the "suffering god." The appropriate Greek

word is *pathea,* "sufferings," and this, connected with rituals
of grief, mourning, and a nocturnal setting, is the proper
content of *mysteria* already in Herodotus.[46] We do find the
abduction of Persephone, and indeed the death of Dionysus,
Attis, and Osiris. There is a sequence of mourning followed
by joy in the mysteries, whether those of Eleusis, Meter, or
Isis. The grief of Demeter ends with the return of Persephone, and "the festival ends with exaltation and the brandishing of torches";[47] at the festival of Mater Magna, the *dies
sanguinis* is followed by the Hilaria, the day of joy;[48] the
mourning rituals of Isis end with the finding of Osiris, the
water of the Nile: "We have found, we rejoice together."[49]
Firmicus Maternus describes a mystery scene in which, after
days of lament in the presence of an idol lying on a litter,
light is brought in and a priest anoints the throats of the
mourners, saying in a whispering voice: "Be confident, *mystai,* since the god has been saved: you too will be saved from
your toils."[50] It is unclear to which cult he is referring, but it
is evident that the fate of the initiate is modeled on the fate of
the god as represented in myth and ritual, following the
peripety from catastrophe to salvation.

Nevertheless, some caution and qualification are called
for. The Frazerian construct of a general "Oriental" vegeta-
tion god who periodically dies and rises from the dead has
been discredited by more recent scholarship.[51] There is no
evidence for a resurrection of Attis; even Osiris remains with
the dead; and if Persephone returns to this world every year,
a joyous event for gods and men, the initiates do not follow
her. There is a dimension of death in all of the mystery
initiations, but the concept of rebirth or resurrection of
either gods or *mystai* is anything but explicit.[52] On the other
hand, tales about suffering gods, who may die and still come
back, are not confined to institutional mysteries. The most
striking case is that of Adonis, whose myth is largely parallel
to and probably related to the Attis myth, and whose festivals
imply ritual lament and nocturnal rites but never had the
organization of mysteries reserved for initiates of either

sex.[53] Likewise, the Heracles cult did not develop into any mysteries of Heracles, even though everyone knew about his sufferings, his death, and his ascent to heaven; it was the mysteries of Eleusis that claimed Heracles as their most prominent initiate. In Egypt and Babylonia, the suffering gods Osiris and Marduk[54] did not give rise to mysteries of the Greco-Roman type. Finally, even if we grant the importance of the "suffering god" myth for mysteries, it is virtually impossible to include Mithras in this company. Ugo Bianchi tried to enlarge or generalize the concept of a suffering god, speaking of *dio in vicenda* instead,[55] but it is difficult to see why Mithras in his adventures should be more subject to change or transformation than Heracles or Hermes in their corresponding exploits—or even Apollo, who was born at Delos, fought the dragon, received purification, served Admetus, and so forth. Once again we must acknowledge the special position of the mysteries of Mithras: they are mysteries without a "suffering god" myth, whereas myths of this type are current even outside of mysteries. The dogmatic Christian theology of "dying with Christ and rising with Christ"[56] imposes too narrow a principle on the variability of ancient mysteries and their myths.

There are indications of another use of myths in mysteries that has an even more archaic ring: not dramatization of vicissitude, but foundation of privilege through genealogy. This is the decisive declaration the initiate has to make in Hades, according to the texts of the Bacchic gold leaves:[57] "I am a son of Earth and starry Heaven." This presupposes a story of generation which the initiate has come to "know," in contrast to the others who are excluded from the secret. An inscription at the entrance to the sanctuary of Meter at Phaistos in Crete proclaims that the goddess is offering "a great miracle" to those "who guarantee their lineage," but is averse to "those who wrongly force themselves into the race of the gods."[58] In Plato's Seventh Letter, true philosophical friendship is contrasted with the comradeship resulting from mysteries, evidently those of Eleusis—which did not prevent Callippus from murdering Dion. Surprisingly enough, this form of community is called "kinship of souls and bodies," *syngeneia psychon kai somaton*—"kinship," we must conclude, of initiates among themselves and probably with gods.[59] In fact in the pseudo-Platonic *Axiochus*, the addressee, a dying man in need of consolation through philosophy, is termed "kinsman of the gods," *gennetes theon,* again in the context of Eleusinian mysteries. These are tiny scraps of evidence, but considering the enormous role of "charter myths" and especially of genealogical myths in archaic society, we must seriously consider these indications of some ancient form of "speaking about gods" through myth, as well as about the effects of the mysteries.[60]

Much more numerous are the testimonies for a loose and playful use of myth in mysteries. Without a need for consistency, but rather with an affection for details, myth communicates living experience. The Eleusinian *mystai* abstain from food, as Demeter did in her grief, and they end their fast when the first star is seen, because Demeter did the same; they carry torches, because Demeter lit them at the flames of Mount Aetna;[61] but they do not sit on the well because Demeter sat there, mourning for her daughter.[62] The hymn to Demeter makes the goddess perform what must have been part of the initiation ritual: sitting down on a stool covered with a fleece, veiling her head, keeping silence, then laughing and tasting the *kykeon*.[63] The worshipers of Isis imitate their goddess, beating their breasts and wailing for Osiris, but bursting into joy when the god has been found again.[64] The castrated *galloi* clearly impersonate Attis. Since Attis is said to have died under a pine tree, this kind of tree is brought into the sanctuary with fillets hanging from its branches; these are said to be the bandages with which Meter tried to stop Attis' bleeding, and she adorned him with spring flowers, like the flowers hanging from the tree.[65] At the same time the tree represents the nymph who lured Attis into infidelity, and for this reason it is cut and "killed" on account of the wrath of Meter.[66] As for Dionysus, things "brought in" in the mysteries are said to correspond to the dismemberment myth;[67] these might include the phallus in the *liknon*. The initiates wear wreaths of black poplar because this tree is said to grow in the netherworld, where Chthonian Dionysus belongs.[68] The enthronement of Chthonian Dionysus by his father Zeus, and especially the playthings and the mirror brought to him in myth and used in ritual, clearly refer to an initiation pattern;[69] once Dionysus himself is called *mystes*,[70] and Attis too is assimilated to his followers.[71] Plutarch says that the sufferings of Isis, as enacted in the *teletai*, should be a lesson in piety and a consolation to men and women caught in "similar sufferings."[72]

Thus in general and in detail, in correspondence and opposition, myth provided a framework for verbalizing more or less important aspects of the mysteries. This is "speaking about god," *theologia*, yet it remains experimental, allusive, and incidental—far from systematic theology.

The second level of explanation to appear regularly in the evidence pertaining to mysteries is that of allegory. This has attracted less attention and sympathy from scholars because it seems a far cry from what is usually considered "mystic," belonging instead to dry rhetorical exercise. We normally take allegory to be a kind of rationalizing sophistry, duly reflected in textbook rhetoric but apt to destroy any genuinely religious feeling or outlook. One ought to keep distinct, however, the two directions of allegorical elaboration. On the one hand there are abstract conceptions secondarily clothed in quasi-mythical garb, from Prudentius' *Psychomachia* to *The Pilgrim's Progress*; on the other hand there is a traditional text or tale that is partially decoded with reference to a more rationalistic system of thought. This was done mainly with Homer, and with the Old Testament in a later period. In the first case the clothes may be thrown away with a change of fashion, whereas in the other case there always remains some unexplained and tantalizing residue.

Allegorical interpretation has been exhaustively dealt with in relation to Stoics, Jews, and Christians.[73] Regarding its use in pre-Hellenistic times, a most important text has come to light with the papyrus of Derveni. In fact it is the pre-Socratic world view, centering on Nature (*physis*), refined but not basically changed by the Stoics, that provides the reference system for this earlier form of Greek allegory. Not very much attention, however, has been paid to the fact that, beginning with the Hellenistic age, allegory has commonly been called "mystic." Most explicit is Demetrius, in his book *On Style*: "What is surmised (but not overtly expressed) is more frightening . . . What is clear and manifest is easily despised, like naked men. Therefore the mysteries too are expressed in the form of allegory, in order to arouse consternation and dread, just as they are performed in darkness and at night."[74] Macrobius concurs: "Plain and naked exposition of herself is repugnant to nature . . . she wishes her secrets to be treated by myth. Thus the mysteries themselves are hidden in the tunnels of figurative expression, so that not even to initiates the nature of such realities may present herself naked, but only an elite may know about the real secret, through the interpretation furnished by wisdom, while the rest may be content to venerate the mystery, defended by those figurative expressions against banality."[75] Macrobius is alluding to the Heraclitean saying, "Nature wishes to be concealed,"[76] which is often used in this context. Thus Strabo, following Posidonius, refers to "concealment in mysteries" which "imitates Nature that shuns direct perception."[77] This concept can also be turned against the mysteries: "You learn more about nature in mysteries than about gods," the Epicurean states in Cicero's *De natura deorum*,[78] and a Christian author mockingly adds: "Why should it have been necessary to hide what is known to all?"[79] It was difficult indeed to justify why mysteries should be superimposed on nature. Interpretation had in fact taken the opposite course, imposing *physis* on the mysteries. In order to make acceptable to a more enlightened mind what the curious experience of shuddering and amazement in ritual and the bizarre details of myth were about, it was gratifying to arrive at "natural" realities. Allegory, therefore, was more needed in mysteries than in less perplexing cults. If nature through these proceedings received some "mysterious" splendor, this was all the more welcome in philosophy.

In consequence, all allegorization in a religious context could be termed "mystic." This is especially true in Philo, who is always prepared to play the mystagogue to the deeper meanings of scripture, guiding those who are "uninitiated to allegory and to nature that wants to be concealed."[80] One long passage in Philo is formally modeled on a mystery *logos:* "We are teaching *teletai* to initiates worthy of the most sacred initiations." His starting point, incidentally, is the explicit mention of "carnal knowledge" in the Bible; his "mystic" allegory, though, does not substitute nature in the Greek sense, but a system of virtues generated by God. Yet no other passage in Philo is so saturated with mystery metaphor.[81] It is hardly less remarkable that the one occurrence of the word *mysterion* in the Gospels is in the context of allegory, the parable of the sower.[82] In this case the imagery taken from nature is used to conceal the dynamics of the divine *logos.* Even in Plotinus the word *mystikos* is used just once, in an allegorical passage that finds some sense in phallic herms.[83]

If we try to focus not on the rhetorical use of mystery metaphors but on the phenomenon itself reflected in this usage, two observations can be made. First, mysteries easily offered themselves to allegorizing in terms of nature, and it was not only officious outsiders who indulged in the method but often the insiders themselves, "priests and priestesses," as it seems, who wanted "to give an account of what they were doing." As for Eleusis, it was no problem to recognize Mother Earth in Demeter, and Persephone consequently became grain or, in a more refined way, the "life breath" which is "transported and killed in the grain."[84] It was also said that the dead returned to the womb of the universal mother, that they were Demetreioi in this sense; if golden ears of grain are buried with the dead, allegory seems to turn into faith.[85] Indeed, the ear of grain exhibited by the hierophant at

Eleusis would perfectly embody these aspects of natural growth—*physis*—and the cycle of life through death.[86] So much for the insiders; the outsiders could speculate as well about the development of culture as contained in the message of the mysteries, the invention of agriculture and of grinding the grain.[87]

Mater Magna too was commonly understood as Mother Earth, and thus was identified with Demeter in a "mystic" (that is, allegorical) way. Bizarre details of her cult were explained along these lines: castration is mowing the ears of grain; the *galli* cutting their arms with knives at the *dies sanguinis* reenact the yearly wounding of the earth with ploughshares; and if the Mother Goddess goes to her bath in the Almo River afterwards, this means that the earth needs irrigation now. These explanations, transmitted by Tertullian,[88] clearly come from the *galli* and their adherents, who need to find method in their madness. In fact, the equation of Attis and the ear of grain—of castration and mowing— recurs even in a hymn invoking Attis himself;[89] allegory has made its way into liturgy. Firmicus Maternus too expressly states that the priests of Meter are anxious to stress the *physica ratio* of their cult.[90] The ears of grain also appear on votive reliefs from the cult of Meter, doubtless expressing the believers' view.[91] Of course, it could not be forgotten that man is dependent on the fertility of the earth; thus allegory in the mysteries would open up the magical dimension of influencing the periodic powers of life through ritual.

The identification of Dionysus with grapes and wine is known everywhere and is anything but a secret; but if the dismemberment myth with all its gory details is made to correspond step by step to the production of wine, this is done by "nature allegorists" (*physiologountes*), who at the same time refer to things "brought in" and exhibited in the mysteries;[92] in other words, these interpreters are initiates in search of a plausible *logos*. A book on *Homeric Allegories* states that the identity of Apollo and the Sun God is clear from the "mystic *logoi*" as told in "the secret *teletai* about the gods."[93] It is difficult to tell which mysteries the author has in mind, yet some thought they could identify both Dionysus and Apollo with the sun.[94]

We find nature allegory no less developed with regard to the cult of Isis and Osiris. Such allegory is the normal explanation of the whole cult in its Hellenized form, not just of mysteries. In fact, authentic Egyptian tradition has linked Osiris to the Nile, the life-giving water that dwindles away and yet comes back with the flood in summer. The vessel with Nile water was exhibited in the ceremonies and carried in processions, and some kind of artificial Nile flood could be produced in the sanctuaries.[95] Hence the simplest "philosophizing" account, according to Plutarch,[96] portrayed Isis as the earth (she had been identified with Demeter as early as Herodotus), Osiris as the Nile, and Typhon as the sea into which the river is dispersed. The romance of Heliodorus has the same equations: these things are told to the *mystai*, he says, but withheld from the profane by those "natural philosophers and theologians" who function as priests in Egypt.[97] The same account, with refinements, is found in a text of Porphyry which probably derives from Chairemon, an Egyptian priest writing at the time of Nero;[98] thus for once we can identify one of these allegorizing priests advertising Egyptian lore to an educated public. According to Chairemon, Isis is the fruit-bearing power in both the earth and the moon, whereas Osiris is the fruit-producing power of the Nile. Plutarch in turn represents Osiris as the procreative power of moisture in general, while Isis remains the power that governs the earth; this more elaborate theory is explicitly attributed to "the priests."[99] The peripety from mournful to joyous festivals was thus correlated to the change of the seasons, "the guarantee of the crops coming back, the elements living, the year replicating itself."[100] One could also make Osiris the grain, dispersed and found again.[101] All these explanations were secondary compared to the immutable ritual tradition, but it was the possibility of a "natural" meaning combined with the ambiguous duality of unspoken and rational elements that fascinated people and was felt to be "mystical" in a special, if derivative, sense.

Mithras was identified with the sun at an early date, and Mithras Helios or Mithras Sol is invoked in countless Mithraic inscriptions.[102] In the iconography of Mithraic monuments, however, Mithras and Helios are kept distinct. But the reference to Nature—to the whole cosmos—is made plain in this cult by an elaborate symbolism. Whereas in the cults of Meter and Demeter and those of Dionysus and Isis the naturalistic interpretations clearly are a secondary and intermittent layer covering a more ancient and sometimes recalcitrant structure of anthropomorphic myth, in Mithraism Hellenistic cosmology seems to be present at the foundations of the system. There is the cave mirroring the cosmos, covered by the vault of heaven with the zodiac; there are the seven planets governing the seven grades of initiation. The sacrifice of the bull always has a cosmic setting, between the rising sun and the setting moon.[103] Yet the identification of the bull and the moon seems secondary again; it does not exhaust the meaning of the sacrifice. The movement of the sun in the cycle of the year directly enters the ceremonies; some Mithraea had openings through which a ray of the sun would penetrate on certain days right to the central panel, illuminating the head of the god.[104] Agriculture is inaugurated once again by the god as the tail of the collapsing bull turns into ears of grain.[105] Mithras is also a gardener, guarding fruit trees and providing water, but we unfortunately have no texts to give us the details of what is in the pictures. Nevertheless, there are some flaws and contradictions in the cosmic elements that point to the conclusion that even here these references are secondary compared to an autonomous ritual-religious system. There is no uniformity in the correlation of initiation grades and the planets, but instead conflicting sequences,[106] and Helios plays such a prominent role in the mythical scenes that he cannot be considered just one of the seven planets, as science would require. The "seven stars" appear as an addition to the sun and moon, as if they were not a part of them. Older, prescientific categories still loom large in Mithraism.

A special offshoot of Hellenistic science is astrology. This too made its impact on the cult of Mithras—whereas there is hardly a trace of it in the other mysteries. An inscription at the central Mithraeum of Rome at Santa Prisca refers to astrological data.[107] One literary text explains the killing of the bull in astrological terms as the sun passing through the sign of Taurus. This is the "esoteric philosophy" of these mysteries, the author says, admitting that this is not the accepted meaning, but at the same time claiming that it comes from the insiders of the cult.[108] Some modern scholars have tried to take further steps along this path and derive more and more details of myth and cult from astrological data.[109] I must confess my skepticism. Astrology can be developed to such a level of subtlety and sophistication that it will fit practically anywhere, and thus its explanatory value will be almost nil. Yet it must be acknowledged that astrology provides another level or "code" with which one can make sense of what was going on—another attempt at *logos*, agreeable to some and unintelligible to others. The mysteries themselves probably antedate these explanations too.

A new and third level of interpreting mysteries was inaugurated by Plutarch's book on Isis and Osiris, in which, instead of plain "nature," metaphysics in the wake of Plato is made the reference system. Retelling and analyzing the myth of Isis and Osiris, Plutarch first repeats the current interpretations along the lines of nature allegory, which he expressly attributes to the priests,[110] but then he raises his analysis to a higher level. It is impossible that the principles of the universe should be corporeal; neither earth nor water can be divine in themselves, but at best are permeated by suprasensual potencies. He invokes "*teletai* and sacrifices"[111] by non-Greeks and Greeks for his thesis that there is a basic metaphysical dualism involving the good and unifying principle and its antagonist, the principle of dispersion and annihilation, working together on "matter" which "receives"

their impact, *hyle dektike:* this is Isis, between Osiris and
Typhon. Nature allegory, by comparison, is coarse and
clumsy.[112]

Following Plutarch, many Platonic writers invoked the
mysteries for confirmation of the basic tenets of their philosophy, for illustration, or for the addition of a religious dimension to the exercises of philosophical dialectic. This went
so far that Numenius once felt he had betrayed the secret of
Eleusis through philosophy.[113] Personal connections began
to play a role, too; Plutarchus, the founder of the last
Academy of Athens, was the son or grandson of Nestorius
the hierophant.[114] We still have only a faint idea of what
Platonic Eleusis was about; apparently it was less concerned
with the fate of Kore and sowing grain than with some procedures of the hierophant at the great nocturnal festival. The
Naassene Gnostic equates the ear of grain exhibited by the
hierophant in the Telesterion with the castrated Attis;[115] this
is not just his private and perverse fantasy, because in an
allusive but unmistakable way the Isis-hymn of Mesomedes
gives the same indication.[116] The movement toward generation thus is interrupted, and the return to higher origins is
made to start; this Gnostic interpretation is basically Platonic.

It is even more with regard to the mysteries of Meter and
Attis that the Gnostics, the emperor Julian, and Sallustius
join in strange fascination with the castration phenomenon.
The most disgusting and absurd detail becomes integrated
into the most sublime evolution of transcendent being. The
One, generating the spiritual and the psychic world as a
father, continues to create even the material world until
finally it has to come to a stop, lest it lose itself in unlimited
profusion. Progress suddenly has to turn into regression:
this is cutting the genitals.[117] Procreation comes to a halt, and
the stability of being is secured as it is made to turn back to
the origin. Whatever psychologists may think about these
sublimations of sexual fantasies, the historian of ideas should
take these explanations seriously, as Julian did, even if they
seem to indicate a loss of life force and the desperate attempt

by a dying paganism to stop the flux of change that was transforming the world.

In a similar way the most bizarre myth of Dionysus, the god's dismemberment by the Titans, was transported into Platonic metaphysics. A starting point was provided by the famous passage in Plato's *Timaeus* about the creation of the world soul from an "undivided" and a "divided" principle mixed with intermediate being.[118] The mixing bowl of Dionysus, the krater, is mentioned for illustration in this context. Some interpreters went further. The combination with the Dionysiac dismemberment myth occurs in Plutarch and in Plotinus[119] and is most fully developed in the later Neoplatonists from Proclus to Damascius.[120] Mythical Dionysus is said to stand for the divine principle that is divided up in the plurality of real bodies in this world of ours, to be reassembled again and restored to the primordial unity.

A Platonizing perspective is also apparent in the mysteries of Mithras. This is not the place to summarize the studies of Robert Turcan and Reinhold Merkelbach.[121] That the caves of ritual where the *mystai* met, and the cave of myth where the bull was slaughtered, indeed represent the cosmos contained by the vault of heaven and governed by the planets is evident from the iconography, and this is expressly stated by Porphyry on the authority of Eubulus.[122] Mithras is the creator, *demiurgos,* of the universe. No further details about either the myth or its interpretations are to be found in our texts; it is not even clear to what extent Mithras promised salvation from this cosmos or preservation and superiority within the world ordained by Mithraic powers.[123]

This much, however, is made plain by the words of Porphyry: if the Mithraic authors Eubulus and Pallas saw the doctrine of transmigration enacted in the mysteries, this was their own opinion, which for them was the "true and exact" one, but the "general tendency" of belief (belief of the *mystai,* of course) was unaware of it all.[124] This leads one to reflect on the very special status of *logoi* about the human soul in mysteries. In fact, we meet with a paradox: in the perspective of "religions of salvation," concern and doctrines about the soul should be the very center of interest; yet in the evidence there is hardly even a faint indication of this, whether in the mysteries of Eleusis,[125] Dionysus,[126] Meter, Isis, or Mithras. Ancient mysteries were a personal, but not necessarily a spiritual, form of religion.

Compared to the *logoi* in mysteries discussed so far, a doctrine about the soul, and in particular the doctrine of transmigration, is of a quite different order. In essence, such a doctrine is not *theologia* but anthropology, fantastic and yet recalling alleged experiences and predicting future ones; it thus lays claim to truth in the most direct sense, in contrast to the playful experimentation that is always apparent in the interpretation of myth.

Transmigration of souls is a doctrine that suddenly appeared in the Greek world toward the end of the sixth century B.C. We find the name of either Pythagoras or Orpheus attached to it,[127] and we have the word of Plato that it was told in mysteries, *teletai*, and found "strong believers" there.[128] The indications of Pindar, the oldest and most extensive witness, are compatible with this.[129] The gold leaves, related to Bacchic mysteries, seem to imply transmigration too, even if this is not expressly asserted.[130] In addition there are the cryptic statements, to be found mainly in Plato, about the soul enclosed in the "prison" of the body, being punished for unspeakable ancient crimes, waiting for release ordained by the god. Orpheus is mentioned in this connection, as well as "the priests of mysteries."[131]

It is all the more remarkable that beyond this evidence, which is concentrated in the fifth and fourth centuries, there is nothing to suggest that belief in transmigration was a basic or essential tenet of mysteries as practiced. There remains the impression of a "drop of foreign blood"[132] that had its impact on some forms of Bacchic mysteries and may have been connected with books of Orpheus at an early date. It was a transient symbiosis of mysteries and spiritual doctrine that developed in this way, in which neither part was essentially dependent upon the other. The idea of transmigration lived on mainly on the authority of Plato, as an incentive to speculation for Platonists, Gnostics, and Christians. In this way, even the potentiality of dogma remained experimental in the sphere of mysteries. In a similar way and even more, the form of *theologia* associated with them was to remain distinct from the theology of later times.

IV

🎝🎝🎝🎝🎝🎝🎝🎝🎝🎝🎝🎝🎝🎝🎝🎝🎝🎝🎝🎝🎝🎝🎝🎝🎝🎝🎝🎝🎝

The Extraordinary Experience

"FORGET ABOUT THE AUGUST MYSTERIES" was the parents'
cry of despair at the loss of their child, indicating that they
had relied on the practical effect of mystery rites; "awaken
the memory of the solemn *telete* in the *mystai*" is the prayer of
initiates in the Orphic hymn to *Mnemosyne*, the goddess of
Memory, pointing toward an effect of a different order.[1]
Mystery festivals should be unforgettable events, casting
their shadows over the whole of one's future life, creating
experiences that transform existence. That participation in
mysteries was a special form of experience, a *pathos* in the
soul, or *psyche*, of the candidate, is clearly stated in several
ancient texts; given the underdeveloped state of introspec-
tion in the ancient world, as seen from a modern vantage
point, this is remarkable. Aristotle is said to have used the
pointed antithesis that at the final stage of mysteries there
should be no more "learning" (*mathein*) but "experiencing"
(*pathein*), and a change in the state of mind (*diatethenai*).[2]

Dio of Prusa, in an elaborate simile, is more explicit: "If
one would bring a man, Greek or barbarian, for initiation
into a mystic recess, overwhelming by its beauty and size, so
that he would behold many mystic views and hear many
sounds of the kind, with darkness and light appearing in
sudden changes and other innumerable things happening,
and even, as they do in the so-called enthronement cere-

mony [*thronismos*]—they have the initiands sit down, and they
dance around them—if all this were happening, would it be
possible that such a man should experience just nothing in
his soul, that he should not come to surmise that there is
some wiser insight and plan in all that is going on, even if he
came from the utmost barbary?" The intended reference is
to the cosmos, the dance of stars and sun around the earth
and other marvels of nature that surpass the artful contriv-
ances of mystery ceremonies; the comparison of the cosmos
with a huge mystery hall goes back to the Stoic philosopher
Cleanthes, who lived in Athens and in all probability was
thinking of Eleusis, which is less clear in the case of Dio. Dio's
text nevertheless gives an impression of what went on at a
mystery festival, and what the expected effect was: "something is bound to happen in the soul," so that initial bewilder-
ment is changed into wonder, and acceptance of sense.[3] In
religious terms, mysteries provide an immediate encounter
with the divine. Let us remember that Marcus Aurelius put
mysteries between dream visions and miraculous healing as
one of the forms in which we may be certain of the care of
the gods.[4] In psychological terms, there must have been an
experience of the "other" in a change of consciousness, moving far beyond what could be found in everyday life. "I came
out of the mystery hall feeling like a stranger to myself"—
this is a rhetor's description of the experience at Eleusis.[5]

It is here that objective scholarship has to face insur-
mountable difficulties. The secret of the mysteries has usually been guarded. At best, we are in the situation of eaves-
droppers, of strangers at the gate, as described by Dio in
another simile:[6] "Servants of the mysteries, who outside, at
the doors, adorn the porches and the altars set in public . . .
but never get indoors . . . they will perceive some of the
things inside, be it that one mystic word is cried out, or that
fire is seen above the walls"—but they remain "servants," not
"*mystai*." But if we had a fuller account, or even a filmed
record such as modern anthropologists provide to document
exotic customs, we would still be baffled. The gap between

pure observation and the experience of those involved in the real proceedings remains unbridgeable. Who can tell what the experience is like without having undergone days and days of fasting, purifications, exhaustion, apprehension, and excitement?[7] The secret of Eleusis was violated in a provocative way by Diagoras of Melos, who is said to have told it in the streets to everyone[8]—and he made it look vile and unimportant by doing this. The secret was also exposed by a Gnostic writer from the "Snake Sect," a "Naassene" whose sermon is quoted by Hippolytus.[9] Hence we have two glimpses of the celebration: "The Athenians, celebrating the Eleusinian mysteries, show to the *epoptai* the great, admirable, most perfect epoptic secret, in silence, a reaped ear of grain." The second description says: "The hierophant, at night at Eleusis, celebrating the great and unspeakable mysteries beneath a great fire, cries aloud, saying: The Lady has born a sacred son, Brimo has born Brimos." But this too, removed from the context of preparations, of concomitant anxiety and concentration, remains a cipher that may invite flights of fantasy[10] but fails to convey authentic experience.

Much of the remaining evidence is metaphor. The language of mysteries is used to illustrate intellectual or emotional situations of a different kind. Plato had led the way, and rhetoric was eager to exploit even the effects of the *arrheton*. There is still a chance that we can use this language as a mirror in order to catch a glimpse beyond the walls. Most impressive is a text of Plutarch that attempts to describe the presumed process of dying in terms of a mystery initiation.[11] At the moment of death, "the soul suffers an experience similar to those who celebrate great initiations . . . Wanderings astray in the beginning, tiresome walkings in circles, some frightening paths in darkness that lead nowhere; then immediately before the end all the terrible things, panic and shivering and sweat, and amazement. And then some wonderful light comes to meet you, pure regions and meadows are there to greet you, with sounds and dances and solemn, sacred words and holy views; and there the initiate, perfect by now, set free and loose from all bondage, walks about, crowned with a wreath, celebrating the festival together with the other sacred and pure people, and he looks down on the uninitiated, unpurified crowd in this world in mud and fog beneath his feet." It is plausible that Plutarch has Eleusis in mind, but the Telesterion building has disappeared, since elements of the real proceedings are fused with Platonic reminiscences and free speculation. We find once more the "sacred views" and "sacred sounds" as in Cleanthes and Dio, but in this text the emphasis is on the exhausting and terrifying events that precede the amazing light.

By far the most influential text about the experience of mysteries is in Plato's *Phaedrus*; imitated again and again by Philo and later Platonists down to Dionysius the Areopagite in "mystic" language, it has in fact become the basic text of mysticism in the true sense. The revelation of true Being brought about by Eros had already been described in the language of mysteries in the *Symposium*, where the distinction between "preliminary initiation" (*myein*) and "perfect and epoptic mysteries" clearly refers to Eleusis.[12] The *Phaedrus* adds the unforgettable image of the soul's chariot ascending to the sky in the wake of the gods, up to the highest summit where a glance beyond heaven is possible. Some dim memory of this view remains in certain souls, to be resuscitated suddenly by images of beauty encountered in this world. All at once we remember how "then resplendent beauty was to be seen, when together with the blessed chorus they . . . saw a joyous view and show, and were initiated by initiations that must be called the most blessed of all . . . celebrating these . . . encountering, as *mystai* and *epoptai*, happy apparitions in pure splendor, being pure ourselves."[13] Although the enchanting quality of the Greek text is inevitably lost in translation, its lasting force is proved by the unique effect it had on the Greek Platonic-mystic tradition. Plato himself, while creating his vision, uses details that clearly refer to Eleusis. The terms *mystai* and *epoptai* are unequivocal; the dancing "chorus" celebrating the *orgia* and the sacred views that convey unforgettable bliss recur in the texts of Dio and Plutarch just quoted, while the "sacred sounds" are omitted because Plato is concentrating on *eide*. There is an oblique allusion to terrifying events, *deimata*, preceding the veneration of the divine.

The allusiveness of these texts stimulates fantasy. Although they fail to provide hard evidence, they do provide a framework for empathy, if not for understanding what mysteries may have meant to participants. The experience is patterned by antithesis, by moving between the extremes of terror and happiness, darkness and light. There are other texts that substantiate and illustrate this ambivalence: Eleusis is both "the most frightening and the most resplendent of all that is divine for men," Aelius Aristides states.[14] If the Eleusinian divinities appear in a dream, this means "for the uninitiated that they bring first some kind of terror and danger, but then nevertheless they bring to perfection what is good."[15] According to Plutarch, "in mystery initiations one should bear up to the first purifications and unsettling events and hope for something sweet and bright to come out of the present anxiety and confusion"; there even is a special kind of "joy, such as the initiands experience, mixed with confusion and depression but full of pleasant hope."[16] Quite common and in fact one of the main characteristics of mysteries is the *makarismos*, the praise of the blessed status of those who have "seen" the mysteries.[17] As the initiate is accepted and hailed by a chorus of those who have gone through the same peripeties of experience, his feelings of relief will rise to the heights of exultation. Yet the texts insist that the true state of blessedness is not in this emotional resonance but in the act of "seeing" what is divine.[18]

We have only some piecemeal information about the details of mystery initiations, which, although it does not add up to form a satisfactory picture, still strikes the imagination with the charm of the fragmentary. For Eleusis we have at least five sets of divergent evidence: the topography of the sanctuary;[19] the myth of Demeter's advent, as told especially in the Homeric hymn;[20] a relief frieze with initiation scenes, known in several replicas;[21] the *synthema*, "password," as transmitted by Clement of Alexandria;[22] and the two testimonies of the Naassene (see n. 9), which clearly pertain to the concluding festival. These testimonies are not totally isolated: an earlier pagan witness—Mesomedes, a poet of the Hadrianic epoch[23]—brings confirmation. In his "Hymn to Isis," he refers with cryptic allusions to the "marriage underground" and the "birth of plants"—which clearly recalls Persephone—and to "the desires of Aphrodite, the birth of the little child, the perfect, unspeakable fire, the Kuretes of Rhea, the reaping of Kronos, cities for the charioteer—all (this) is danced through the *anaktora* for Isis." Here we see the birth of the child and the great fire, the reaping of grain with a background of castration, and finally a reference to Triptolemus, the charioteer: clearly an Eleusinian scenario, which even provides a definite sequence rather than unconnected glimpses. Still, this rapid résumé is not a substitute for experience.

The preparations for initiation are summed up in the *synthema*, which again is intentionally cryptic: "I fasted, I drank the *kykeon*, I took out the covered basket [*kiste*], I worked and laid back into the tall basket [*kalathos*], and from there into the other basket [*kiste*]" (see n. 22). What "working" means has best been explained by a casual remark of Theophrastus about making a secret of pounding grain: the initiand apparently had to pound some grain in a mortar; symbolic meanings of the act are at hand, but remain unconfirmed.

The reliefs from the initiation frieze (see Figs. 2–4) depict three scenes: preliminary sacrifice, purification, and encounter with the goddesses Demeter and Kore; the latter is seen approaching. A snake coils from the *kiste* to Demeter's lap, and the *mystes*, distinguished by his bundle of twigs, is seen touching this snake without fear—having transcended human anxiety, moving free and relaxed in a divine sphere. The purification scene, with the veiled initiand sitting on a ram's fleece, clearly reproduces ritual in realistic detail, while the final scene proceeds to a mythical level and thus hides the secret of the ceremonies.

In the topography of the sanctuary, the most evocative detail is the grotto of Pluto, identified by a few dedications, between the Propylaea and the Telesterion. It is not mentioned in any literary text and apparently remained unknown to outsiders. One might connect it with the "frightening paths in darkness that lead nowhere" (see n. 11). But much remains unclear, especially regarding the relationship between individual, preparatory initiation or purification and participation in the great communal festival.

Regarding initiations to Dionysus, there is a special and intriguing iconography in the later evidence, beginning with the famous fresco of the Villa of the Mysteries at Pompeii from the time of Caesar;[24] the stucco reliefs of the Villa Farnesina in Rome, from the time of Augustus, are hardly less important;[25] in the following centuries there are architectural reliefs,[26] scenes on sarcophagi,[27] and one mosaic from Djemila-Cuicul in Algeria[28] which most likely adorned a cult room. The most striking item in this imagery is a huge erect phallus in a winnowing basket, *liknon*, covered by a cloth, being unveiled either by a kneeling female, as in the Villa painting, or by a silenus in front of a veiled, advancing boy.[29] This evidently is "showing a sacred object"; it is a "hierophantic" scene. It is easy to add interpretations about encountering divine potency, or just sexuality, in the context of some "original" puberty ritual. The tale of Psyche and Eros has been adduced in this connection,[30] which might provide a mythical sequence in the sense of the *psyche* becoming acquainted with eros. The climactic scene occurs when Psyche first beholds her partner unveiled by the light of her lamp; this is followed by a period of tribulation before the happy ending.

It is appropriate to read the Villa frieze (see Fig. 5) as a sequence, beginning with the woman entering on the left and then proceeding through purification and a transient

idyll of satyric life to the mysterious revelation of the god at
the central wall. Two main manifestations of Dionysus on
either side of the god accentuate the elaborate interplay of
sequential and central composition: the satyr boys manipu-
lating a silver bowl and a mask (wine drinking turning into
catoptromancy?)[31] and the girl unveiling the phallus. These
appear to be two forms of revelation that remain enigmatic
to the uninitiated. The sequence then continues with the
flagellation scene[32] and the frantic dance, indicating both
humiliation and the final bliss. No text has been discovered
to give the true key to interpretation. No direct antecedents
of the Villa pictures have come to light so far;[33] they seem to
bear testimony to a comparatively recent influx of reformed
Dionysiac mysteries that came back to Italy, from where they
had been ousted by the repression of the Bacchanalia in 186
B.C. The *liknon* with phallus appears much earlier in Bacchic
contexts, but without any special "mystic" connotations. It is
carried in a Dionysiac thiasos on an Apulian vase painting;[34]
set on a post or pillar, it characterizes a rural landscape in
Pompeiian—and probably Hellenistic—wall paintings and in
neoclassical reliefs.[35] In a general way, phallus processions
had always been present in the worship of Dionysus. A phallus as such was not much more of a secret than an ear of
grain; the mystery is not in the object.

An older stratum of testimonies regarding Dionysiac initiation puts the emphasis on purification and change of status,
even change of identity. Through Demosthenes' invective
against Aeschines we discern a nocturnal ceremony which
includes putting on fawn skins and setting up a krater with
wine. The initiands, seated, are then smeared with a mixture
of clay and chaff; from the dark the priestess appears like a
frightening demon; clean again and rising to their feet, the
initiates exclaim "I escaped from evil, I found the better,"
and the bystanders yell in a high, shrieking voice (*ololyge*) as
though in the presence of some divine agent. In the daytime
there follows the integration of the initiates into the group of
celebrants, with the *thiasos* moving through the streets; peo-

ple are crowned with fennel and white poplar; they dance and utter rhythmic cries, carrying the *kiste* and the *liknon*, and some brandishing live snakes. Terror has become manageable for the initiate.[36] Plato, in an elaborate metaphor, alludes to the change effected in the soul (*psyche*) by initiatory ritual; the "great *tele*" that first make the soul void of all the powers that once haunted it mean "purification," and then a jubilant chorus, crowned with wreaths, brings in new powers to hold sway thereafter.[37] Plato's interest is in the psychological process; he fails to provide details of the ritual, but the outlines he gives are compatible with Aeschines' proceedings.

Initiation to Isis is described in a single text, the famous passage in Apuleius' *Metamorphoses*. It is the only first-person account of a mystery experience that we have. It is not only fiction, though, within a parodistic romance; it is decidedly figurative and playfully allusive: "Dear reader, you may awfully wish to know what was said and done afterwards. I'd tell if it were allowed . . . But I shall not keep you in suspense with perhaps religious desire nor shall I torture you with prolonged anguish." This is the introduction to the most often quoted sentences: "I approached the frontier of death, I set foot on the threshold of Persephone, I journeyed through all the elements and came back, I saw at midnight the sun, sparkling in white light, I came close to the gods of the upper and the nether world and adored them from near at hand."[38] This is what happened at night; the following morning the initiate is presented to an admiring crowd, placed on a podium in the middle of the temple, holding a torch, and wearing a complicated twelve-fold garment and a crown imitating the rays of the sun.[39] For the nocturnal experience one might imagine a fantastic apparatus, elaborate machinery to produce all kinds of apparitions, as some imagined for Eleusis before the excavations revealed the barren soil in the midst of the Telesterion, without any underground passages or room for machinery.[40] It is probably more accurate to think of the power of simple ritual symbolism: there is "purification" by the "elements" of water, air, and fire, as Servius points out.[41] Purification by air is accomplished by the *liknon*, which, in practical life, "purges" grain of husks. For purification with fire, torches are used, and the sparkling light at midnight could be equivalent to the great fire at the Eleusinian hearth on the night of the mysteries. It is left to our imagination as to how the "frontier of death" was reached;[42] there is no further evidence of either a literary or an iconographic kind. Apuleius has succeeded in frustrating our curiosity, just as he intended to do.

For the mysteries of Meter we have an older stratum in the evidence about Corybants, with the enthronement of the initiand occurring while others whirl around him in a frantic dance. Myth has a comparable scene for Dionysus and the Corybants.[43] From late antiquity we get a *synthema*, evidently modeled on the Eleusinian formula: "I ate from the tympanon, I drank from the cymbal, I carried the composite vessel [*kernos*], I slipped under the bedcurtain [*pastos*]" or, in an alternative version, "I became a *mystes* of Attis."[44] *Tympana* and *cymbala* are the ubiquitous emblems of the cult of Meter, but they are put to a strange use or misuse in this text; *pastos* is indicative of marriage. Totally different is the taurobolium in the cult of the Great Mother. As described by Christian authors,[45] the initiand, crouching in a pit, is flooded with 50 liters of blood from the bull agonizing just above. The unforgettable character of this experience is easy to imagine; it would hardly have seemed a blessed state, yet emerging from the pit the initiate is "adored" by the others, as one who has risen to a superior state, and feelings of liberation and a new life would have been overwhelming by contrast, just because of the horrifying procedure undergone before. "I escaped from evil, I found the better" would apply even here; the instrumental and even magical character of the *telete* seems to have been predominant in this case, however.[46]

Mithras stands apart once more. The initiations are more prominent and more sophisticated in these mysteries than anywhere else, since they are multiplied to produce seven grades of initiates: *Korax/corvus*, the raven; *nymphus*, the chrysalis;[47] *stratiotes/miles*, the soldier; *leo*, the lion; *Persa*, the Persian; *heliodromus*, the sun-runner; and *pater*, the father. Each step would have had its own ritual, with preparations, peripeties, and integration,[48] but there is extremely little evidence about the details in either literature or iconography, and the little we do have—some badly preserved frescoes at the Mithraeum of Capua Vetere[49] and some controversial remarks in Christian authors that lead to the problem of initiation tortures[50]—is not clearly correlated to the seven grades.

The basic idea of an initiation ritual is generally taken to be that of death and rebirth. A well-known book of Mircea Eliade has appeared in successive editions under the title of either *Rites and Symbols of Initiation* or just *Birth and Rebirth*.[51] Being essentially initiation ceremonies, ancient mysteries should conform to this pattern, which at the same time seems to supply the best explanation of why this ritual is believed to overcome the threat of real death.[52] Yet, as in the corresponding case of the "dying god" myth,[53] the evidence is less explicit and more varied than the general hypothesis would postulate.

Most telling, for all its allusiveness, is the passage of Apuleius. The mysteries of Isis are to be accepted, the priest says, "in the form of a voluntary death and salvation by grace";[54] the phrase "I set foot on the threshold of Persephone" in the following account seems to correspond to this. The Osiris myth tells how the god was put to death: Seth with his "conspirators" enticed Osiris to lie down in a coffin, and they suddenly shut the lid.[55] This could easily be enacted in an impressive ritual, but there is no corroborating evidence.[56] In any event, the day following the night of initiation is reckoned as a new birthday;[57] Isis has the power to change fate and to grant a new life.[58] This promise of the goddess was to be turned into experience through initiation, in some form or other.

In a similar way, inscriptions at the Santa Prisca Mith-

raeum of Rome[59] and some taurobolium inscriptions[60] indicate that the day of the initiation ritual was a new birthday;
the *mystes* was *natus et renatus*. Birth should in fact be the
proper activity of a Mother Goddess. There is a graphic image in Plato's myth, that of passing "through the throne" of
the Great Goddess Ananke on the way to rebirth, but this is
without clear reference to cultic reality. What we know about
the corybantic *telete* is totally different. The taurobolium
could also suggest an act of birth, when the initiate emerges
from a cave in a garment dripping with blood;[61] but there is
no explicit confirmation.

Least telling is the evidence for Eleusis. Alfred Koerte had
found a ritual of rebirth in the oblique hints of the *synthema*
in combination with a remark in Theodoretus.[62] His theory
had some success, but it collapsed with the discovery of the
passage in Theophrastus about the secrets of grinding grain.
The birth of a divine child is celebrated in the mysteries
according to the Naassene,[63] and there is a much earlier
reference to "tending children" in the recess of Eleusis.[64] But
there are other suggestions and images as well, which seem
to be parallel codes to express the paradox of life in death:
Persephone carried off by Death personified and still coming
back as a joy for gods and men; the ear of grain, cut to
provide seed; the child in the fire, burned to become immortal. This multiplicity of images can hardly be reduced to a
one-dimensional hypothesis, one ritual with one dogmatic
meaning: death and rebirth of "the" god and the initiand.

The myth about Chthonian Dionysus—the child set on the
throne, encircled by Corybants, enticed by Titans, killed,
torn to pieces, and yet born again[65]—is some kind of initiation scenario, and we have evidence that the playthings reminiscent of the god's fate (balls, tops, knucklebones) were used
in the ritual and even kept by the initiates as a token of their
experience and hope.[66] But there is no reason to assume that
the myth was reenacted exactly in this form in ritual. Other
ritual signs—for example, the wearing of a poplar wreath, a
tree said to grow in Hades[67]—indicate the dimension of

death, and the "caves" often mentioned as localities for Dionysiac reveling[68] may have been seen and experienced as a kind of netherworld. But there was nothing as elaborate as the Mithraea. At the Roman Bacchanalia some people were drawn by machines into subterranean caves, we are told, and thus purportedly carried off by the gods; this was actually ritual murder, the accusation said.[69] Such testimony belongs to the eccentricities of these infamous events. There is no word about rebirth.

To sum up, there is a dynamic paradox of death and life in all the mysteries associated with the opposites of night and day, darkness and light, below and above, but there is nothing as explicit and resounding as the passages in the New Testament, especially in Saint Paul and in the Gospel of John,[70] concerning dying with Christ and spiritual rebirth. There is as yet no philosophical-historical proof that such passages are directly derived from pagan mysteries; nor should they be used as the exclusive key to the procedures and ideology of mysteries.

It is appropriate to emphasize in this connection that there is hardly any evidence for baptism in pagan mysteries, though this has often been claimed.[71] Of course there are various forms of purification, of sprinkling or washing with water, as in almost all the other cults as well. But such procedures should not be confused with baptism proper—immersion into a river or basin as a symbol of starting a new life. We have no way to determine what the *Baptai* of the Thracian goddess Kotyto did in Corinth in the fifth century B.C.[72] A fragmentary votive relief from Eleusis has been used and reproduced again and again as evidence for baptism there,[73] yet iconographic typology makes it clear that the little naked boy beneath the goddess is just the first person in a procession of worshipers advancing toward the goddess. The water receptacles in sanctuaries of Isis, again suggestive of baptism to our eyes, were used to represent the flood of the Nile, as Wild's study has shown.[74] We are left with some remarks of Tertullian about *lavacrum* in cults of Isis and

Mithras. This is not to deny that there are some features in early Christian baptism that irresistibly remind one of pagan mystery initiations: the individual ritual upon application, often thwarted by *oknos;* the preparation and instruction; the nocturnal celebration, preferably on the eve of the great common festival, which is Easter; the use of milk and honey; and the curious detail of "stamping on goatskins" (the Eleusinian *mystes* is shown sitting on a ram's fleece).[75] These are probably not just parallels in the common context of initiation patterns but rather some direct borrowings that took place; they are clearly additions to what John the Baptist did at the Jordan. But connections or influences of this kind do not justify large-scale reconstructions. Another ritual firmly rooted in the Jewish tradition, anointing, is likewise scarcely seen in mysteries.[76]

Secrets are meant to arouse curiosity, and once it is aroused, people will not be satisfied with negative answers. Three questions in particular continue to be asked about mysteries: What about tortures? What about sex in the "orgies"? What about the use of drugs? In a way these are legitimate questions, but the attempt to answer calls for differentiation once more.

To harass novices by causing humiliation, pain, or even serious injuries is common practice in initiations, from those of Australian aborigines to those in American universities— at least until recent times. The unsettling experience has the effect of shaking the foundations of personality and making it ready to accept new identities. Pertinent testimonies exist in connection with the mysteries of Mithras: some scornful remarks of Gregory of Nazianzus,[77] some elaborations of his scholiast,[78] and a text of Pseudo-Augustine called "Ambrosiaster."[79] Franz Cumont, the founding father of Mithraic studies, flatly refused to believe the scholiast's information;[80] "fifty days of fasting, two days of flogging, twenty days in the snow" seems too much indeed, and how could there be snow at Dura-Europos or in Africa? A delicate orator such as Himerius could undergo a Mithraic initiation without too much exertion, as it seems, in order to please Julian.[81] Yet it is curious that in the Avestan Mithra Yašt there are days not only of washing but also of "flogging" in preparation for a Mithraic ceremony.[82] More graphic and hence less likely to reproduce mere fantasy is "Ambrosiaster's" account, according to which the candidates, blindfolded, hear the sounds of ravens and of lions, and "some" (most likely those at a certain grade) have their hands tied with chicken guts and are made to stumble into a water basin, whereupon a man comes with a sword to cut the bonds and calls himself "liberator." The frescoes at Capua Vetere,[83] though not well preserved, seem to represent scenes of this very kind. Dangerous encounters with fire must have occurred as well. Some of the lion headed statues are constructed in such a way as to breathe fire through an opening in the stone, and an epigram from Santa Prisca refers to the "lions who burn incense," "through whom we are consumed ourselves."[84] Apparently there were other forms of mock death as well. A curious implement found at the Mithraeum of Riegel in Germany has been explained as a kind of theatrical sword used to represent a man stabbed right through the heart with a spear.[85] Commodus is said to have committed actual murder in the context of a Mithraic cult, and rumors of human sacrifice were occasionally substantiated by skulls found on the spot.[86] Whatever the facts were, the historian of religion may note with satisfaction that Mithraic mysteries conform to the general, well-known patterns of initiation rituals much better than the other ancient mysteries. Mithras appears as a stranger again, more primitive and more authentic, as it were, in the *dromena*.

In the other mysteries, humiliating or painful experiences of this sort seem to be conspicuously absent. Their place is taken in a way by "purification," which may function as a euphemism for saving face even in embarrassing circumstances (for example, while being smeared with clay). Psychological terror, however, is well attested: "all those terrible things, panic and shivering and sweat," to quote Plutarch once more.[87] A man devoted to Mater Magna, a Gallus or

Archigallus, it seems, had to receive a tattoo mark on his body, burned into the skin with hot needles, according to Prudentius.[88] A comparable practice is described for Hellenistic mysteries of Dionysus in the reign of Ptolemy IV Philopator, but this seems to be an exceptional case.[89]

There remains the intriguing depiction in the Villa of the Mysteries of what is no doubt a flagellation scene (see Fig. 5).[90] A kneeling girl, keeping her head in the lap of a seated woman and shutting her eyes, the seated woman grasping her hands and drawing back the garment from the kneeling girl's bare back, while a sinister-looking female behind is raising a rod—these are all quite realistic details of caning. But the threatening figure wielding the rod has black wings; she is not from this world but rather an allegorical personality. Some allusions to flogging in Bacchic contexts have been collected, from Plautus to late sarcophagi.[91] On these we find Pan or satyr-boys being disciplined with a sandal, but the situation and the iconography are quite different. On the other hand, madness is described as feeling the strokes of a whip as early as in Attic tragedy; Lyssa, as "frenzy" personified, appears with a whip in vasepainting,[92] and in any event *mania* is the special province of Dionysus. Not even Aphrodite would disdain a *sublime flagellum* to make an arrogant girl move to her command, as Horace suggests.[93] This would dissolve the flagellation scene into pure symbolism; at the critical moment, with a stroke, divine madness will take possession of the initiate, and the kneeling girl, changed into a true bacchant, will rise and move freely in a frenzied dance just like the other dancer next to this scene. Yet symbolism does not exclude ritual practice, and there are suggestions that one form of purification, *katharsis*, could in fact be flogging.[94] Once more art has succeeded in remaining intentionally ambiguous as to what actually occurred in mysteries.

The modern use of the word "orgies," from *orgia*,[95] reflects the puritan's worst suspicions about secret nocturnal rites. There is no doubt that sexuality was prominent in mysteries. We have the word of Diodorus that Priapos Ithyphallos played a role in nearly all the mysteries, though it was "with laughter and in a playful mood" that he was introduced,[96] and this was hardly the core of the mystery. Processions with a huge phallus were the most public form of Dionysus festivals, the great Dionysia themselves.[97] In puberty initiations, of course, the encounter with sexuality is normal and necessary. The change from childhood through puberty to maturity and marriage is the natural, archetypal model for change of status, and elements of this sequence may well be preserved in mysteries, especially in Dionysiac mysteries. There are indications that only married women, not virgins, could be *bakchai* in the full sense.[98] Plutarch, in the consolation to his wife, refers to their common initiation into the mysteries of Dionysus.[99] The frescoes in the Villa of the Mysteries have also been interpreted as preparations for marriage or a form of Roman Matronalia;[100] the encounter with the phallus unveiled, so prominent in the initiation scenes, perfectly fits such a perspective.[101] The Apulian vases of the fourth century, mainly destined for funerary use and hence most probably related to mysteries of Dionysus, usually depict the encounter of male and female in a Bacchic environment. This type of iconography has been interpreted as referring to a hope for "eschatogamy" in Elysium,[102] the final bliss in the beyond; but these pictures, which have no indications of Hades, may just as well hint at initiations, or at both initiations and afterlife, since the festival of the initiates is going on after death.[103]

Direct and coarse, by contrast, is Livy's testimony regarding the Bacchanalia of 186 B.C.: with as much explicitness as Augustan prudery would allow, he says that the initiands suffered homosexual rape, *simillimi feminis mares*.[104] Scholars at one time gave advice not to believe in slander of this sort, but we can hardly be sure. Parallels from initiations elsewhere are not difficult to find.[105] One might be tempted to make some associations with the curious fact that markedly androgynous representations of Eros become quite prominent in late Apulian vase painting, toward 300 B.C. But if homosexual practice of this kind ever came to exist in closed circles of Italiote mysteries, it evidently could not endure. What we find after the catastrophe of the Bacchanalia is definitely symbolism—sexual symbolism, no doubt, but in a form that could not violate the bodily integrity of any of the participants, and hardly the integrity of their fantasy either, even if there was some emotional response to the phallus in the *liknon*. It is symbolism that shapes the more durable forms of ritual, not the "real" orgies.

One special form of initiation with significant sexual symbolism is reported in connection with the mysteries of Sabazius: a snake made of metal was made to pass beneath the initiand's clothes. This is the "God through the lap," *Theos dia kolpou.*[106] Scholars agree that this is a form of sexual union with the god; in myth Persephone is impregnated by Zeus in the form of a snake, and legend has associated the snakes of Dionysus' *orgia* with the impregnation of Olympias, mother of Alexander, by a god.[107] But in the Sabazius ritual this is transformed through double symbolism—snake for phallus, and artifact for snake. The ritual must have remained impressive enough, but the real dread would come not so much from sexual associations as from the anticipation of touching a snake, especially since the initiand by the light of flickering torches could hardly know for certain what was real and what was artifact. Even here, sexuality in itself is not the secret in question.

The Eleusinian mysteries were notable for their "purity,"[108] which still does not exclude sexual encounters or exhibitions. Iacchus was equated with Dionysus. But so far as we know there was no phallic symbolism, and if there were further "unspeakable manipulations" in the context of the nocturnal ceremonies, the secret has been guarded.[109] Even more in the Mithraic mysteries, warlike virility seems to have suppressed any sexual intimacy; anyhow, it was said that "Mithras hates women."[110] We may still wonder at the attention devoted to the dying bull's genitals in the well-known reliefs, which depict semen being collected in a krater, a scorpion grabbing at the testicles, and the tail turning into ears of grain. This seems to hint at themes of fertilization, castration, and miraculous procreation for which we have no text. Castration remains a fascinating center of interest in the mysteries of Meter; in a way, through its radical negation, sexuality becomes more obsessive here than elsewhere. There is, in addition, the enigmatic hint at a "bridal curtain" in mysteries of Attis.

The picture presented by the cult of Isis is a strange one. There are no overt sexual symbols. Shaved heads and linen clothes, processions, prayers, water, incense, and sistrums all look severe and puritan; if the sacred water of the Nile is identical with the procreative power of the rediscovered Osiris, this is definitely the most diluted form of sexual symbolism. Yet the cult of Isis had a great attraction and a considerable influence not only on *hetairai*; in Rome even a noble matron, Paulina, went to the temple of Isis to spend the night with the god Anubis, who had called her. The god was no god, of course, but rather the Roman *eques* Decius Mundus hiding under a jackal's mask.[111] But one cannot draw many conclusions from this scandal, which caused the emperor Tiberius to ban the priests of Isis from Rome once more; comparable scandals have happened even in Christian sects down to the present day, without affecting, let alone revealing, Christian theology. On the other hand, the very prominence of sexual abstinence in the preparation for the Isis ceremonies[112] draws attention to a center that is veiled. A priest of Isis from Prusa, in a recently published epigram, is praised for having arranged "the bed, covered with linen, which is unspeakable for the profane"; the word used for bed, *demnion*, does not suggest a dining couch.[113] An "unspeakable" ritual of sacred marriage seems to emerge; its correspondences in the Isis-Osiris myth are well known.

To speak of the mysteries of Eros became routine mainly under the impact of Plato's *Symposium*. In later romances and related literature, many a lover is prone to propose to his partner initiation into the mysteries of this special god.[114]

Parallel to this there developed the possibility of making obscene allusions or insinuations by using the language of mysteries;[115] what else could the secrets of night be about? Petronius has a parody of Priapus mysteries in the house of Quartilla that leaves little to be desired in terms of explicitness—except for the fragmentary text.[116] Gnostics were credited by their adversaries with mystery celebrations involving carnal knowledge.[117] If this was true, it was once again a short-lived experiment. Of course sexual abstinence is a normal prerequisite for participation in practically all the mysteries, as it is in certain other cults.[118] This would stimulate expectations and attentiveness to certain signals. Sexuality becomes a means for breaking through to some uncommon experience, rather than an end in itself.

The easy way to uncommon experience is through the use of drugs. The role of drugs in religious contexts has been eagerly explored in recent years; in fact, there are many who will never be persuaded that there could have been mysteries without drugs. Kerényi once thought that the ingredient in the *kykeon* drunk at Eleusis, pennyroyal (*glechon*), may have been mildly hallucinogenic,[119] and others found mushrooms represented in unexpected places.[120] A more sophisticated guess in regard to Eleusis is that ergot (horned rye; *Mutterkorn* in German), a fungus growth on ears of grain, was used. We are told that among its water-soluble constituents are ergonovine and sometimes traces of LSD.[121] But even if the Rharian plain at Eleusis might have been infected by this pest, as Wasson and his adherents surmise, one may wonder about the quantities needed for thousands of participants in order to provide happy visions for all; in addition, ergot poisoning is normally described as quite an unpleasant and not at all a euphoric state. A case could be made for the use of opium at Eleusis, since the poppy, together with the ears of grain, is the constant attribute of Demeter. The Subminoan goddess of Gazi in Crete, adorned with poppies, has been unmasked as a true opium goddess,[122] and an opium pipe is said to have been found at a sanctuary of Kition,

Cyprus, from about the same time.[123] Ovid depicts Demeter putting the Eleusinian child, Triptolemus, to sleep with the use of poppy juice.[124] Thus all the elements are present, but there remains the problem of how opium could have been procured for thousands of initiates who did not even smoke. Speculation might trace a way from an Indo-Iranian Soma cult to the mysteries of Mithras, but evidence is nonexistent.[125]

What is perhaps more important is that the use of drugs, as our time has been doomed to see, does not create a true sense of community but rather leads to isolation. If Carlos Castaneda, with whatever degree of authenticity, has given an account of something resembling drug mysteries,[126] the impressive feature is the long and difficult period of apprenticeship under the direction of a unique master, the "teachings of Don Juan." On a typological level, this is equivalent to the succession of magicians or charismatic "craftsmen," but not to the communal experience of ancient mysteries, open to the public upon request within a few days. A week would have sufficed for Eleusis, and less for Samothrace. For a ceremony such as R. G. Wasson claims to have experienced in Mexico,[127] in which he lay down in a sleeping bag while a shaman kept on singing, the steps of the Telesterion would have been utterly unsuited. A king who wished to do a favor for his *hetaira* during the nights of Eleusis provided her with a seat next to the hierophant,[128] not with a sleeping bag. Thus it is by contrast rather than by analogy that the drug hypothesis helps in the understanding of ancient mysteries.

There is reason to emphasize a more down-to-earth form of communal bliss that was present in all the ancient mysteries: that of feasting or sharing an opulent meal. This again arouses the suspicions of the more puritan observer, as if religion were made a pretext for clearly secular desires. Nilsson denounced the "Pseudo-mysteries of late antiquity."[129] No doubt the krater with wine was at the center of most Bacchic *orgia*,[130] and roast meat was not absent either. But even at the mysteries of Eleusis, following the night of visions, it seems, there were sacrifices of bulls in which the ephebes proved their strength by "lifting up the bulls" for slaughter,[131] which were then to be consumed by the happy crowd. The servants of Meter, the *galloi*, were not allowed to eat cereals but gladly lived on the meat of sacrifices they urged people to offer;[132] a *kriobolion* and even more a *taurobolion* must have been a happy event for them. When the cult of Meter came to Rome, worshipers immediately organized in groups for common feasting.[133] As for Isis and Sarapis, the *deipna* are among the best established facts: adherents of the cult would assemble in an *oikos* on the couches, *klinai*, prepared in a special way for ceremonial eating and drinking.[134] In excavated Mithraea the remnants of animal bones of different species clearly show that the couches were not used for kneeling down in prayer, as Cumont imagined, but for consuming substantial meals.[135] In Mithraic iconography, Mithras and Helios feast together at a table covered with the slaughtered bull's hide—consuming his meat, no doubt, while the lower grades, Raven to Lion, are serving the table.[136] In all these cases the sacrificial meals are realistic, enjoyable festivities with plenty of food, in contrast to the rather parsimonious everyday life. There is no reduction to a purely symbolic level, as is characteristic of Christian communion. The simplicity of the latter alone made mass religion possible, while mysteries remained costly clubs with restricted membership; they were too expensive to be available to all.

The Christian perspective, however, raises the question of whether there was anything corresponding to the Eucharist, some form of communion or sacrament, in pagan mysteries. Justin reports that in mysteries of Mithras bread and a cup of water were set up in imitation of Christian practice;[137] we know nothing about the position or function of this detail in the complex of sevenfold initiations and reunions. Drinking the *kykeon*, a kind of barley soup, was an important event at the Eleusinian mysteries; it marked the end of fasting[138] and represented the aboriginal form of a cereal diet that came into practice once "cannibalism" had come to an end. Again we are ignorant of the position of this act within the ceremonies. In Bacchic mysteries "happiness" itself, *makaria,* was presented to the initiated in the form of a cake,[139] just as *Hygieia,* "Health," could be eaten in the cult of Asclepius.[140] The motif of "eating the god" which has especially fascinated Christian observers,[141] is explicit only in a single and famous version of the Dionysus myth in which the Titans, the ancestors of man, tasted their divine victim, whom they had killed, cooked, and roasted.[142] One scholion on Clement of Alexandria brings this into connection with the more commonly described Dionysiac ritual of "eating raw meat," *omophagia,* but the incompatibility of raw versus cooked was noticed even before Lévi-Strauss.[143] Sacramental drinking of wine in correspondence with myths of death and dismemberment may be surmised from the ritual of the Attic Anthesteria, but these were public rites, not mysteries.[144] A recurrent motif in rumors surrounding secret, "unspeakable" ceremonies is the suspicion of cannibalism, the most horrible common crime that holds together weird participants. This suspicion was turned against Jews and Christians; it struck sanctuaries of Mithras and Ma Bellona;[145] and it is skillfully developed in a scene of the romance of Lollianus.[146] Even if such scenes were more than fantasies, they did not amount to "eating the god."

It is probably preferable to look for a more general background to these real, symbolic, and fantastic forms of the communal feast. The aboriginal institution of animal sacrifice, with the inevitable antinomy of killing and eating— life presupposing death and rising from its counterpart—is enacted by playing out antitheses of renunciation and fulfillment, mourning and rejoicing, searching and finding, the fast and the feast.[147] Mysteries evidently take part in this more general rhythm. Among the inscriptions found in the Mithraeum of Santa Prisca, Rome, one hexameter, incompletely preserved, is uncommonly suggestive and has become famous: "You saved us . . . by shedding the blood" (*et nos servasti . . . sanguine fuso*).[148] The word in the middle cannot be read with certainty; *eternali,* "eternal," has been read and rejected again. But even so we find the concept of salvation by killing, referring no doubt to the god slaying the bull, and this makes sense at various levels. It was "salvation" for the race of men to turn to hunting big animals in a changing environment; it was "salvation" to substitute the cultivation of cereals for the hunt at a later stage, as represented by the tail of the bull turning into grain. Thus the deed of the god is the basic image of salvation as such, prefiguring the hopes of the individuals integrated in this cult for the present as for the future. This concept is as primitive as it is fundamental, and it is not easily superseded by spiritualization.

It is true, nevertheless, that a more special kind of experience beyond the general sacrificial pattern was expected from mysteries. A veritable change of consciousness in ecstasy is typical of two major divinities of mysteries, Dionysus and Meter; they often appear together in this aspect.[149] "Madness" is a distinctive feature of *bakcheia* in its full sense,[150] and those devoted to the Phrygian Mother become *entheoi* or *theophoretoi,* "carried by the divinity," especially under the effect of certain kinds of music.[151] This, however, is not identical with mystery ritual in general. The well-known saying that "many are the narthex-bearers, but few are *bakchoi*"[152] seems to indicate just this fact, that "to be taken by the god"[153] is an event that will happen in an unforeseeable way, and probably only to a few special individuals. There are mediumistic gifts that are beyond the reach of many. Even the most common drug often identified with Dionysus, wine, is not sufficient to induce true *bakcheia*: anyone can get drunk, but not all are *bakchoi*.

There are certain techniques to control experience even here, of course. "Like the bacchic and corybantic ecstatics," Philo writes, "they [the Therapeutae] continue in their possession until they see the object of their desire."[154] This describes the quest for a vision, be it illusion or reality, and suggests that something similar happens to Bacchants and

Corybants. Plutarch declares himself convinced that ghosts, *daimones,* take part in the mystery celebrations.[155] We even have a clinical description of ecstasy in the cult of Meter, as seen by a doctor: the *galloi* "are turned on by flute music and gladness of heart [thymedie], or by drunkenness, or by the instigation of those present"—an interesting observation of the interdependence of performers and onlookers. "This madness is divine possession. When they end the state of madness, they are in good spirits, free of sorrow, as if consecrated by initiation to the god."[156] More simple is the account that Aristides Quintilianus, the musicologist, gives of Bacchic initiation; he follows to some extent Aristotle's concept of *katharsis:* "This is the purpose of Bacchic initiation, that the depressive anxiety [*ptoiesis*] of less educated people, produced by their state of life, or some misfortune, be cleared away through the melodies and dances of the ritual in a joyful and playful way." This, then, is a form of psychotherapy that would be compatible even with the latest trends of today. The condescending reference to the "uneducated" is indicative of a social dimension that is not often found in the evidence.[157] Still more deprecating and purportedly realistic is the explanation given by Livy for the ecstasy and miracles experienced at the Bacchanalia: it was just the lack of sleep, he writes, and the wine and the musical sounds and cries throughout the night that stunned people.[158] This is a collection of stimuli that every rationalist may endorse. But this interpretation closes the doors of the secret rather than revealing it.

No ecstasy in the full sense can be credited to Eleusis,[159] and even less to the cult of Isis or Mithras. It would be just as misleading to think of mysticism in the true sense as to accept the drug hypothesis. We are left with a remarkable passage of Proclus, head of the Academy in the fifth century A.D. Eleusis had been destroyed some fifteen years before he was born, and pagan sacrifice was forbidden by law in his times; still, he knew the daughter of Nestorius, the Eleusinian hierophant, and admired her as a guardian of the most sacred traditions.[160] Thus what he writes about mysteries should be taken seriously as containing authentic tradition. Proclus writes the following about the *teletai:*[161] "They cause sympathy of the souls with the ritual [*dromena*] in a way that is unintelligible to us, and divine, so that some of the initiands are stricken with panic, being filled with divine awe; others assimilate themselves to the holy symbols, leave their own identity, become at home with the gods, and experience divine possession." The very fact that the reactions described here are not uniform but vary between perplexity and exaltation indicates that this is not free speculation based on postulates, but a description of what has been observed: *sympatheia* of souls and rituals, some form of resonance which does not come in every case but which, once it is there, will deeply move or even shatter the constructs of reality. Being ignorant of the ritual and unable to reproduce it, we cannot recreate this experience, but we may acknowledge that it was there. There was a chance to "join the *thiasos* with one's soul," *thiaseuesthai psychan,* and this meant happiness.[162]

Mysteries were too fragile to survive as "religions" on their own. They were options within the multiplicity of pagan polytheism, and they disappeared with it. There remains a strange fascination even in the glimpses and guesses at evocative fragments: the darkness and the light, the agony and the ecstasy, the wine, the ear of grain. *Logoi* remained tentative, without reaching for the level of system or creed. It was enough to know there were doors to a secret that might open up for those who earnestly sought it. This meant that there was a chance to break out of the enclosed and barren ways of predictable existence. Such hopes were attempts to create a context of sense in a banal, depressing, and often absurd world, providing the experience of a great rhythm in which the resonances of the individual psyche could be integrated through an amazing event of *sympatheia.*

Abbreviations

Bibliography

Notes

Index of Greek Terms

General Index

Abbreviations

Common periodicals cited in the notes are referred to by standard abbreviations. For full titles of classical works cited in abbreviated form in the notes, see the *Oxford Classical Dictionary*.

ANRW	*Aufstieg und Niedergang der römischen Welt,* ed. H. Temporini and W. Haase (Berlin 1972–)
CCCA	M. J. Vermaseren, *Corpus Cultus Cybelae Attidisque* (Leiden; II, 1982; III, 1977; IV, 1978; V, 1986; VII, 1977 = *EPRO* 50)
CE	P. Roussel, *Les cultes égyptiens à Délos du IIIe au Ier siècle av. J.-C.* (Paris-Nancy 1916)
CIMRM	M. J. Vermaseren, *Corpus inscriptionum et monumentorum religionis Mithriacae,* 2 vols. (The Hague 1956–60)
CLE	*Carmina Latina Epigraphica*
CMG	*Corpus Medicorum Graecorum*
DK	H. Diels and W. Kranz, *Die Fragmente der Vorsokratiker,*[6] 2 vols. (Berlin 1951/52)
EPRO	*Etudes préliminaires aux religions orientales dans l'Empire romain,* ed. M. J. Vermaseren (Leiden 1961–)
GGR	M. P. Nilsson, *Geschichte der griechischen Religion* (Munich; I^3, 1967; II^2, 1961)
GR	W. Burkert, *Greek Religion* (Cambridge, Mass., and Oxford 1985; German ed. Stuttgart 1977)
Hansen	P. A. Hansen, *A List of Greek Verse Inscriptions Down to 400 B.C.* (Copenhagen 1975)
HN	W. Burkert, *Homo Necans: The Anthropology of Ancient Greek Sacrificial Ritual and Myth* (Berkeley 1983; German ed. Berlin and New York 1972)

IG   *Inscriptiones Graecae*
IGBulg   *Inscriptiones Graecae in Bulgaria repertae,* ed. G. Mihailov
         (Sofia 1956–; 1: 1956. ²1970; 2: 1958; 3: 1961. 1964; 4:
         1966)
IGRom   R. Cagnat, *Inscriptiones Graecae ad res Romanas pertinentes,*
         vols. I–IV (Paris 1901–27)
ILS   H. Dessau, *Inscriptiones Latinae Selectae,* vols. I–III (Berlin
         1892–1916)
JDAI   *Jahrbuch des Deutschen Archäologischen Instituts*
Kaibel   G. Kaibel, *Epigrammata graeca ex lapidibus conlecta* (Berlin
         1878)
L&S   W. Burkert, *Lore and Science in Ancient Pythagoreanism*
         (Cambridge, Mass. 1972; German ed. 1962)
LSAM   F. Sokolowski, *Lois sacrées de l'Asie Mineure* (Paris 1955)
LSCG   F. Sokolowski, *Lois sacrées des cités grecques* (Paris 1969)
LSS   F. Sokolowski, *Lois sacrées des cités grecques, Supplément*
         (Paris 1962)
OE   W. Burkert, *Die orientalisierende Epoche in der griechischen
         Religion und Literatur,* Sitzungsber. (Heidelberg 1984,1)
OF   O. Kern, *Orphicorum Fragmenta* (Berlin 1922)
OGI   *Orientis Graeci Inscriptiones Selectae,* ed. W. Dittenberger
         (Leipzig 1903–05)
Peek   W. Peek, *Attische Grabinschriften,* 2 vols. (Berlin 1954/58)
PG   J. P. Migne, *Patrologia Graeca* (Paris 1857–1936)
PGM   *Papyri Graecae Magicae,* ed. and trans. K. Preisendanz,
         2 vols. (Leipzig 1928–1941; 2nd ed. rev. A. Henrichs,
         Stuttgart 1973/74)
PL   J. P. Migne, *Patrologia Latina* (Paris 1844–1900; *Suppl.*
         1958–1974)
PW   *Pauly's Realencyclopädie der classischen Altertumswissenschaft,*
         ed. G. Wissowa et al.
RGVV   *Religionsgeschichtliche Versuche und Vorarbeiten*
RML   W. H. Roscher, *Ausführliches Lexikon der griechischen und
         römischen Mythologie* (Leipzig 1884–1937)
RVAp   A. D. Trendall and A. Cambitoglou, *The Red-Figured
         Vases of Apulia,* 2 vols. (Oxford 1978/82)
Sammelb. *Sammelbuch griechischer Urkunden aus Aegypten,* I/II ed. F.
         Preisigke (Strassburg, Berlin, Leipzig 1913–22); III/IV/V
         ed. F. Bilabel (Heidelberg 1931–34)
SEG   *Supplementum Epigraphicum Graecum*
S&H   W. Burkert, *Structure and History in Greek Mythology and
         Ritual* (Berkeley 1979)

SIG   *Sylloge Inscriptionum Graecarum*[3], ed. W. Dittenberger, 4 vols. (Leipzig 1915–24)

SIRIS   *Sylloge inscriptionum religionis Isiacae et Sarapiacae*, ed. L. Vidman (Berlin 1969)

SVF   *Stoicorum Veterum Fragmenta*, ed. H. von Arnim, 3 vols. (Leipzig 1903–21)

Bibliography

Alföldi, A. 1979. "Redeunt Saturnia regna VII: Frugifer-Triptolemos im ptolemäisch-römischen Herrscherkult," *Chiron* 9, 553–606.

Altmann, W. 1905. *Die römischen Grabaltäre der Kaiserzeit*, Berlin.

Alviella, G. d'. 1981. *The Mysteries of Eleusis: The Secret Rites and Rituals of the Classical Greek Mystery Tradition*, Wellingborough.

Anrich, G. 1894. *Das antike Mysterienwesen in seinem Einfluss auf das Christentum*, Göttingen.

Assmann, J. 1979. "Isis und die ägyptischen Mysterien," in W. Westendorf, ed., *Aspekte der spätägyptischen Religion*, Wiesbaden, 93–115.

Baratte, F. 1974. "Le sarcophage de Triptolème au musée du Louvre," *Rev. Arch.*, 271–290.

Baslez, M. F. 1977. *Recherches sur les conditions de pénétration et de diffusion des religions orientales à Délos*, Paris.

Bastet, F. L. 1974. "Fabularum dispositas explicationes," *BABesch* 49, 207–240.

Beck, R. 1984. "Mithraism since Franz Cumont," *ANRW* II, 17(4), 2002–2115.

Bérard, C. 1974. "Silène porte-van," *Bull. Assoc. pro Aventico* 22, 5–16.

Berner, W. D. 1972. "Initiationsriten in Mysterienreligionen, im Gnostizismus und im antiken Judentum," diss. Göttingen.

Beskow, P. 1979. "Branding in the Mysteries of Mithras?" in Bianchi 1979, 487–501.

Bianchi, U. 1975. "Mithraism and Gnosticism," in Hinnells 1975, 457–465.

—— 1976. *The Greek Mysteries,* Leiden (Iconography of Religions XVII, 3).

—— ed. 1979. *Mysteria Mithrae,* Leiden (*EPRO* 80).

—— 1980. "Iside dea misterica. Quando?" in *Perennitas: Studi A. Brelich,* Rome, 9–36.

—— and M. J. Vermaseren, eds. 1982. *La soteriologia dei culti orientali nell' Impero Romano,* Leiden (*EPRO* 92).

—— 1984. "La tipologia storica dei misteri di Mithra," *ANRW* II, 17(4), 2116–2134.

Bidez, J., and F. Cumont. 1938. *Les mages hellénisés: Zoroastre, Ostanès et Hystaspe d'après la tradition grecque,* 2 vols., Paris.

Bleeker, C. J., ed. 1965. *Initiation,* Leiden (*Numen* Suppl. 10).

Bösing, L. 1968. "Zur Bedeutung von 'renasci' in der Antike," *MH* 25, 145–178.

Bouyer, L. 1953. "Le salut dans les religions à mystères," *RSR* 27, 1–16.

Boyancé, P. 1960/61. "L'antre dans les mystères de Dionysos," *RPAA* 33, 107–127.

—— 1966. "Dionysiaca," *REA* 68, 33–60.

Brelich, A. 1963. "Politeismo e soteriologia," in S. G. F. Brandon, ed., *The Saviour God: Comparative Studies in the Concept of Salvation, Presented to E. O. James,* Manchester, 37–50.

—— 1969. *Paides e Parthenoi,* Rome.

Bremmer, J. N. 1984. "Greek Maenadism Reconsidered," *ZPE* 55, 267–286.

Brendel, O. J. 1966. "Der grosse Fries in der Villa dei Misteri," *JDAI* 81, 206–260.

Bruhl, A. 1953. *Liber Pater: Origine et expansion du culte dionysiaque à Rome et dans le monde romain,* Paris.

Bultmann, R. 1963. *Das Urchristentum im Rahmen der antiken Religionen*[3], Zurich (1st ed. 1949).

Burg, N. M. H. van den, 1939. "Aporreta Dromena Orgia," diss. Utrecht.

Burkert, W. 1972. *Lore and Science in Ancient Pythagoreanism,* Cambridge, Mass. (German ed. 1962).

—— 1975. "Le laminette auree: da Orfeo a Lampone," in *Orfismo in Magna Grecia. Atti del XIV Convegno di studi sulla Magna Grecia,* Naples, 81–104.

—— 1979. *Structure and History in Greek Mythology and Ritual,* Berkeley.

—— 1982. "Craft versus Sect: The Problem of Orphics and Pythagoreans," in Meyer-Sanders 1982, 1–22.

—— 1983. *Homo Necans: The Anthropology of Ancient Greek Sacrificial Ritual and Myth*, Berkeley (German ed. 1972).

—— 1985. *Greek Religion*, Cambridge, Mass., and Oxford (German ed. 1977).

Casadio, G. 1982/83. "Per un'indagine storico-religiosa sui culti di Dioniso in relazione alla fenomenologia dei misteri," I: *SSR* 6 (1982) 209–234, II: *SMSR* 7 (1983) 123–149.

Clemen, C. 1913. *Der Einfluss der Mysterienreligionen auf das älteste Christentum*, Giessen (*RGVV* 13, 1).

—— 1924. *Religionsgeschichtliche Erklärung des Neuen Testaments*[2], Giessen (1st ed. 1909).

Clinton, K. 1974. *The Sacred Officials of the Eleusinian Mysteries*, Philadelphia.

Coche de la Ferté, E. 1980. "Penthée et Dionysos: Nouvel essai d'interprétation des 'Bacchantes' d'Euripide," in R. Bloch, ed., *Recherches sur les religions de l'antiquité classique*, Geneva, 105–257.

Cole, S. G. 1980. "New Evidence for the Mysteries of Dionysos," *GRBS* 21, 223–238.

—— 1984. *Theoi Megaloi: The Cult of the Great Gods of Samothrace*, Leiden (*EPRO* 96).

Colpe, C. 1961. *Die religionsgeschichtliche Schule: Darstellung und Kritik ihres Bildes vom gnostischen Erlösermythos*, Göttingen.

—— 1969. "Zur mythologischen Struktur der Adonis, Attis- und Osirisüberlieferungen," in *lišān mithurti: Festschrift W. von Soden*, Neukirchen-Vluyn, 23–44.

—— 1975. "Mithra-Verehrung, Mithras-Kult und die Existenz iranischer Mysterien," in Hinnells 1975, 378–405.

Cosi, D. M. 1976. "Salvatore e salvezza nei misteri di Attis," *Aevum* 50, 42–71.

—— 1979. "Attis e Mithra," in Bianchi 1979, 625–638.

—— 1982. "Aspetti mistici e misterici del culto di Attis," in Bianchi 1982, 482–502.

Cumont, F. 1896/99. *Textes et monuments figurés aux mystères de Mithra*, 2 vols., Brussels.

—— 1923. *Die Mysterien des Mithra*[3], Leipzig (French ed. 1900).

—— 1931. *Die orientalischen Religionen im römischen Heidentum*[4], Stuttgart (repr. 1981[8]), trans. of *Les religions orientales dans le paganisme romain*, Paris 1929[4] (1st ed. 1907); English trans., *Oriental Religions in Roman Paganism*, Chicago 1911.

—— 1933. "Un fragment de rituel d'initiation aux mystères," *HThR* 26, 153–160.

———— 1975. "The Dura Mithraeum," ed. E. D. Francis, in Hinnells 1975, 151–214.

Daniels, C. M. 1975. "The role of the Roman army in the spread and practice of Mithraism," in Hinnells 1975, 249–274.

Deubner, L. 1932. *Attische Feste*, Berlin.

Devereux, G. 1974. "Trance and Orgasm in Euripides: Bakchai," in A. Angoff and K. D. Barth, eds., *Parapsychology and Anthropology*, New York, 36–58.

Diakonoff, I. M. 1977. "On Cybele and Attis in Phrygia and Lydia," *AAntHung* 25, 333–340.

Dibelius, M. 1917. "Die Isisweihe bei Apuleius und verwandte Initiations-Riten," *Sitzungsber. Heidelberg* 1917, 4.

Dieterich, A. 1891. *Abraxas, Studien zur Religionsgeschichte des späteren Altertums*, Leipzig.

———— 1923. *Eine Mithrasliturgie*[3], Leipzig (1st ed. 1903).

Diez, E. 1968/71. " 'Horusknaben' in Noricum," *OeJh* 49, 114–120.

Dihle, A. 1980. "Zur spätantiken Kultfrömmigkeit," in *Pietas, Festschrift B. Kötting*, Münster, Westfalen, 39–54.

Dodds, E. R. 1951. *The Greeks and the Irrational*, Berkeley.

Dowden, K. 1980. "Grades in the Eleusinian Mysteries," *RHR* 197, 409–427.

Duchesne-Guillemin, J., ed. 1978. *Etudes mithriaques. Actes du 2*[e] *congrès international*, Teheran (*Acta Iranica* 17).

Dunand, F. 1973. *Le culte d'Isis dans le bassin oriental de la Méditerranée*, 3 vols. (I: *Le culte d'Isis et les Ptolémées*; II: *Le culte d'Isis en Grèce*; III: *Les culte d'Isis en Asie Mineure: Clergé et rituel des sanctuaires isiaques*), Leiden (*EPRO* 26).

Duthoy, R. 1969. *The Taurobolium: Its Evolution and Terminology*, Leiden (*EPRO* 10).

Egger, R., and H. Vetters. 1950. *Dacia Ripensis. Der Grabstein von Čekančevo*, Vienna (Schriften der Balkankommission, Antiquar. Abt. 11).

———— 1951. "Zwei oberitalienische Mystensarkophage," *MDAI* 4, 35–64.

Eisler, R. 1925. *Orphisch-Dionysische Mysteriengedanken in der christlichen Antike*, Leipzig.

Eliade, M. (1958/65): *Birth and Rebirth*, New York 1958; reprinted as *Rites and Symbols of Initiation*, New York 1965.

Engelmann, H. 1975. *The Delian Aretalogy of Sarapis*, Leiden (*EPRO* 44).

Farnell, L. R. 1896–1909. *The Cults of The Greek States* I–V, Oxford.

Fauth, W. 1984. "Plato Mithriacus oder Mithras Platonicus? Art und Umfang platonischer Einflüsse auf die Mithras-Mysterien," *Göttingische Gelehrte Anzeigen* 236, 31–50.

Fehrle, E. 1910. *Die kultische Keuschheit im Altertum*, Giessen (*RGVV* 6).

Ferguson, J. 1970. *The Religions of the Roman Empire*, London.

Festugière, A. J. 1954. *Personal Religion among the Greeks*, Berkeley (Sather Classical Lectures 26).

——— 1972. *Etudes de religion grecque et hellénistique*, Paris.

Ibid. 13–63: "Les mystères de Dionysos" (orig. 1935).

Ibid. 89–113: "Ce que Tite-Live nous apprend sur les mystères de Dionysos" (orig. 1954).

Foucart, P. 1873. *Des associations religieuses chez les Grecs*, Paris.

——— 1914. *Les mystères d'Eleusis*, Paris.

Foucher, L. 1964. *La maison de la procession dionysiaque à 'El Jem*, Paris.

——— 1981. "Le culte de Bacchus sous l'empire Romain," *ANRW* II, 17(2), 684–702.

Francis, E. D. 1975. "Mithraic Graffiti from Dura-Europos," in Hinnells 1975, 424–445.

Fraser, P. M. 1972. *Ptolemaic Alexandria*, 3 vols., Oxford.

Frickel, J. 1984. *Hellenistische Erlösung in christlicher Deutung. Die gnostische Naassenerschrift*, Leiden (Nag Hammadi Studies 19).

Gennep, A. van. 1909. *Les rites de passage*, Paris (*The Rites of Passage*, Chicago 1960).

Geyer, A. 1977. *Das Problem des Realitätsbezuges in der dionysischen Bildkunst der Kaiserzeit*, Wurzburg.

Giversen, S. 1975. "Der Gnostizismus und die Mysterienreligionen," in J. P. Asmussen and J. Laessøe, eds., *Handbuch der Religionsgeschichte*, Göttingen, 255–299.

Gonzenbach, V. von. 1957. *Untersuchungen zu den Knabenweihen im Isiskult der römischen Kaiserzeit*, Bonn.

Goodwin, J. 1981. *Mystery Religions in the Ancient World*, London.

Gordon, R. L. 1972. "Mithraism and Roman Society: Social Factors in the Explanation of Religious Change in the Roman Empire," *Religion* 2, 92–121.

——— 1975. "Franz Cumont and the Doctrines of Mithraism," in Hinnells 1975, 215–248.

——— 1976. "The Sacred Geography of a Mithraeum: The Example of Sette Sfere," *JMS* 1, 119–165.

——— 1980. "Reality, Evocation and Boundary in the Mysteries of Mithras," *JMS* 3, 19–99.

Graf, F. 1974. *Eleusis und die orphische Dichtung Athens in vorhellenistischer Zeit*, Berlin (*RGVV* 33).

―――― 1985. *Nordionische Kulte. Religionsgeschichtliche und epigraphische Untersuchungen zu den Kulten von Chios, Erythrai, Klazomenai und Phokaia*, Rome (Bibliotheca Helvetica Romana 21).

Graillot, H. 1912. *Le culte de Cybèle, mère des Dieux, à Rome et dans l'Empire romain*, Paris.

Grandjean, Y. 1975. *Une nouvelle arétalogie d'Isis à Maronée*, Leiden (*EPRO* 49).

Gressmann, H. 1923/24. "Die Umwandlung der orientalischen Religionen unter dem Einfluss hellenischen Geistes," *Vortr. d. Bibl. Warburg* III, 5 (1926) 170–195.

Griffiths, J. G. 1976. *Apuleius, The Isis-Book (Metamorphoses, Book XI)* with intro., trans., and comm., Leiden (*EPRO* 39).

Guarducci, M. 1983. *Scritti scelti sulla religione greca e romana e sul cristianesimo*, Leiden (*EPRO* 98).

Hamilton, J. D. B. 1977. "The Church and the Language of Mystery: The First Four Centuries," *Ephem. Theol. Lovan.* 53, 479–494.

Harder, R. 1943. *Karpokrates von Chalkis und die memphitische Isispropaganda*, Abh. Berlin 14.

Heilmann, W. 1985. "Coniuratio impia. Die Unterdrückung der Bacchanalia als Beispiel für römische Religionspolitik," *Altsprachl. Unterricht* 28(2), 22–37.

Henrichs, A. 1972. *Die Phoinikika des Lollianos. Fragmente eines neuen griechischen Romans*, Bonn.

―――― 1978. "Greek Maenadism from Olympias to Messalina," *HSCP* 82, 121–160.

―――― 1982. "Changing Dionysiac Identities," in Meyer-Sanders 1982, 137–160.

―――― 1984a. "Male Intruders among the Maenads: The So-called Male Celebrant," in H. D. Evjen, ed., *Mnemai: Classical Studies in Memory of K. K. Hulley*, Chicago, 69–91.

―――― 1984b. "Loss of Self, Suffering, Violence: The Modern View of Dionysus from Nietzsche to Girard," *HSCP* 88, 205–240.

Hepding, H. 1903. *Attis, seine Mythen und sein Kult*, Giessen (*RGVV* 1, repr. Berlin 1967).

Herbig, R. 1958. *Neue Beobachtungen am Fries der Mysterien-Villa in Pompeji*, Baden-Baden (Deutsche Beiträge zur Altertumswissenschaft 10).

Hinnells, J. R., ed. 1975. *Mithraic Studies: Proceedings of the First International Congress of Mithraic Studies*, I–II, Manchester.

———— 1976. "The Iconography of Cautes and Cautopates, 1: The Data," *Journal of Mithraic Studies* 1, 36–67.

Hölbl, G. 1979. *Beziehungen der ägyptischen Kultur zu Altitalien*, Leiden (*EPRO* 62).

Hommel, H. 1983. "Antike Bussformulare. Eine religionsge-schichtliche Interpretation der ovidischen Midas-Erzählung," in *Sebasmata* 1, Tübingen, 351–370.

Horn, H. G. 1972. *Mysteriensymbolik auf dem Kölner Dionysosmosaik*, Bonn.

Hornbostel, W. 1973. *Sarapis. Studien zur Ueberlieferungsgeschichte, den Erscheinungsformen und Wandlungen der Gestalt eines Gottes*, Leiden (*EPRO* 32).

Janko, R. 1984. "Forgetfulness in the Golden Tablets of Memory," *CQ* 34, 89–100.

Jeanmaire, H. 1939. *Couroi et Courètes*, Lille.

———— 1951. *Dionysos: Histoire du culte de Bacchus*, Paris.

Johnson, S. E. 1984. "The Present State of Sabazios Research," *ANRW* ii, 17 (3), 1583–1613.

Kane, J. P. 1975. "The Mithraic Cult Meal in Its Greek and Roman Environment," in Hinnells 1975, 313–351.

Karageorghis, V. 1984. "Dionysiaca and Erotica from Cyprus," *RDAC*, 214–220.

Kater-Sibbes, G. J. F. 1973. *Preliminary Catalogue of Sarapis Monuments*, Leiden (*EPRO* 36).

Kerényi, K. 1967. *Eleusis: Archetypal Image of Mother and Daughter*, London.

———— 1976. *Dionysos, Urbild des unzerstörbaren Lebens*, Munich (*Dionysos, Archetypal Image of Indestructible Life*, Princeton 1976).

Keuls, E. C. 1974. *The Water Carriers in Hades*, Amsterdam.

Klimkeit, H. J., ed. 1978. *Tod und Jenseits im Glauben der Völker*, Wiesbaden.

Köster, H. 1980. *Einführung in das Neue Testament im Rahmen der Religionsgeschichte und Kulturgeschichte der hellenistischen und römischen Zeit*, Berlin (*Introduction to the New Testament*, 2 vols., Philadelphia, New York, Berlin 1982).

Kraemer, R. S. 1979. "Ecstasy and Possession: The Attraction of Women to the Cult of Dionysus," *HThR* 72, 55–80.

———— 1981. "Euoi, Saboi in Demosthenes' *De Corona*: In Which Honor Were the Women's Rites?" *Seminar Papers Soc. Bibl. Lit.*, 229–236.

Lambrechts, P. 1957. "L'importance de l'enfant dans les religions à mystères," in *Hommages W. Deonna*, Brussels, 322–333.

Laum, B. 1914. *Stiftungen in der griechischen und römischen Antike* I–II, Berlin.

Leclant, J. 1984. "Aegyptiaca et milieux isiaques: Recherches sur la diffusion du matériel et des idées égyptiennes," in *ANRW* II, 17(3), 1692–1709.

Leclant, J., and G. Clerc. 1972/74/85. *Inventaire bibliographique des Isiaca (IBIS)* I–III, Leiden (*EPRO* 18).

Le Corsu, F. 1977. *Isis: Mythe et Mystères*, Paris.

Leipoldt, J. 1923. *Sterbende und auferstehende Götter*, Leipzig.

——— 1961. *Von den Mysterien zur Kirche. Gesammelte Aufsätze*, Leipzig.

Lentz, W. 1975. "Some Peculiarities not Hitherto Fully Understood of 'Roman' Mithraic Sanctuaries and Representations," in Hinnells 1975, 358–377.

Lévêque, P. 1982. "Structures imaginaires et fonctionnement des mystères grecs," *SSR* 6, 185–208.

Linforth, I. M. 1946a. "The Corybantic Rites in Plato," *Univ. of Calif. Publ. in Class. Philol.* 13, 121–162.

——— 1946b. "Telestic Madness in Plato, *Phaedrus* 244 DE," *Univ. of Calif. Publ. in Class Philol.* 13, 163–172.

Lobeck, C. A. 1829. *Aglaophamus sive de theologiae mysticae Graecorum causis* I–II, Königsberg.

Lohse, E. 1974. *Umwelt des Neuen Testaments*, Göttingen.

Loisy, A. 1930. *Les mystères paiens et le mystère chrétien*[2], Paris (1st ed. 1919).

MacMullen, R. 1981. *Paganism in the Roman Empire*, New Haven.

——— 1984. *Christianizing the Roman Empire (AD 100–400)*, New Haven.

Malaise, M. (1972): *Les conditions de pénétration et de diffusion des cultes égyptiens en Italie*, Leiden (*EPRO* 22).

——— 1984. "La diffusion des cultes égyptiens dans les provinces européennes de l'empire romain," in *ANRW* II, 17(3), 1615–1691.

Matz, F. 1963. "Dionysiake Telete. Archäologische Untersuchungen zum Dionysoskult in hellenistischer und römischer Zeit," *Abhandlungen der Akademie Mainz*, 1963 no. 15.

Merkelbach, R. 1962. *Roman und Mysterium in der Antike*, Munich.

——— 1965. "Die Kosmogonie der Mithrasmysterien," *Eranos Jb.* 34, 219–257.

——— 1968. "Der Eid der Isismysten," *ZPE* 1, 55–73.

——— 1974. "Mystery Religions," in *Encyclopaedia Britannica*[15], London 1974, 778–785.

———— 1982. *Weihegrade und Seelenlehre der Mithrasmysterien,* Opladen (Rhein.-Westfäl. Ak. d. Wiss., Geisteswiss., Vorträge G 257).

———— 1984. *Mithras,* Meisenheim.

Metzger, B. M. 1955. "Considerations of Methodology in the Study of the Mystery Religions and Early Christianity," *HThR* 47, 1–20.

———— 1984. "A Classified Bibliography of the Graeco-Roman Mystery Religions 1924–73 with a Supplement 1974–77," in *ANRW* II, 17(3), 1259–1423.

Metzger, H. (1944/45): "Dionysos chthonien d'après les monuments figurés de la période classique," *BCH* 68/9, 296–339.

———— 1965. *Recherches sur l'imagerie athénienne,* Paris.

Meyer, B. F., and E. P. Sanders, eds. 1982. *Self-Definition in the Graeco-Roman World,* London (cf. Sanders 1980–82).

Mylonas, G. E. 1961. *Eleusis and the Eleusinian Mysteries,* Princeton.

Naumann, F. 1984. *Die Ikonographie der Kybele in der phrygischen und griechischen Kunst,* Tübingen.

Nilsson, M. P. 1950. "Kleinasiatische Pseudo-Mysterien," *Ephem. Inst. Arch. Bulgarici* 16, 17–20.

———— 1952. *Opuscula selecta* II, Lund.

———— 1957. *The Dionysiac Mysteries of the Hellenistic and Roman Age,* Lund.

———— 1961/67. *Geschichte der griechischen Religion,* Munich.

Nock, A. D. 1933. *Conversion: The Old and the New in Religion from Alexander the Great to Augustine of Hippo,* Oxford.

———— 1937. "The Genius of Mithraism," *JRS* 27, 108–113 (= Nock 1972, 452–458).

———— 1952. "Hellenistic Mysteries and Christian Sacraments," *Mnemosyne* 4,5, 177–214 (= Nock 1972, 791–820).

———— 1972. *Essays on Religion and the Ancient World,* ed. Z. Stewart, 2 vols., Oxford.

Ohlemutz, E. 1940. *Die Kulte und Heiligtümer der Götter in Pergamon,* Würzburg.

Oppermann, H. 1924. *Zeus Panamaros,* Giessen (*RGVV* 19,3).

Otto, W. 1905/08. *Priester und Tempel im hellenistischen Aegypten,* 2 vols., Leipzig.

———— 1949. "Beiträge zur Hierodulie im hellenistischen Aegypten," *Abh. München, Phil. hist. Kl.* 29.

Pailler, J.-M. 1982. "La spirale de l'interprétation: les Bachanales," *Annales ESC* 37, 929–952.

Perdelwitz, R. 1911. *Die Mysterienreligion und das Problem des 1. Petrusbriefes,* Giessen (*RGVV* XI, 3).

Pettazzoni, R. 1954. "Les mystères grecs et les religions à mystères de l'antiquité. Recherches récentes et problèmes nouveaux," *Cahiers d'Histoire Mondiale* 11(2), 303–312, 661–667.

Phythian-Adams, W. J. 1912. "The Problem of the Mithraic Grades," *JRS* 2, 53–64.

Piccaluga, G. 1982. "Salvarsi ma non troppo. Il rischio di un valore assoluto nella religione romana," in Bianchi 1982, 403–426.

Poland, F. 1909. *Geschichte des griechischen Vereinswesens*, Leipzig.

Pringsheim, H. G. 1905. "Archäologische Beiträge zur Geschichte des Eleusinischen Kultes," Munich (diss. Bonn).

Prümm, K. 1937. " 'Mysterion' von Paulus bis Origenes," *Zeitschr. f. Kath. Theol.* 61, 391–425.

———— 1943. *Religionsgeschichtliches Handbuch für den Raum der altchristlichen Umwelt*, Freiburg i. Br.

———— 1960. "Mystères," in *Supplément au Dictionnaire de la Bible* 6, Paris, 10–173.

Quandt, W. 1912. "De Baccho ab Alexandri aetate in Asia minore culto," diss. Halle.

Rahner, H. 1945. "Das christliche Mysterium und die heidnischen Mysterien," in *Griechische Mythen in christlicher Deutung*, Zurich, 21–123.

Reitzenstein, R. 1927. *Die hellenistischen Mysterienreligionen nach ihren Grundgedanken und Wirkungen*[3], Leipzig (1st ed. 1910); English trans., *Hellenistic Mystery Religions: Their Basic Ideas and Significance*, London 1978.

Richardson, N. J. 1974. *The Homeric Hymn to Demeter*, Oxford.

Riedweg, Chr. 1987. *Mysterienterminologie bei Platon, Philon und Klemens von Alexandrien*, Berlin.

Ries, J. 1979. *Le culte de Mithra en Orient et en Occident*, Louvain-la-Neuve.

———— 1980. *Osirisme et monde hellénistique*, Louvain-la-Neuve.

Rohde, E. 1898. *Psyche*[2], 2 vols., Tübingen (1st ed. 1893).

Rouse, W. H. D. 1902. *Greek Votive Offerings: An Essay in the History of Greek Religion*, Cambridge.

Rousselle, R. J. 1982. "The Roman Persecution of the Bacchic Cult, 186–180 B.C.," diss. Ann Arbor.

Rusajeva, A. S. 1978. "Orfizm i kult Dionisa b Olbii" [Orphism and the Dionysos Cult in Olbia], *Vestnik Drevnej Istorii* 143, 87–104.

Rutter, J. B. 1968. "The Three Phases of the Taurobolium," *Phoenix* 22, 226–249.

Sabbatucci, D. 1979. *Saggio sul misticismo greco*[2], Rome (1st ed. 1965).

Sanders, E. P., ed. 1980–82. *Jewish and Christian Self-Definition*, 1: *The Shaping of Christianity in the Second and Third Centuries*, London 1980; II: *Aspects of Judaism in the Greco-Roman Period*, Philadelphia 1981. For III see Meyer and Sanders 1982.

San Nicolo, M. 1913/15. *Aegyptisches Vereinswesen zur Zeit der Ptolemäer und Römer*, I (1972²), II, Munich.

Schmidt, M., A. D. Trendall, and A. Cambitoglou. 1976. *Eine Gruppe apulischer Grabvasen in Basel*, Basel.

Schneider, C. 1939. "Die griechischen Grundlagen der hellenistischen Religionsgeschichte," *ARW* 36, 300–347.

——— 1954. *Geistesgeschichte des antiken Christentums*, Munich.

——— 1979. *Die antiken Mysterien in ihrer Einheit und Vielfalt. Wesen und Wirkung der Einweihung*, Hamburg.

Schneider-Hermann, G. 1977/78. "Unterschiedliche Interpretationen süd-italischer Vasenbilder des 4. Jh.v.Chr.," *BaBesch* 52/3, 253–257.

Schwertheim, E. 1975. *Die Denkmäler orientalischer Gottheiten im römischen Deutschland*, Leiden (*EPRO* 40).

——— 1979. "Mithras. Seine Denkmäler und sein Kult," *AW Sondernr.* VII, Feldmeilen.

Seaford, R. 1981. "Dionysiac Drama and the Dionysiac Mysteries," *CQ* 31, 252–275.

Seyrig, H. 1974. "Pseudo-Attideia," *Bagd. Mitt.* 7, 197–203.

Sfameni Gasparro, G. 1971. "Le religioni orientali sul mondo ellenistico-romano," in G. Castellani, ed., *Storia della religioni*[6], Torino 1971, vol. III, 423–564.

——— 1978. "Connotazioni metroache di Demetra nel coro dell' 'Elena' (vv. 1301–1365)," in M. B. de Boer and T. A. Edridge, eds., *Hommages à M. J. Vermaseren*, 3 vols., Leiden (*EPRO* 68), 1148–87.

——— 1979a. "Il Mitraismo nell' ambito della fenomenologia misterica," in Bianchi 1979, 299–348.

——— 1979b. "Il mitraismo; una struttura religiosa fra tradizione e invenzione," in Bianchi 1979, 349–384.

——— 1979c. "Reflessioni ulteriori su Mithra dio mistico," in Bianchi 1979, 397–408.

——— 1981. "Interpretazioni Gnostiche e misteriosofiche dei miti di Attis," in R. van den Broek and M. J. Vermaseren, eds., *Studies G. Quispel*, Leiden, 376–411.

——— 1985. *Soteriology and Mystic Aspects in the Cult of Cybele and Attis*, Leiden (*EPRO* 103).

Sharpe, E. J., and J. R. Hinnells, eds. 1973. *Man and His Salvation*, Manchester.

Siber, P. 1971. *Mit Christus leben. Eine Studie zur paulinischen Auferstehungshoffnung*, Zurich.

Simon, E. 1961. "Zum Fries der Mysterienvilla bei Pompeji," *JDAI* 76, 111–172.

Smith, H. R. W. 1972. *Funerary Symbolism in Apulian Vase-Painting,* Berkeley.

Smith, J. Z. 1978. *Map Is Not Territory: Studies in the History of Religions,* Leiden.

✗ Smith, M. 1973. *Clement of Alexandria and a Secret Gospel of Mark,* Cambridge.

Soden, H. von. 1911. "Mysterion und sacramentum in den ersten zwei Jahrhunderten der Kirche," *Zeitschr. f. NT Wiss.* 12, 188–227.

Solmsen, F. 1979. *Isis among the Greeks and Romans,* Cambridge, Mass.

Speyer, W. 1981. *Büchervernichtung und Zensur des Geistes bei Heiden, Juden und Christen,* Stuttgart.

Stewart, Z. 1977. "La religione," in R. Bianchi Bandinelli, ed., *Storia e civiltà dei Greci,* vol. IV, Bari, 501–616.

Straten, F. T. van. 1981. "Gifts for the Gods," in H. S. Versnel, ed., *Faith, Hope and Worship,* Leiden, 65–151.

Teixidor, J. 1977. *The Pagan God. Popular Religion in the Greco-Roman Near East,* Princeton.

Thomas, G. 1984. "Magna Mater and Attis," in *ANRW* II, 17(3), 1500–1535.

Totti, M. 1985. *Ausgewählte Texte der Isis- und Sarapis-Religion,* Hildesheim.

Tran Tam Tinh, V. 1964. *Essai sur le culte d'Isis à Pompéi,* Paris.

—— 1984. "Etat des études iconographiques relatives à Isis, Sérapis et Sunnaoi Theoi," in *ANRW* II, 17(3), 1710–1738.

Turcan, R. 1965. "Du nouveau sur l'initiation dionysiaque," *Latomus* 24, 101–119.

—— 1969. "La démone ailée de la Villa Item," in *Hommages à M. Renard* III, Brussels, 586–609.

—— 1975. *Mithras Platonicus,* Leiden (*EPRO* 47).

—— 1981a. *Mithra et le mithriacisme,* Paris.

—— 1981b. "Le sacrifice mithriaque: innovations de sens et de modalités," in *Le sacrifice dans l'antiquité,* Entretiens sur l'antiquité classique 27, Vandoeuvres/Geneva, 341–373.

Vermaseren, M. J. 1963. *Mithras, The Secret God,* London.

—— 1966. *The Legend of Attis in Greek and Roman Art,* Leiden (*EPRO* 9).

—— 1971. *Mithriaca I: The Mithraeum at St. Maria Capua Vetere,* Leiden (*EPRO* 16).

———— 1974. *Der Kult des Mithras im römischen Germanien*, Stuttgart.

———— 1977. *Cybele and Attis: The Myth and the Cult*, London.

———— eds. 1981. Die orientalischen Religionen im Römerreich, Leiden (*EPRO* 93).

Vermaseren, M. J., and C. C. van Essen, 1965. *The Excavations in the Mithraeum of the Church of Santa Prisca in Rome*, Leiden.

Vidman, L. 1970. *Isis und Sarapis bei den Griechen und Römern*, Berlin.

Wagner, G. 1962. *Das religionsgeschichtliche Problem von Römer 6, 1–11*, Zurich (English ed., *Pauline Baptism and the Pagan Mysteries*, Edinburgh 1967).

Wasson, G. R., A. Hofman, and C. A. P. Ruck. 1978. *The Road to Eleusis: Unveiling the Secret of the Mysteries*, New York.

Wedderburn, A. J. M. 1982. "Paul and the Hellenistic Mystery Cults: On Posing the Right Questions," in Bianchi 1982, 817–833.

West, M. L. 1983. *The Orphic Poems*, Oxford.

Widengren, G. 1980. "Reflections on the Origin of the Mithraic Mysteries," in *Perennitas, Studi in onore di Angelo Brelich*, Rome, 645–668.

Wiens, D. H. 1980. "Mystery Concepts in Primitive Christianity and in Its Environment," in *ANRW* II, 23(2), 1248–84.

Wilamowitz-Moellendorff, U. von. 1931/32. *Der Glaube der Hellenen*, 2 vols., Berlin.

Wild, R. A. 1981. *Water in the Cultic Worship of Isis and Sarapis*, Leiden (*EPRO* 87).

———— 1984. "The Known Isis-Sarapis-Sanctuaries from the Roman Period," in *ANRW* II, 17(4), 1739–1851.

Wilson, R. McL. 1981. "Gnosis and the Mysteries," in R. van den Broek and M. J. Vermaseren, eds., *Studies G. Quispel*, Leiden, 451–457.

Wissowa, G. 1912. *Religion und Kultus der Römer*[2], Munich.

Witt, R. E. 1971. *Isis in the Graeco-Roman World*, Ithaca.

Zijderveld, C. 1934. "Telete," diss. Utrecht.

Zuntz, G. 1963a. "Once More the So-called 'Edict of Philopator on the Dionysiac Mysteries' (BGU 1211)," *Hermes* 91, 228–239 (= Zuntz 1972, 88–101).

———— 1963b. "On the Dionysiac Fresco in the Villa dei Misteri at Pompei," *Proc. Brit. Acad.* 49, 177–202.

———— 1971. *Persephone*, Oxford.

———— 1972. *Opuscula Selecta*, Manchester/Cambridge.

Notes

꛰꛰꛰꛰꛰꛰꛰꛰꛰꛰꛰꛰꛰꛰꛰꛰꛰꛰꛰꛰꛰꛰꛰꛰꛰꛰꛰꛰꛰꛰꛰꛰꛰꛰

Introduction

1. See Reitzenstein 1927 (1910[1]; English trans. 1978); Cumont 1931 (original French ed. 1907; English trans. 1911). The work of Reitzenstein developed into a *religionsgeschichtliche Schule* exploring mainly the influence of Iranian religion on Gnosticism; see Colpe 1961. For the influence of Reitzenstein in theology see, for example, Dibelius 1917; Bultmann 1963 (1949[1]); Schneider 1954; J. Leipoldt, *Von den Mysterien zur Kirche* (Leipzig 1961), for whom early Christianity is a form of "mystery religion" (81). A mirage of Jewish mystery religion was created by J. Pascher, *He basilike Hodos: Der Königsweg zu Wiedergeburt und Vergottung bei Philon von Alexandreia* (Paderborn 1931), and in a more subtle way by E. R. Goodenough, *By Light, Light: The Mystic Gospel of Hellenistic Judaism* (New Haven 1935). An independent study claiming the influence of mysteries on Christianity was Loisy 1930 (1919[1]), based largely on Cumont. A scholar who maintained a cautious and critical position was A. D. Nock; see, for example, Nock 1952. For a more recent, cautious assessment, see Köster 1980 (English trans. 1982), sec. 4d, who still speaks of an "age of mystery religions" (209) and is inclined to include Christianity among them (206). As pertinent surveys, Prümm 1960 and Nilsson *GGR* II[2] (1961) should still be mentioned. For a bibliography see Metzger 1984. Schneider 1979 (edited posthumously) lacks references; Goodwin 1981 is a syncretistic picture book.

2. This series (Leiden: Brill) started in 1961, reached its one hundredth volume in 1984, and is still continuing; it includes *CCCA* (vol. 50), Bianchi 1979 (vol. 80), Bianchi-Vermaseren 1982 (vol. 92); it was preceded by *CIMRM* (1956/60).

3. See Hinnells 1975; Duchesne-Guillemin 1978; *Journal of Mithraic Studies* 1–3 (1976–1980).

4. Especially in vol. II, 17(3/4, 1984); see Beck, Johnson, Leclant, Malaise, Metzger, Thomas.

5. See Sabbatucci 1979; Bianchi 1979, 1980; Cosi 1976, 1982; Casadio 1982, 1983; Sfameni Gasparro 1979, 1981, 1985; Lévêque 1982; for criticism of Cumont's picture of Mithraism, see Gordon 1975, cf. n. 29; for Reitzenstein, see n. 1 above.

6. Reitzenstein 1927, 94–108, tried to establish, against E. Meyer and others, that the "mystery religions" date from the Hellenistic epoch, not from later antiquity, but excluded the old Greek mysteries as insignificant (3n.; 133). In the same vein, Giversen 1975 treats gnosticism and "mystery religions" together without regard to Eleusis or Dionysus.

7. See n. 22 below.

8. Reitzenstein 1927, 2: "Ich bezeichne dabei mit dem Worte 'Hellenistisch' Religionsformen, in denen orientalische und griechische Elemente sich mischen"; 3n.: "die dem Orient entlehnten, also hellenistischen Mysterienvorstellungen."

9. This was stated by Wilamowitz 1932, 368–387; cf. Schneider 1939. This is not the place to discuss the various phenomena of Egyptian or Mesopotamian religion that have been called "mysteries" by modern scholars at one time or another. For Isis, see chap. II, n. 66 below; for the mirage of *Iranisches Erlösungsmysterium* created by Reitzenstein, see Colpe 1961, 1975. M. Adriani, *Misteri e iniziazione in oriente* (Florence 1978), is nothing but a popularized survey of so-called mystery religions.

10. Reitzenstein 1927, 9: "Um Unsterblichkeit, also im allerweitesten Sinne um 'Erlösung,' handelt es sich bei dem eigentlich religiösen Teil dieser Mysterien immer."

11. This begins with Justin Martyr *Apol.* 1.54, 1.66.4; *Dial. c. Tryph.* 70, 78; Tertullian *Cor.* 15, *Bapt.* 5, *Praescr. haer.* 40; see also Firmicus *Err.* 22.1, 27; Ambrosiaster *PL* 35.2279; Augustine *In Ioh. tract.* 7.1.6, *PL* 35.1440, etc.; Cosi 1976, 66. Lucian *Mort. Per.* 11 calls Christianity a "new *telete*," as Origen, adopting his opponent's terms, calls Christianity "the *teletai* which are with us," *Cels.* 3.59.

12. The most explicit testimony is Irenaeus *Haer.* 1.21.3 (1.14.2 p. 185 Harvey): "They prepare a bridal chamber and celebrate mysteries." Clement repeatedly says the Gnostics celebrate sexual intercourse as mysteries, *Strom.* 3.27.1,5, cf. 3.10.1; 3.30.1. A homosexual encounter is insinuated in the "Secret Gospel of Mark," Smith 1973, 115–117; 185; 452. See also R. M. Grant, "The Mysteries of Marriage in the Gospel of Philip," *Vig. Christ.* 15 (1961) 129–140. Cf. chap. III at nn. 6–7; chap. IV at nn. 114–118.

13. Von Soden 1911; Prümm 1937; in general, see Rahner 1945; Nock 1952; Hamilton 1977; Wiens 1980; Riedweg 1987.

14. E. Renan, *Marc Aurèle et la fin du monde antique* (Paris 1882), 579 (= *Oeuvres complètes*, Paris 1947, v, 1107; quoted by Cumont 1923, 188):

"On peut dire que, si le christianisme eût été arrêté dans sa croissance par quelque maladie mortelle, le monde eût été mithriaste."

15. Cf. Sanders 1980–82; Meyer-Sanders 1982.

16. Pride of place is due to Samothrace (see Cole 1984; *GR* 282–285); mention should be made of the Kabirion near Thebes (*GR* 281f.) and, in Caria, of Zeus of Panamara (Oppermann 1924; the evidence now in M. C. Şahin, *Die Inschriften von Stratonikeia*, Cologne 1981/82). Nilsson 1950 claims that *mysteria* is used in a loose and uncharacteristic way in the later period, but he shows unjustified prejudice against dancing and feasting in mysteries.

17. The old standard work was Foucart 1914, outdated by the excavations; for the material evidence, see Mylonas 1961; for a serious attempt at understanding, see Kerényi 1967; basic for prosopography and history is Clinton 1974. See also *HN* 248–256; *GR* 285–290.

18. See Casadio 1982, 1983; *GR* 290–295; a basic study was Quandt 1912. Nilsson 1957 is still quite useful, even if the evidence for the older period, partly ignored in his book, has considerably increased since then; see also Festugière 1972, 13–63 (originally 1935); Kerényi 1976.

19. See chap. II, n. 11 below.

20. *GR* 286–301; cf. chap. III at n. 127.

21. Wissowa 1912, 317.

22. The old standard work is Graillot 1912; *CCCA* is far from completion; a careful survey is given by Thomas 1984; see also Vermaseren 1977; for the historical development of the cult see *S&H* 102–122, *GR* 177–179; for the reading *matar kubileya* in Phrygian see C. Brixhe, *Die Sprache* 25 (1979) 40–45.

23. See Sfameni Gasparro 1985.

24. Rutter 1968; Duthoy 1969; *S&H* 1979, 201f.; cf. chap. IV, n. 45 below.

25. The material on the cults of the Egyptian gods is enormous. For a bibliography, see Leclant-Clerc 1972, 1974, 1985; for the diffusion of the cults, see esp. Dunand 1973; Vidman 1970; Malaise 1972, 1984; Leclant 1984. Recent general accounts are Witt 1971; Le Corsu 1977; Solmsen 1979.

26. Herodotus 2.42.2, 2.59.2, 2.144.2, 2.156.5; he is probably following Hecataeus.

27. Hornbostel 1973; Kater-Sibbes 1973; Fraser 1972, 246–276.

28. Commentary: Griffiths 1976.

29. The basic work was Cumont 1896/1899, of which Cumont 1923 (original French ed. 1900) is an excerpt. The archaeological evidence was brought up to date by Vermaseren in *CIMRM*, followed by his synthesis, Vermaseren 1963. In the 1970s there were three major congresses on Mithraic studies, published by Hinnells 1975, Duchesne-Guillemin 1978, Bianchi 1979; for an excellent short survey see Turcan 1981a; a major new

synthesis is Merkelbach 1984; a careful survey of scholarship is given by Beck 1984. For the name Mithra see A. Meillet, *Journal Asiatique* x, 10 (1907) 143–159; P. Thieme, "Mitra and Aryaman," *Transactions of the Connecticut Academy of Arts and Sciences* 41 (1957) 1–96; Merkelbach 1984, 4f. On the Mitanni evidence for Mithra, see P. Thieme, *Kleine Schriften* I (Wiesbaden 1971), 396–412; M. Mayrhofer, *Die Indo-Arier im alten Vorderasien* (Wiesbaden 1966); *Die Arier im Vorderen Orient—ein Mythos?* (Vienna 1974). On theophoric names such as Mitradata see Cumont 1896, II, 75–85; R. Schmitt in Duchesne-Guillemin 1978, 395–455.

30. Mark 4.11 and Pauline epistles; cf. Bornkamm in *Kittels Theologisches Wörterbuch zum Neuen Testament*, IV, 823–831; see also Smith 1973, 178–188.

31. For the *kiste* at Eleusis, see Pringsheim 1905, 49–64, esp. the *synthema*, chap. IV, n. 22; in connection with Dionysus, Demosthenes 18.260, Theocritus 26.7, "cistophoric" coins of Pergamon (F. S. Kleiner and S. P. Noe, *The Early Cistophoric Coinage*, New York 1977), see also A. Henrichs, *ZPE* 4 (1969) 230f.; in connection with Attis, Catullus 64.259; see Fig. 10; in connection with Isis, see chap. II, n. 62 below. The *kiste* does not appear in Mithraic contexts.

32. See L. Bouyer, "Mystique: Essai sur l'histoire d'un mot," in *La vie spirituelle, ascétique et mystique*, S.9 (1949) 3–23; Casadio 1982, 210–212.

33. The bilingual inscription from Samothrace, late Hellenistic period, published by J. R. McCredie in *Hesperia* 48 (1979) 16f. (= *SEG* 29, 799) has *initiatei* corresponding to *mystai*. Samothracum initia, Varro *De lingua lat.* 5.58; Cicero *De legibus* 2.36 (referring to Eleusis); Livy 31.14.7 (Eleusis), 39.9.4 (Bacchanalia); *initiari*, Cicero *De nat. deorum* 1.119 (Eleusis), *Tusculans* 1.29; *initiare*, Livy 39.9.4 (Bacchanalia). Following Latin usage, the word "initiand" will be used here to designate the candidate for initiation, in contrast to the "initiate," who has already undergone initiation.

34. Fundamental was van Gennep 1909; see, in general, Eliade 1958, Bleeker 1965; for the concept of "status dramatization," see F. W. Young, *Initiation Ceremonies: A Cross-cultural Study of Status Dramatization* (Indianapolis 1965); V. Popp, ed., *Zeremonien der Statusänderung und des Rollenwechsels* (Frankfurt 1969); see also Berner 1972.

35. Theophrastus *Characters* 16.12 has the superstitious man getting himself initiated every month; this is comic exaggeration of a real possibility. On taurobolium see chap. I, n. 27; on Lucius-Apuleius' repeated initiations, chap. I at nn. 23–26. At Eleusis and Samothrace those who come back become *epoptai*, "watching" the rites instead of undergoing them. See also Dodds 1951, 75f.; Nock 1972, 796. Repetition is essential in Plato's metaphorical transposition, *Phaedrus* 249c.

36. PY Un2,1, cf. L. Baumbach *Glotta* 49 (1971) 174; M. Gérard-Rousseau, *Les mentions religieuses dans les tablettes mycéniennes* (Rome 1968),

146f. The connection with *myo*, "to shut one's eyes or lips," may be just popular etymology.

37. *GR* 44f. n. 13; 31.

38. Mylonas 1961, 29–54; a note of caution is struck by P. Darcque, *BCH* 105 (1981) 593–605.

39. A. Leukart in *Flexion und Wortbildung: Akten der V. Fachtagung der Indogermanischen Gesellschaft* (Wiesbaden 1975), 175–191.

40. Mycenaean *tereta* (evidently = Greek *telestes*) disproved the connection with a root *kwel-*, cf. P. Chantraine, *Dictionnaire étymologique de la langue grecque* (Paris 1957–1980), 1103; F. M. J. Waanders, *The History of TELOS and TELEO in Ancient Greek* (Amsterdam 1983).

41. Zijderveld 1934; Kern, *PW* v A 393–397; Dowden 1980, 415f.; Coche de la Ferté 1980, 233–241; Casadio 1983, 124–126. Athenaeus 40d, though, defines *teletai* as "festivals with some mystical tradition" (*paradosis*, cf. chap. III at n. 14).

42. Herodotus 4.79.1; *telein toi Dionysoi LSAM* 48.18 and in the edict of Philopator, see chap. II, n. 10; galli *teloumenoi tei theoi Et. M.* 220.25; cf. *epi Demetran tetelentai LSCG* 96.22; *Bakcheia telesthenai* Aristophanes *Frogs* 357. *Telein* is also used for the initiation of a king (Plutarch *Artoxerxes* 3.1) and of priests, *GR* 98 n. 46. Following the Greek usage, "to initiate to a god" will be used here in the sense of "to initiate into the mysteries of a divinity."

43. Cf. Burg 1939; A. Henrichs, *ZPE* 4 (1969) 226–229. First in *Homeric Hymn to Demeter* 273; 476 (Eleusis); *ta myston orgia* Euripides *Heracles* 613 (Eleusis); *Demetros kai Kores mysteria kai orgia* Ps.-Thessalos *Presb.* in Hippocrates, ed. Littré, IX, 420; *Eleusinia e Samothrakia orgia* Galen *De usu part.* 7.14 XVII 1, 366 K.

44. *Arrhetos telete* (Eleusis) in a fifth-century epigram from the Eleusinion *Agora* III, 226 = *IG* I³953 = Hansen no. 317; *arrhetos Kore* Euripides *fr.* 63, *Helen* 1307; *arrheta orgia* Euripides *Bacchae* 470–472; *arrheta hiera* Aristophanes *Clouds* 302; *mysteria aporrheta* Euripides *Rhesus* 943, Aristophanes *Ecclesiazusae* 442; *ta aporrheta tes kata ta mysteria teletes IG* II/III² 1110 = *SIG* 873 (epistle of Commodus); *teletai aporrhetoi* (Mithras) Plutarch *Pompey* 24.7.

45. *GR* 251–254.

46. Plutarch *Pericles* 13.7, cf. n. 44 above.

47. Heraclitus B 14 Diels-Kranz = 87 Marcovich; for Hipponion, see chap. I, n. 49, *GR* 293; for *telein*, see n. 42 above; Dionysus is the lord of *telestike mania*, Plato *Phaedrus* 265b; *tes teletes kai ton Dionysiakon mysterion* Diodorus 1.23.2; *mysteria kai teletas kai bakcheias* Diodorus 3.63.2; *mysteria* in Pergamon, *Inschriften von Pergamon* 248 = *OGI* 331.38; 55; Ohlemutz 1940, 109–116; in Kyme, *Epigraphica Anatolica* 1 (1983) 34, line 13; *teletai* Euripides *Bacchae* 22, etc. The term *teletai* occurs also in the Lycurgus story as attributed to Eumelus, *Europia* in *Schol. A Il.* 6.131, but we cannot be sure about the author, much less about his words.

48. See Sfameni Gasparro 1985, 21–25; *mysteria* of Sabazius, Agdistis and Ma at Sardis, *SEG* 29, 1205, see chap. II, n. 110; *Metros Megales mysteria* Hippolytus *Ref.* 5.9.10; *mystai Anth. Pal.* 6.51; *telete, teloumenoi* at Amorgos, *LSCG* 103 B 11f.; *telesteres* at Troizene, *IG* IV, 757 = *CCCA* II, 479; *telete Metros* Pausanias 2.3.4. *Schol. Pind. Py.* 3.137b has *teletai,* 140 *mysteria; koinon ton myston* at Argos, *IG* IV, 1,659 = *CCCA* II, 469. A *tauroboliatus* as *mystipolos teleton IG* XIV, 1018 = *CIL* VI, 509 = *CCCA* III, 236 = Duthoy 1969 no. 22, cf. *CCCA* III, 237, *tauroboli . . . dux mystici sacri CCCA* III, 243 = Duthoy no. 24; *teletai IG* XIV, 1019 = *CCCA* III, 238 = Duthoy no. 31, cf. no. 28. "I became a *mystes* of Attis" Firmicus *Err* 18.1, see at chap. IV, n. 44; *myein,* Suda s.v. *metragyrtes.*

49. Apuleius *Metamorphoses* 11.22, 24, 27, 30; *mysteria* Artemidorus 2.39, Hippolytus *Ref.* 5.7.22; *mystes SIRIS* 295, 390; see chap. II at n. 62.

50. Justin Martyr *Apol.* 1.66.9; Pallas, *Peri ton tou Mithra mysterion* in Porphyry *Abst.* 2.56, cf. 4.16; *myoumenoi* Porphyry *Antr.* 15; *initiantur* Tertullian *Cor.* 15; *he tou Mithra telete* Origen *Cels.* 6.22, *Persika mysteria* ibid; *mysta booklopies* in a formula, Firmicus *Err.* 5; *hai Persikai hai tou Mithra teletai* Proclus *In remp.* II, 345, 4 Kroll.

51. Apuleius *Metamorphoses* 11.17.

52. Livy 39.11.1.

53. Herodotus 8.65.4, 4.79.1; cf. M. West, *ZPE* 45 (1982) 25.

54. Euripides *Bacchae* 474.

55. Painting of Polygnotus at Delphi, Pausanias 10.29.1f.; an earlier Lekythos at Palermo, C. H. Haspels, *Attic Black-Figured Lekythoi* (Paris 1936), 66 pl. 19, 5, cf. Graf 1974, 188–194. A penitential inscription from Asia Minor (*MAMA* 4, 1933, n. 281) states that the dedicant was punished by the god "because he did not wish to come and take part in the mystery when he was called."

56. Tertullian *Apol.* 8.7, sarcastically describing the cannibalistic mysteries of Christianity in the pagans' fantasy, still making use of the pagans' knowledge about the appropriate procedure; *pater* points to mysteries of Mithras; cf. *petitor CIMRM* 41; Francis 1975, 439.

57. See B. Snell, *The Discovery of the Mind* (New York 1960; original German ed. 1946). For the tendency to make mysteries Mycenaean, see n. 38. Herodotus 2.171, on pre-Dorian *thesmophoria* in Arcadia, is important but inconclusive in this respect.

58. Plato *Laws* 815cd, 909d–910c; Cicero *De legibus* 2.21; Philo *Spec.* 1.319–323, cf. the speech of Maecenas in Dio Cassius 52.36.

59. This tentative definition largely coincides with the term *misterico* in the typology of Bianchi (in Bleeker 1965, 154–171; Bianchi 1976, 1–8; Bianchi 1979, 5–9, 1980, 11; cf. Cosi 1976, 54; Sfameni Gasparro 1981, 377, 1985, 6). Bianchi wishes to distinguish this from *mistico* in the sense of *esperienza di interferenza* between god, world, and self (that is, a somewhat larger concept than mysticism proper, cf. n. 32), and from *misteriosofico,* the speculative elaborations of Orphism or Platonism (see chap. III).

I. Personal Needs

1. "Personal religion" is the subject of Festugière 1954. He does not discuss votive religion.

2. Plato *Laws* 909e. The term "votive religion" has been used, for example, by Q. F. Maule and H. R. W. Smith, *Votive Religion at Caere: Prolegomena* (Berkeley 1959). The basic work, outdated but not replaced, is Rouse 1902. A valuable collection of materials is van Straten 1981; for Christian practice, see L. Kriss-Rettenbeck, *Ex Voto. Zeichen, Bild und Abbild im christlichen Votivbrauchtum* (Zurich 1972). Cf. also *GR* 68–70. "Votive religion," like "personal religion," signifies a special form of worship within ancient religion, not a separate religion; in the same sense the term "mystery religion" (singular) would be unobjectionable.

3. See W. Eisenhut, *PW* suppl. xiv, 964–973 s.v. *votum*.

4. D. Wachsmuth, "Pompimos ho Daimon," diss. Berlin 1965.

5. Hansen no. 227 = *IG* I³728.

6. Visions: Plato *Laws* 910a; *kat' onar*: cf. F. T. van Straten, *BABesch* 51 (1976) 1–38.

7. Diogenes Laertius 6.59; Cicero *De nat. deorum* 3.89; Diagoras Melius (ed. M. Winiarczyk, Teubner 1981) T 36–37.

8. Attested in Isis contexts: *Pap. Ox.* 1380, 152 ὁρῶσί σε οἱ κατὰ τὸ πιστὸν ἐπικαλούμενοι; *plena fiducia*, Apuleius *Metamorphoses* 11.28; *crede et noli deficere*, *SIRIS* 390. Asclepius of Epidaurus punishes a reluctant believer by renaming him Apistos, *SIG* 1168, 29–33; A. Henrichs *HSCP* 82 (1978) 210f. See F. Chapouthier, "De la bonne foi dans la dévotion antique," *REG* 45 (1932) 391–396.

9. See, for example, J. D. Frank, *Persuasion and Healing*² (Baltimore 1973; *Die Heiler*, Stuttgart 1981).

10. Nock 1933, 7.

11. See above, n. 3.

12. To give just a few examples: for Isis, *SIRIS* p. 68, *CE* 72 "saved from many great dangers," cf. *SIRIS* 198, 406, 538 (*salus*); Egyptian gods in general as *soteres:* Artemidorus 2.39. For Meter, *Matri deum salutari, CCCA* III, 201; *conservatoribus suis, CCCA* III, 229; saved from captivity: E. Schwertheim in *Studien zur Religion und Kultur Kleinasiens: Festschrift F. K. Dörner* (Leiden 1978), 811. For Mithras, *CIMRM* 171 (*soteria*); "saved from water" *CIMRM* 568. See esp. Piccaluga 1982.

13. *CIMRM* 568, cf. *CCCA* VII 69. See also Lucian *De merc. cond.* 1 (Isis); cf. n. 4 above.

14. *SIRIS* 5, 106, 107, 269, 308; *pro salute coniugis pientissimi, CCCA* IV, 219; *pro salute amici karissimi, CIMRM* 1873, cf. 144, 804, 819, 916, 567, 658, etc.

15. *SIRIS* 404, 405, 535, 552, 560, 702; *pro amore patriae, SIRIS* 779; *CCCA* III, 9, 401; in connection with taurobolium *CCCA* III, 405–407; 417; *CCCA* IV, 172, see Cosi 1976, 68; very common with Mithraists, *CIMRM* 53, 54, 142, 146, etc.

16. Diodorus 1.25.4, cf. Diogenes Laertius 5.76 on Demetrius of Phaleron; *iatreia*, *IDélos* 2116, 2117, 2120; Isis Hygieia, *SIRIS* p. 71, *CE* 124 = *IDélos* 2060; *SIRIS* 16 (Athens, Asclepieum); on Asclepius-Sarapis, see *SIRIS* 7 with notes; on incubation, Dunand 1973, II, 102f.; limbs as votives, Dunand 1973, I, 63, 170; II, 106; van Straten 1981, 105–151.

17. Tibullus 1.3.23–32.

18. In the cult of Isis, Ovid *Epistulae ex Ponto* 1.1.52–56, Juvenal 6.535–541, cf. Hommel 1983, and in general F. S. Steinleitner, "Die Beicht im Zusammenhange mit der sakralen Rechtspflege in der Antike," diss. Munich 1913.

19. Aelius Aristides 45.18; *SIRIS* 389, cf. 513; tax reduction, *SIRIS* 574.

20. For example, *CIMRM* 423 (*spelaeum*), 1242f. (*aram*), 1948 (*signum*).

21. *CIMRM* 2307.

22. *CIMRM* 423; for *syndexioi*, see Firmicus *Err.* 5.2; Bidez-Cumont 1938, II, 153f.; Merkelbach 1984, 107.

23. Nock 1933, 138–155: "The Conversion of Lucius," explicitly drawing the parallel to "a man received into the Catholic church," 155. I see no special justification for the Pauline formula "living in the world but not as of the world" being applied to Lucius.

24. Apuleius *Metamorphoses* 11.28.5: *nec minus etiam victum uberiorem subministrabat . . .* , cf. 30.2. On the sudden appearance of *Madaurensem* in 11.27.8, see R. Th. van der Paardt, *Mnemosyne* IV, 34 (1981) 96–106.

25. Apuleius *Metamorphoses* 11.30.4: *incunctanter gloriosa in foro redderem patrocinia nec extimescerem malevolorum disseminationes.*

26. Apuleius *Metamorphoses* 11.21.6; cf. J. Bergman in H. Ringgren (ed.), *Fatalistic Beliefs* (Stockholm 1967), 37f. Griffiths 1976, 166 is puzzled about *novae*. Tibetans, on recovery from serious illness, take a new name.

27. *CIL* VI, 504 = *CIMRM* 514 = *CCCA* III, 233 = Duthoy 1969 no. 17; *iterato viginti annis expletis taurobolii sui*, *CIL* VI, 512 = *CCCA* III, 244 = *SIRIS* 447 = Duthoy no. 25 (Rome, 390 A.D.); cf. *CIL* X, 1596 = Duthoy no. 50 = *CCCA* IV, 11.

28. *CCCA* III, 239 = Duthoy no. 33.

29. On the background of this collection of hymns, see R. Keydell, *PW* XVIII, 1330–1332. Health and wealth: 15.10f.; 17.10; 40.20; hymn to Health, no. 68; a good year, 43.10; fruit, 56.12; seafaring, 74.10; salvation on land and sea, 75.5; "pleasant life" granted by the Sun god, 8.20; Hestia should keep the *mystai* "ever flourishing, rich in fortune, in good spirits, and pure," 84.

30. Athens, Nat. Mus. no. 1390; *RML* III, 2124; Preisendanz, *RML* V, 327–329, *contra* Kern, *PW* V A 396f.; E. Kunze in E. Langlotz, *Aphrodite in den Gärten* (Sitzungsber. Heidelberg 1953/4, 2), 49 n. 32; S. Karusu, *Römische Mitt.* 76 (1969) 256, pl. 83, 2. Interpretation remains controversial.

31. Plato *Phaedrus* 244f.,265b; *Laws* 815c. In Sophocles *Antigone* 1144 and *Oedipus Tyrannus* 203ff. Dionysus is to chase off pollution and disease. See Linforth 1946b; *OE* 66f.

32. Aristotle *Politics* 1341 b 32 through 1342 a 18, connected with the definition of tragedy at *Poetics* 1449 b 24–28 since J. Bernays, *Grundzüge der verlorenen Abhandlung des Aristoteles über Wirkung der Tragödie* (Breslau 1857). Bernays, however, disliked the "charlatans" and tried to make *katharsis* a concept of "pure" medicine. The terms "possessed" (*katokochimoi*) and "sacred tunes" in Aristotle (1342 a 8f.) clearly refer to the Corybants, of whom we learn most from Plato, *Ion* 534a, *Euthydemus* 277d. See Linforth 1946a; Dodds 1951, 77–80; Jeanmaire 1951, 131–138; Cosi 1983, 134f.

33. Aristophanes *Wasps* 118–124 (*teletai*, 121); see K. J. Reckford, "Catharsis and Dream-Interpretation in Aristophanes' *Wasps*," *TAPA* 107 (1977) 283–312.

34. Demosthenes 18.259–260, 19.199, 249, 281; Aristotle *Politics* 1342 a 14f. Cf. H. Wankel, *Demosthenes, Rede für Ktesiphon über den Kranz* (Heidelberg 1976), 1132–1149. Aeschines was born in 390, and the activities described are thus dated to ca. 380/375. This is the most detailed description of *telete* in the classical period. Fragments of an ancient commentary on the passage survive in Harpocration s.vv. *apomatton, Attes, enthrypta, euoi, kittophoros, leuke, liknophoros, nebrizon, neelata, pareiai opheis, streptous,* with interesting details about Dionysiac mysteries; cf. chap. IV, n. 36. See also *OE* 45f.

35. *Schol. Ap. Rh.*1.916b; cf. Introduction, n. 16.

36. *LSCG* 7; *IG* I^3 7 = *LSCG* 5; cf. Graf 1974, 159, 180f. Pictures with Plutos, "Wealth," born amidst Eleusinian divinities: Kerényi 1967, 163–165; Metzger 1965, pl. 16.

37. Votive relief of Eucrates, Athens Nat. Mus. A 11386, Kerényi 1967, 96–98; van Straten 1981, fig. 56; *Anth. Pal.* 9.298.

38. *Homeric Hymn to Demeter* 219–274; cf. Richardson 1974, esp. 231–238, 242f. On the date of the hymn see *Gnomon* 49 (1977) 442f.

39. "Metternich Stele" rev. 48ff., in C. E. Sander-Hansen, *Die Texte der Metternich-Stele* (Copenhagen 1956), 35–43; a parallel text in A. Klasens, *A Magical Statue Base [socle Bétague] in the Museum of Antiquities at Leiden* (Leiden 1952), 52f., 64–78. The Metternich Stele is dated to the 30th dynasty, fourth century B.C.; the single charms are older. German translation of the text in G. Roeder, *Urkunden zur Religion des alten Aegypten* (Jena 1915), 87–89; paraphrase in E. A. W. Budge, *Egyptian Magic* (London 1899), 130–133.

40. Egyptian parallels in Klasens (see n. 39), 75. A Greek charm about Horos burning: *PGM* 20, II^2 145, 265; H. D. Betz (ed.), *The Greek Magical Papyri in Translation* (Chicago 1986), 258; L. Koenen, *Chronique d'Egypte* 37 (1962) 167–174 (without reference to the Metternich Stele).

The text has *mystodokos,* clearly referring to mysteries, possibly to the child in the fire at Eleusis.

41. The tale about the child in the fire is transposed to Isis at Byblos, Plutarch *Isis* 357bc; this is probably "Greek influence": Richardson 1974, 238 with lit.

42. On Eastern healing magic influencing archaic Greece, see *OE* 57–77.

43. The examples of "putting children on the fire" adduced by J. G. Frazer, *Apollodorus II* (Loeb 1921), 311–317, center on magical protection. For the connection of charms and afterlife see nn.66–69.

44. *Homeric Hymn to Demeter* 480–482, cf. Richardson ad loc.; Pindar *fr.* 137a; Sophocles *fr.* 837 Radt; Isocrates *Panegyricus* 28; Krinagoras *Anth. Pal.* 11.42.

45. *IG* II/III² 3661, 6; Clinton 1974, 42.

46. Cicero *De legibus* 2.36.

47. *Odyssey* 24.74f.; Stesichorus 234 Page; represented on the François vase as Dionysus' wedding gift for Thetis, A. Rumpf, *Gnomon* 25 (1953) 469f., E. Simon, *Die griechischen Vasen* (Munich 1976), 70f. (T. H. Carpenter, *Dionysian Imagery in Archaic Greek Art,* Oxford 1986, 11 raises doubts about this interpretation.)

48. Plato *Republic* 365a; for the threat of punishment in the beyond, cf. Plato *Laws* 870de; in Dionysiac mysteries, Plutarch *Cons. ad ux.* 611d; Nilsson 1957, 122f.; see also n. 69 below.

49. G. Pugliese Carratelli and G. Foti, *PP* 29 (1974) 108–126; M. L. West *ZPE* 18 (1975) 229–236; Cole 1980; *GR* 295. Aristophanes *Frogs* 448–455, cf. Graf 1974, 79–94.

50. E. Schwyzer, *Dialectorum Graecarum exempla epigraphica potiora* (Leipzig 1923), no. 792; L. H. Jeffery, *The Local Scripts of Archaic Greece* (Oxford 1961), 240 no. 12; Nilsson 1957, 12f.

51. Herodotus 2.81; for the text see *L&S* 127f.

52. Rusajeva 1978, 96–98.

53. Pindar *fr.* 131a.

54. Pausanias 10.31.9,11; Amphora Munich 1493, *ABV* 316, 7 and Lekythos Palermo, see Introduction n.55; Graf 1974, 110–120; Keuls 1974, 34–41.

55. This equivalence resounds in the ode in Sophocles *Antigone* 1117–1121 (keeping 1119 *Italian* against the conjecture of R. D. Dawe in the Teubner edition, 1979).

56. See H. R. W. Smith 1972 (a most unreadable text, but with interesting points); Schmidt, Trendall, and Cambitoglou 1976; Schneider-Herrmann 1977/78. The deceased woman as maenad on an Etruscan sarcophagus lid: Horn 1972, 82 pl. 50.

57. Matz 1963; R. Turcan, *Les sarcophages romains à représentations Dionysiaques* (Paris 1966); F. Matz, *Die dionysischen Sarkophage* (Berlin 1968–1975); Geyer 1977.

58. Geyer 1977, 61–67; cf. chap. iv at n. 27.

59. E. Gàbrici, *MAL* 33 (1929) 50–53; A. M. Bisi, *ACl* 22 (1970) 97–106; for *kalathos* and *kiste* in the Eleusinian synthema, see chap. iv, n. 22.

60. Dioscorides *Anth. Pal.* 7.485; *SEG* 33.563; Nonnos 19.167–197; grapes, wine, tympana, even thyrsoi and satyrs beside the tomb on Apulian vases, cf. n. 56; parody *Anth. Pal.* 7.406. Burial by a Dionysiac *thiasos: IG* ii/iii² 11674 = no. 153 Kaibel = no. 1029 Peek; *IG* vii 686; *SEG* 31, 633; 32, 488; this, however, is a common obligation in clubs, see ibid. 486, 487.

61. *CIL* iii, 686 = *CLE* 1233; Festugière 1972, 30; Horn 1972, 20: "whether the female initiates, marked with the seal of Bromios, wish to have you as a consort of the satyrs on the flowery meadow, or the naiads . . ." Various identifications of a dead child with gods are suggested in *CIL* vi, 21521 = *CLE* 1109 = *CCCA* iii, 334; cf. *Sammelb.* no. 2134 (Nock 1972, 305 n. 145). Identification of a dead child with Dionysus: no. 705 Kaibel = no. 1030 Peek; relief in Bologna, Nilsson 1957, 107, fig. 27; Horn 1972, 52, 46; 91; fig. 49. Cf. n. 80.

62. Plato *Republic* 330d; Plutarch *Non posse* 1105b.

63. See chap. iii.

64. See chap. iv at nn. 51–70.

65. See Introduction at n. 34.

66. Plato *Phaedrus* 244f. (see at n. 31); for Near Eastern connections, see *OE* 65–72.

67. Plato *Republic* 365a; see n. 31.

68. See n. 49.

69. *Homeric Hymn to Demeter* 367–369, cf. Richardson ad loc.; this is not directly related to the institution of the Eleusinian mysteries in 473–482, but there is no contradiction either; it is surprisingly close to the practices criticized by Plato (n. 67).

70. Augustine *City of God* 7.26; but in 7.24 he states, in connection with Magna Mater, that "not even the demons ventured to make any great promises for these rituals." Cf. Nock 1972, 296–305, "Mysteries and the Afterlife"; Cosi 1976, 67; 7of.

71. Common burial ground: *CCCA* iv, 16, cf. iii, 422; private burial: *CCCA* iii, 261, cf. 462; iv, 241; participation of *sodales* in burial (cf. n.60): *CIL* vi, 10098 = *CCCA* iii, 355; *CIL* vi, 2265 = *CCCA* iii, 361.

72. See *CCCA* iii, *praefatio; CCCA* vi, 23–26; iv, 210.

73. Damascius *Vit. Is.* sec. 131 Zintzen; Cumont 1931, 55.

74. *CIL* vi, 510 = *CIMRM* 520 = *CCCA* iii, 242 = Duthoy 1969 no. 23. Cf. chap. iii at n. 56, chap. iv at n. 70.

75. See I. Lévy, "Les inscriptions araméennes de Memphis," *Journal asiatique* 121 (1927) 281–310, who gives seven instances of the Greek formula from Egypt; older is an Aramaic inscription (third century b.c.; Lévy 303; *CIS* i, 141) which has "take water in front of Osiris." From outside Egypt: *SIRIS* 459–462 (Rome); 778 (Carthage); see also Cumont 1931, 93; 250f.

76. Athenagoras 22.8; cf. Plutarch *Isis* 352bc; Damascius *Vit. Is.* sec. 107 (on the Neoplatonic philosopher Heraiscus, who was in fact an Egyptian priest).

77. See Dunand 1973, II, 144–150 with pl. 4; 20, 2; 23; 40, 2, etc.; *SIRIS passim.*

78. *SIRIS* 586; Egger 1951; Vidman 1970, 132–138; H. Gabelmann, *Die Werkstattgruppen der oberitalischen Sarkophage* (Bonn 1973), 147–157.

79. S. Şahin in *Hommages à M. J. Vermaseren* (Leiden 1978), III, 997f., *SEG* 28, 1585; cf. *SIRIS* 42; for the motif "not to Hades, but . . ." cf. *SEG* 26, 1280.

80. See v. Gonzenbach 1957; Diez 1968/71; Vidman 1970, 128f., 131; *SIRIS* 542; 746; 747; *nomen tenebit Isidis nati puer, SIRIS* 585. For identification with Dionysus, see n. 61; in general, H. Wrede, *Consecratio in formam deorum: Vergöttlichte Privatpersonen in der römischen Kaiserzeit* (Mainz 1981). The deification of dead children is not dependent on initiation; a decisive impulse came from Augustus when Germanicus' son died and was made "Eros," Suetonius *Caligula* 7.

81. Apuleius *Metamorphoses* 11.6.5; *SIRIS* 464, on which see H. S. Versnel in *ZPE* 58 (1985) 264f.

82. Text from Maroneia 25 (cf. chap. II, n. 68), Grandjean 1975, 18; Bianchi 1980, 20–27.

83. Cumont 1923, 160. Private burials: *CIMRM* 624, 885, cf. 566, 623, 708.

84. Bianchi 1984, 2131–2134 speaks of *aeternitas,* claiming at the same time that there was an "eighth door" beyond the seven attested grades and steps; *unendlicher Himmelsraum,* Schwertheim 1979, 71. For *aeternali* in the Santa Prisca inscription see chap. IV, n. 148.

85. Origen *Cels.* 6.22; Porphyry *Antr.* 6; *Abst.* 4.16; see Turcan 1975. L. Campbell, *Mithraic Iconography and Ideology* (Leiden 1968), contains wild speculations.

86. Cf. chap. III at nn. 121–123. On an interesting graffito, *magicas invictas cede Degentio,* see H. Solin in Bianchi 1979, 137–140.

87. Julian *Symp.* 336c – Plato *Phaedo* 67c, *Phaedrus* 248a, 250b.

88. "Those around the tombs," Libanius *Or.* 62.10; "those clad in gray," Eunapius *Vit. soph.* 7.3.5; cf. *Iul. or.* 7, 344a.

89. Cicero's formulation, cf. n. 46.

90. *IG* XIV, 1449 = Kaibel 588 = *CCCA* III, 271 = L. Moretti, *Inscriptiones Graecae Urbis Romae* III, 1169 = H. W. Pleket, *Epigraphica* II (Leiden 1969), no. 57. The crucial line is 7: πάνθ᾽ ὑπολανθάνετε τὰ βίου συνεχῶς μυστήρια σεμνά.

91. G. W. H. Lampe, *Patristic Greek Lexicon* (Oxford 1961), s.v. *hypolanthano* refers to *Clementine Homilies* 20.13.

92. Cf. n. 82. *SIRIS* 789 on Felix, priest of Isis: *felix de nomine tantum; SIRIS* 396, an aedituus of Isis: *mulier infelicissuma.*

II. Organizations and Identities

1. J. Z. Smith 1978, 290; cf. R. L. Gordon 1980, 22: ". . . to validate the existence of a purely imaginary world."

2. U. v. Wilamowitz-Moellendorff, *Homerische Untersuchungen* (Berlin 1884), 213 speaks of "eine art kirchliche gemeinde" of Orphics and "die eleusinische kirche." Reitzenstein 1927 (1st ed. 1910) speaks of "Mysteriengemeinden" passim. He also assumed a "Poimandres-Gemeinde" for *Corp. Herm.* 1: see *Poimandres* (Leipzig 1904), 248; criticized by W. Kroll in *Neue Jahrbücher* 39 (1917) 150. See also Burkert 1982, 2 n. 4.

3. Plato *Phaedrus* 248de.

4. *Pap. Derv.* (published in *ZPE* 47, 1982; possibly Stesimbrotos *Peri Teleton,* see *ZPE* 62, 1986, 1–5): *ho technem poioumenos ta hiera.* Cf. the derogatory term *banausie* for miracle healers in Hippocrates *Morb. sacr.* 18, VI, 396 Littré; *to philotechnon* for "Dionysiac and Orphic arts," Strabo 10.3.23 p. 474; see also Burkert 1982 and *OE* 43–48. The term "charismatic" originated in St. Paul's use of *charisma* and was raised to a general category of religious and social studies by Max Weber; see W. E. Mühlmann in *Historisches Wörterbuch der Philosophie* I (Basel 1971), 988f.

5. Hippocrates *Morb. sacr.* 1, VI, 360 Littré; cf. the "Aglaophamos" text in Iamblichus *Vit. Pyth.* 146; the Hippocratic *Nomos* IV, 642 Littré; Introduction, n. 42 above.

6. *Oath,* Hippocrates IV, 628–632 Littré, cf. Ch. Lichtenthaeler, *Der Eid des Hippokrates* (Cologne 1984), esp. 79–110, 261–265; *Nomos,* cf. n. 5.

7. Plato *Republic* 364a–e; the anecdote about the *Orpheotelestes,* Plutarch *Lac. apophth.* 224e; Demosthenes on Aeschines, see chap. I, n. 34; in Latin literature, Plautus *Miles Gloriosus* 692; Ennius, Pacuvius, Naevius in Cicero *De divinatione* 1.132; Cato ibid. 2.51.

8. On Greek priests in general, see R. S. J. Garland, "Religious Authority in Archaic and Classical Athens," *BSA* 79 (1984) 75–123; *GR* 95–98; for Hellenistic Egypt, Otto 1905/08.

9. Marcus Aurelius 9.30. See Foucart 1873; Poland 1909; Laum 1914; San Nicolo 1913/15; Nock 1972, 430–442, "Greek and Egyptian Forms of Association."

10. W. Schubart, *Amtliche Berichte aus den Kgl. Preussischen Kunstsammlungen* 38 (1916/17) 189f.; *Sammelb.* no. 7266; cf. Nilsson 1957, 11f.; Zuntz 1963a; Fraser 1972, II, 345f.; *OE* 46.

11. Livy 39.8–19: *Graecus ignobilis . . . sacrificulus et vates,* 39.8.3; *Pacullam Anniam Campanam sacerdotem omnia tamquam deum monitu immutasse,* 39.13.9; *capita coniurationis . . . M. et C. Atinios de plebe Romana et Faliscum L. Opicernium et Minium Cerrinium Campanum* (son of Paculla, initiated by his mother, 13.9) 39.17.6. Cf. Festugière 1972, 89–109 (originally 1954); D. W. L. van Son, "Livius' behandeling van de Bacchanalia," diss. Amsterdam 1960; Bruhl 1953, 82–116; Nilsson 1957, 14–21; Rousselle 1982; Heilmann 1985.

12. Euripides *Bacchae* 465–474, cf. 232–238. On Euripides blending general Bacchic cult and Dionysiac mysteries, see *GR* 291f.

13. *LSAM* 48.19f.; Nilsson 1957, 6f.

14. Herodotus 4.78–80; *thiasotai*, A. Kocevalov, *Würzburger Jahrbücher* 3 (1948) 265; cf. Rusajeva 1978.

15. See chap. I, n. 34.

16. Plato *Republic* 364b–e; Theophrastus *Characters* 16.2.

17. The most thorough study of the gold plates is given by Zuntz 1971, 277–393, before the discovery at Hipponion (see chap. I, n. 49); an additional text is in the J. Paul Getty Museum, possibly from Thessaly, *ZPE* 25 (1977) 276; on the form of diffusion, see Janko 1984.

18. The inscriptional evidence was collected by Quandt 1912, Nilsson 1957; new findings include *Inscriptiones Graecae in Bulgaria repertae* III, 1517; *IG* x, 2,1, 259 = *SEG* 30,622 (Thessalonike); *Epigraphia Anatolica* 1 (1983) 34 (Kyme); there is no complete up-to-date collection. For the Villa of the Mysteries, the Farnesina house, and related iconography, see chap. IV at nn. 24 and 25. See Henrichs 1978; Geyer 1977; Cole 1980; Casadio 1982/83.

19. O. Kern, *Die Inschriften von Magnesia* (Berlin 1900), no. 215a; Henrichs 1978 has defended the authenticity of this text.

20. Plato *Phaedo* 69c = *OF* 5, 235.

21. A. Vogliano and F. Cumont, *AJA* 37 (1933) 215–263; Nilsson 1952, 524–541; 1957, 46f.; 51f.; middle of the second century A.D.

22. Mysteries of Lerna, *IG* IV, 666 = Kaibel no. 821; *IG* III/III², 4841 = Kaibel no. 822; *IG* II/III², 3674; *CIL* VI, 1779; 1780; *Anth. Pal.* 9.688; these are unique among Bacchic mysteries by being bound to one place. A mosaic from Cyprus, A.D. 325/50, shows the birth of Dionysus in a pattern evidently modeled on Christ adored by the magi: W. A. Daszewski, *Dionysos der Erlöser* (Mainz 1985).

23. Semonides *fr.* 36 West, cf. Hipponax *frr.* 127, 156 West.

24. See Introduction at n. 22; Cyzicus, Herodotus 4.76; graffito from Locri, Italy, seventh century B.C., M. Guarducci, *Klio* 52 (1970) 133–138.

25. Cratinus *fr.* 66 Kassel-Austin; Aristotle *Rhetoric* 1405a20.

26. E. W. Handley, *BICS* 16 (1969) 96; S. Charitonidis, L. Kahil, and R. Ginouvès, *Les mosaiques de la Maison du Ménandre à Mytilène* (Bern 1970), pl. 6. On performances of *galloi* as a kind of show business, see M. C. Giammarco Razzano, "I 'Galli di Cibele' nel culto di età ellenistica," *Ottava Miscellanea Greca e Romana: Studi pubblicati dall' Istituto Italiano per la Storia Antica* 33 (1982) 227–266.

27. Clearchus *fr.* 47 Wehrli = Athenaeus 541cd. The ancestor of the earlier tyrants of Syracuse had been an "effeminate" priest of the "Chthonic gods," Herodotus 7.153f.; Zuntz 1971, 136f.

28. On Bronze Age tradition at Pessinus, the myth of Agdistis recalling Ullikummi, see *Würzburger Jahrbücher* 5 (1979) 253–261. Ancient tradi-

tion links the *galloi* to the river Gallos at Pessinus, mentioned already by Callimachus *fr.* 411. The name must antedate the arrival of the Celtic Galatai in 278 B.C. For a possible connection with Sumerian-Akkadian *gallu*, see *S&H* 110f. Galloi from Pessinus winning the favor of the Romans in 190 B.C.: Polybius 21.37.5; cf. Plutarch *Marius* 17. Cult of emperors at Pessinus: *OGI* 540. See also Thomas 1984, 1525–1528.

29. Documents in *CCCA* III, 1–200 and 225–245.

30. *Erra* 4.55f. (L. Cagni, *L'epopea di Erra*, Rome 1969, 110), referring to Ishtar of Uruk.

31. *CCCA* III, 289; IV, 47; Livy 37.9.9; 38.18.9; Juvenal 2.112; Prudentius *Peristeph.* 10.1061; with reference to Bellona, Juvenal 4.123; to Bacchanalia, Livy 39.15.9; to Isis, *CIL* VI, 2234 = *SIRIS* 373. Cf. Wissowa 1912, 350.

32. Wissowa 1912, 320f.

33. *CIL* X, 3698 = *CCCA* IV, 7; *CIL* X, 3699 = *CCCA* IV, 2; *CIL* XIII, 1751 = Duthoy 1969 no. 126; see H. Cancik in J. Taubes (ed.), *Gnosis und Politik* (Paderborn 1984), 173.

34. *Sodalitates* with ceremonial feasts, Cicero *De senectute* 45; cf. chap. IV at n. 133; Wissowa 1912, 318.

35. *CCCA* III, 362–449; *archigallus*, 446; *dendrophori*, 364, etc.; *cannophori*, 398, etc.; many other sanctuaries in Italy in *CCCA* IV.

36. Farnell 1907, III, 199–205; Graf 1985, 274–277. The diffusion of the cult is attributed to the period of the Ionian migration, Herodotus 9.97.

37. Excellent collection of the evidence: Clinton 1974. A new inscription on Kerykes: D. J. Geagan, *ZPE* 33 (1979) 93–115.

38. Inscription of a *daduchos*, first century B.C., in Clinton 1974, 50–52, line 64.

39. Aristotle *Constitution of Athens* 57.1; *epistatai*, *IG* I^3, 32.

40. For example, lekythos from Kertch, Louvre CA 2190, in Metzger 1965 pl. 15; Kerényi 1967, 157; Triptolemus arriving at the Nile, Apulian volute crater Leningrad 586, *RVAp* 8/6; cf. Fraser 1972, II, 341; Alföldi 1979, 567.

41. Fraser 1972, II, 340f.; H. Laubscher, *JDAI* 89 (1974) 249f. (bibliography); Alföldi 1979, 570–572.

42. Graf 1974, 180f.; Burkert 1975, 100–104.

43. Plutarch *Isis* 362a; Tacitus *Histories* 4.83.2; Arnobius 5.5; Fraser 1972, I, 200; 251; Clinton 1974, 9; 43; 92.

44. Detailed discussion in Fraser 1972, I, 200f., II, 340–342, with negative result; *contra*, Alföldi 1979, 554–558, cf. n. 46. Clinton 1974, 8f. points out that Porphyry *Peri agalmaton* 10, p. 22* Bidez = Eusebius *P.E.* 3.12.4 describes the "mysteries of Eleusis" in a purely Egyptian context. Porphyry in Proclus *Tim.* I 165.19–23 is different, clearly referring to Attica.

45. Callimachus *Hymn* 6.128f.; cf. the regulation at Mykonos, *LSCG* 96.

46. Epiphanius *Panar.* 51.22.8–10; E. Norden, *Die Geburt des Kindes* (Leipzzig 1924), 28f.; R. Merkelbach, *Isisfeste in griechisch-römischer Zeit* (Meisenheim 1963), 47–50; Fraser 1972, II, 336–338; Alföldi 1979, 561. E. Alföldi-Rosenbaum discovered representations of a temple called Eleusinion on Alexandrian *tesserae*, *Chiron* 6 (1976) 215–231, pl. 21, which she identifies with the Koreion. Dedication of a statue of Aion at Eleusis: *IG* II/III², 4705.

47. This uniqueness is stated in a rhetorical text, *Pap. Ox.* 1612, on which see L. Deubner, *Kleine Schriften zur klassischen Altertumskunde* (Königstein 1982), 198–201; cf. Epictetus 3.21.11–14; Fraser 1972, II, 339f.

48. See chap. I, n. 55.

49. *IG* XI, 4,1299; cf. *SIRIS* p. 62–87; Engelmann 1975.

50. Egyptians had established their sanctuary in Piraeus by the fourth century B.C., *IG* II/III², 337 = *SIRIS* 1, cf. Eretria *SIRIS* 73.

51. Cf. *SIRIS* Index; Vidman 1970, 66–94.

52. Apuleius *Metamorphoses* 11.30.5; cf. Otto 1905, I, 94–98; Griffiths 1976, 255f.; H. B. Schoenborn, *Die Pastophoren im Kult der ägyptischen Götter* (Meisenheim 1976).

53. See Tran Tam Tinh 1964.

54. See Wissowa 1912, 351–359; Malaise 1972, 362–401.

55. This statement is made by Dionysius of Halicarnassus *Roman Antiquities* 2.19.3 as a general principle.

56. *SIRIS* 291 (Priene); cf. *SIRIS* 75, 100, 255, 286, 356, 398, 613, 708; for evidence from the pictures, see Le Corsu 1977, 136.

57. See chap. I, n. 17.

58. See *SIRIS* Index; Vidman 1970, 61f., 72–74.

59. *Grege linigero circumdatus et grege calvo*, Juvenal 6.533; *turba linigera*, Ovid *Metamorphoses* 1.747; Plutarch *Isis* 352c (see n. 95).

60. Apuleius *Metamorphoses* 11.19.1, cf. 3; Vidman 1970, 69–75. Cf. *therapeutai* of Asclepius at Pergamon: Ch. Habicht, *Altertümer von Pergamon* VIII, 3 (1969) pp. 114f.

61. *SIRIS* 390, 295, 326; *telestini* (a hapax), *SIRIS* 587, see H. Solin in Bianchi 1982, 132. Cf. Vidman 1970, 125–138; Dunand 1973, III, 243–254; Bianchi 1980; M. Malaise, "Contenue et effets de l' initiation isiaque," *ACl* 50 (1981) 483–498.

62. Tibullus 1.7.48: *cista* in connection with Osiris (cf. also chap. I at n. 17); not mentioned by Bianchi 1980, who refers to *SIRIS* 448 as the earliest appearance of the *cista* in the context of Isis. See, on *cista*, Introduction, n. 31; on *mysteria* of Isis, Introduction, n. 49.

63. *SIRIS* 435–443 (Rome); 467 (Brundisium); *hieroi*, *SIRIS* 154, 307, 315a; *turbae sacrorum*, Apuleius *Metamorphoses* 11.23.4; see Vidman 1970, 80f., 88f. Cf. *hieroi* at the mysteries of Andania, *LSCG* 65, *GR* 279; in Dionysiac mysteries, see n. 21.

64. Cf. L. Delekat, *Katoche, Hierodulie und Adoptionsfreilassung* (Munich 1964).

65. See chap. I at nn. 24–25.

66. Cf. Griffiths 1976, 189.

67. Herodotus 2.171: from Egyptian *mysteria* to Arcadian *thesmophoria;* Hecataeus of Abdera *FGrHist* 264 F 25 = Diodorus 1.22.4 (Dionysiac festivals, *mysteria, teletai*); 1.96.4f. (Osiris = Dionysus, Isis = Demeter).

68. Grandjean 1975; *SEG* 26,821. Lines 35–41 read: "You have honored Athens most of all in Greece. There you first brought the grain to light, Triptolemus yoked your sacred dragons and thus on his chariot distributed the grain to all the Greeks. Therefore in Greece we are eager to see Athens, and in Athens Eleusis." The reconstructed archetype of the later versions has instead: "I showed initiations to men" (sec. 22, Harder 1943, 21). For the origin of Isis aretalogies, see A. Henrichs, *HSCP* 88 (1984) 152–158; for Mesomedes, see chap. III, n. 116.

69. On the number of caves in Rome and Ostia and corresponding numbers of Mithraists, see F. Coarelli in Bianchi 1979, 76f.; Merkelbach 1984, 184–186.

70. On the seven grades, see Merkelbach 1984, esp. 77–86; a structural interpretation is in Gordon 1980; for ritual details see at chap. IV, n. 48 and 77–84; for correlations with the planets, chap. III, n. 106.

71. *CIMRM* 57, 336, 400–403, etc.; Index *CIMRM* I, p. 352.

72. *CIMRM* 1315, 2296; *ex permissu sanctissimi ordinis* in a new inscription (San Gemini, Umbria), U. Ciotti in *Hommages à M. J. Vermaseren* (Leiden 1978), 233–239, cf. C. A. Spada in Bianchi 1979, 647; a dedication *patre prostante, CIMRM* 1598, cf. *antistante, CIMRM* 413a.

73. The funerary inscriptions of a *leo* and a *lea* in Africa, *CIMRM* 114–115, are hardly related to Mithras. Eubulus in Porphyry *Abst.* 4.16 says women were called hyenas (*hyainai;* wrongly changed to *leainai* in Nauck's edition) by Mithraists; this is not a compliment, and they are explicitly contrasted with "those who take part in the mysteries"; this context is misunderstood, for example, by Schwertheim 1979, 63. Slaves: *CIMRM* Index I, p. 354, II, p. 429.

74. Herodotus 4.79.5 (see Introduction at n. 53); Demosthenes 18.260 (see chap. I, n. 34); Aristophanes *Wasps* 118–124 (see chap. I, n. 33).

75. *IGBulg* III, 1864 (Bacchic); for *symmystai* see *OGI* 541 = *IGRom* III, 541 (Pessinus, Meter); *IG* XII, 8, 173.13 (Samothrace); G. Kazarow, *AA* 30 (1915) 88 (Zeus Dionysus); *synbakchoi, SEG* 31,983. *Symmystai* was taken over by the Christians: martyrs are *Paulou symmystai,* Ignatius *Eph.* 12.2; Paul wrote about his vision "for the *symmystai ton apokryphon,*" Mani in the Cologne Mani Codex, *ZPE* 19 (1975) p. 62, 8.

76. Lawsuits: *IG* II/III², 1275 = *LSS* 126; funerals: ibid., and see chap, I, n. 60.

77. Andocides 1.132; Plato *Epistles* VII 333e; Plutarch *Dio* 56; Sopatros *Rhet. Gr.* VIII, 123,26.

78. Plato *Epistles* VII, 333e, alluding to the fact that later Dion was murdered by Callippus, Plutarch *Dio* 56.

79. Philo *Cher.* 48, adopting mystery metaphors for the allegorical interpretation of the Bible. For *symbola* see nn. 84–85 below and chap. IV at nn. 22, 66.

80. See n. 21.

81. *SIRIS* 413 (Rome).

82. Apuleius *Metamorphoses* 11.27.2, 29.5.

83. *Orph. hymn.* 77.9f., to Mnemosyne: "Awaken in the *mystai* the memory of the holy *telete*."

84. *Symbola,* Plutarch *Cons. ad ux.* 611d; *crepundia,* Apuleius *Apol.* 56, cf. 55; see chap. IV at n. 66 and, for *synthema, chap.* IV at n. 22.

85. W. Müri, "SYMBOLON: Wort- und sachgeschichtliche Studie," in *Griechische Studien* (Basel 1976), 1–44, esp. 37–44.

86. Reitzenstein 1927, 23: "dass feste Bekenntnisse die Gemeinden zusammenhalten."

87. Plato *Laws* 782c; Plutarch *Q. conv.* 635e; already Euripides *Hippolytus* 951–953; *GR* 301–304.

88. Rusajeva 1978; West 1983, 17f.; scarcity of "Orphics": Wilamowitz 1932, II, 199f. On the special position of Orphism see chap. III at nn. 127–131.

89. Proclus *Tim.* III, 297.8f. Diehl. On *bakchoi* see chap. IV, nn. 150, 152f.

90. *ZPE* 14 (1974) 77 (Smyrna).

91. E. Renan (cf. Introduction, n. 14) used "Mithriaste," cf. *Sarapiastai;* "mithriaque" is patterned on *Isiacus.*

92. Julian *Symp.* 336c, cf. chap. I, n. 87.

93. Tertullian *Cor.* 15: *idque in signum habet ad probationem sui . . . statimque creditur Mithrae miles.* Cf. I. Toth, "Mithram esse coronam suam," *Acta Classica Univ. Scient. Debrecinensis* 2 (1966) 73–79.

94. Vidman 1970, 89–94; *Isiaci coniectores,* Cicero *De divinatione* 1.132; *Isiaci* (substantive), Valerius Maximus 7.3.8; *sacerdos . . . et ceteri Isiaci, SIRIS* 560 (Portus); for Pompeii, see n. 97.

95. Plutarch *Isis* 352b, cf. Epictetus 3.22.9ff. on the "true cynic."

96. See chap. I, n. 79.

97. *SIRIS* 487, cf. 488; see J. L. Franklin, *Pompeii: The Electoral Programmata, Campaigns and Politics, A.D. 71–79* (Rome 1980).

98. See chap. I, nn. 45, 60, 61, 76, 79. A golden laurel leaf, found in a tomb at Aigion, Achaia, is inscribed *mystes* (*Arch. Rep.* 1985/86, 38).

99. For example, at Delos, Serapeum C, dedications to the Eleusinian gods, *SIRIS* p. 66, *CE* 44; p. 77, *CE* 206; to Men, *SIRIS* p. 67 *CE* 63, cf. p. 65 *CE* 34; Venus Genetrix in a Meter sanctuary, *CCCA* III, 5; Sarapis and Isis dedicated to Zeus of Panamara and Hera, *SIRIS* 279 = *Inschriften von Stratonikeia* 207; Cybele, Isis, and Mithras in a sanctuary of Zeus Bronton, *CIMRM* 634; cf. also *SIRIS* 528; 530.

100. Cumont 1896/99, I, 137ff., 142ff.; 1923, 99f. See esp. *CIMRM* 1176–1188 (Stockstadt).

101. Apuleius *Metamorphoses* 11.22.3.

102. *CCCA* III, 366, cf. 367, 385; *CIMRM* 509, 378; *SIRIS* 286; *CIMRM* 1971; *SIRIS* p. 67 *CE* 50.

103. *SIRIS* 16; p. 72 *CE* 141; *SIRIS* 54; cf. 88.

104. On Praetextatus, see *PW* XXII, 1515–1579; *CIL* VI, 1778 = *CIMRM* 420; *CIL* VI, 1779 = *CCCA* III, 246; his wife, *CIL* VI, 1780 = *SIRIS* 450 = *CCCA* III, 295.

105. Plato *Phaedrus* 247a.

106. *Pap. Ox.* 1380, Totti 1985 no. 20 with bibliography.

107. Apuleius *Metamorphoses* 11.5.2–3; *una quae es omnia, SIRIS* 502 (Capua); see Dunand 1973, I, 80, 103; in general, E. Peterson, *HEIS THEOS: Epigraphische, formgeschichtliche und religionsgeschichtliche Untersuchungen* (Göttingen 1926).

108. R. Merkelbach, *ZPE* 1 (1967) 72f.; Totti 1985 no. 8 with bibliography; the text beyond the oath formula is hopelessly fragmentary. It is most remarkable that there are two exemplars, separated by nearly two centuries (first/third century A.D.). "Local oath": Thucydides 5.18.9; 47.8. By contrast, in Aristophanes *Clouds* 423–426 Strepsiades has to declare that he will no longer recognize any other god: Socrates' "mysteries" of atheism foreshadow uncommon possibilities (with an Orphic-Pythagorean background? See *L&S* 291 n. 73; *HN* 268f.).

109. Eunapius *Vit. Soph.* 7.3.2–4, cf. Clinton 1974, 43.

110. Polarity of Demeter and Hera cult, Servius auctus *Aen.* 4. 58, *HN* 274; Sardis inscription, L. Robert, *CRAI* 1975, 306–330, *SEG* 29, 1205; for an interpretation from an Iranian point of view, see J. Wiesehöfer, *Gnomon* 57 (1985) 565f.

111. See K. L. Schmidt in *Kittels Theologisches Wörterbuch* III (Stuttgart 1938), 502–539; Matthew 16.18; 18.17; St. Paul, Acts of the Apostles; in the Septuagint, *ekklesia* is synonymous with *synagoge*.

112. For *politeia*, see Philo *Spec.* I, 319; Josephus *Jewish Antiquities* 4.45; Ephesians 2.12; 1 Clement 2.8; 54.4; *Ep. Diogn.* 5.4; *spiritalis populus*, Augustine *De vera rel.* 37.

113. *Didache* 4.9.

114. On incipient analogs in the Pythagorean "movement," see Burkert 1982; cf. n. 108.

115. Bacchic: Nilsson 1957, 106–115; Lambrechts 1957; F. Matz, *Gnomon* 32 (1960) 545–547; Horn 1972, 89–92; Geyer 1977, 67 f.; Eleusis: *HN* 280; Clinton 1974, 98–118. Klea is dedicated (*kathosiomene*) to the Egyptian gods "from father and mother," Plutarch *Isis* 32, 364e. A father initiates his son to Mithras, *CIMRM* 405.

116. *Apostates, apostasia* are political concepts, never used in pagan religion. See Joshua 22.22.2; 1 Maccabees 2.15; Acts 21.21; James 2.11 *v.l.;* 2 Thessalonians 2.3. The Egyptian guild of Zeus Hypsistus (see

Nock 1972, 414–443) forbids members "to leave the brotherhood of the president for another"; this is to avoid factions, but it is a far cry from "apostasy."

117. Livy 39.13.14; number of executions: 39.17.6. One may add a reference to 3 Maccabees 2.30: King Ptolemy IV is said to have made participation in Dionysiac *teletai* a prerequisite to full citizenship; Bacchic mysteries as state religion: it is no coincidence that this comes from a Jewish source.

118. Diodorus 34.2, following Posidonius.

119. Augustine *De vera rel.* 14.

120. For the problems of European witches, see the helpful survey of M. Eliade, "Some Observations on European Witchcraft," *History of Religions* 14 (1975) 149–172.

III. Theologia and Mysteries

1. Cumont 1931, 10f.

2. K. Kerényi, *Die griechisch-orientalische Romanliteratur in religionsgeschichtlicher Beleuchtung* (Tübingen 1927); Merkelbach 1962. The discussion was revived by the discovery of the Lollianos romance with an elaborate mystery scene: Henrichs 1972, esp. 28–79; *contra*, advocating a purely literary approach, J. Winkler, "Lollianos and the Desperadoes," *JHS* 100 (1980) 155–181.

3. On tale patterns and initiation, see *S&H* 5–7, 16, 57.

4. A complete translation became available in 1977: J. M. Robinson (ed.), *The Nag Hammadi Library in English* (Leiden); index: F. Siegert, *Nag-Hammadi-Register* (Tübingen 1982); there is also *The Facsimile Edition of the Nag Hammadi Codices* (Leiden 1972–1979), and the project in progress, *The Coptic Gnostic Library, Edited with English Translation, Introduction and Notes* (Leiden), with III, 5 (ed. S. Emmel) published in 1984, in the series *Nag Hammadi Studies* (Leiden 1972–).

5. B. A. Pearson, "Jewish Elements in *Corpus Hermeticum* I (*Poimandres*)," in R. van den Broek and M. J. Vermaseren (eds.), *Studies in Gnosticism and Hellenistic Religions Presented to G. Quispel* (Leiden 1981), 336–348; cf. R. McL. Wilson, "Gnosis and the Mysteries," *ib.* 451–457; J. Büchli, "Der Poimandres—ein heidnisches Evangelium," diss. Zürich 1986 (in course of publication); see also W. C. Grese, *Corpus Hermeticum XIII and Early Christian Literature* (Leiden 1979); in general, R. van den Broek, "The present state of Gnostic Studies," *Vigiliae Christianae* 37 (1983) 41–71. Totti 1985 nos. 80–81 includes two Gnostic prayers in the documents of Isis-Sarapis worship: this juxtaposition brings out the basic difference.

6. On mystery metaphors in philosophy, see E. des Places, "Platon et la langue des mystères," in *Etudes Platoniciennes* (Leiden 1981), 83–98; *HN* 250f.; Riedweg 1987.

7. See Introduction, n. 12.

8. Dieterich 1891; 1923. The text of the "Mithras Liturgy" is *PGM* 4, 475–829, translation with notes in H. D. Betz (ed.), *The Greek Magical Papyri in Translation* I (Chicago 1986), 48–54.

9. See chap. I at nn. 38–43.

10. Zosimus 4.18.2f.; Clinton 1974, 43f.

11. See Introduction, n. 44.

12. See chap. IV, n. 161.

13. Aristotle *fr.* 15 = Synesius *Dio* 10 p. 48a, to be read in connection with Plutarch *Isis* 382de = Aristotle *Eudemus fr.* 10 Ross and Clement *Strom.* 5.71.1. Apparently Aristotle systematized the steps of Diotima's speech in Plato's *Symposium* and made the highest step of philosophy analogous to *epopteia;* this still presupposes various forms of "teaching" and "learning." See Riedweg 1987, 127–130.

14. A Hellenistic inscription from a sanctuary of Dionysus at Halicarnassus invites the reader to join the rites "in order that you may know the whole *logos,*" which is partly secret, partly not, *SEG* 28, 841 (some restorations remain doubtful, but the words quoted are clear). "To know clearly" is contrasted with indications overheard by chance, Dio *Or.* 36.33. *Didaskalia* is placed between "purification" and *epopteia,* Clement *Strom.* 5.71.1 (cf. nn. 13 and 18; Clement's reference to "Lesser Mysteries" is misleading; two dichotomies, Lesser/Greater Mysteries and teaching/ *epopteia,* have become conflated). *Paradosis* appears between "purification" and *epopteia* in Theon of Smyrna, p. 14; *mystike paradosis,* Athenaeus 40a, cf. Diodorus 3.65.6; 5.77.3. The terms *paradosis, paradidonai* can be used in a narrower sense, referring to instruction, and in a larger one, referring to instruction plus ritual. At Andania, *paradosis* means the transmission from one generation of "sacred persons" to the next, *LSCG* 65.13. In the Eleusinian *Lex Sacra IG* I³, 6 = *LSS* 3 C 23, *myen* refers to an action performed on individuals that differs from the collective festival at Eleusis, that is, to personal instruction plus ritual, to a form of *paradosis,* cf. Clinton 1974, 13. The joke about the hierophant "telling" the mysteries implies personal instruction too (Diogenes Laertius 2.102).

15. The term first occurs in Herodotus, 2.51 (Samothrace); 2.63, 2.81 (Egypt), hence Diodorus 1.98.2 (Pythagoras); edict of Ptolemy IV, n. 20 below; in later literature, for example, Plutarch *Isis* 353d; *Q. conv.* 636d; Pausanias 2.13, 8.15.4; Lucian *Syr. D.* 88, 93, 97; with regard to immortality, Plato *Epistles* VII 335a; *carmen sacrum* in the Bacchanalia, Livy 39.18.3. Isis herself wrote down the *hieros logos,* the fearsome one, for the mystai: Hymn from Andros, Totti 1985 no. 2, 12. *Hieros logos* in Orphic and Pythagorean pseudepigraphy: *OF* pp. 140–143; H. Thesleff, *The Pythagorean Texts of the Hellenistic Period* (Åbo 1965), pp. 158–168.

16. Chrysippus *fr.* 42, *SVF* II, 17.

17. Empedocles B 6 takes the form of a "first" instruction in names of gods, to be followed later by a "good *logos* about the blessed gods" (B 131, belonging to *Peri Physeos:* M. R. Wright, *Empedocles: The Extant Frag-*

ments, New Haven 1981, 83). On the revelation received by Parmenides, see W. Burkert, "Das Proömium des Parmenides und die Katabasis des Pythagoras," *Phronesis* 14 (1969) 1–30. Empedocles B 131 contains one of the first formulations of the concept of *theologia* (cf. also Xenophanes B 34.3); the word *theologia* itself first occurs in Plato *Republic* 379a. See V. Goldschmidt, "Theologia," *REG* 63 (1950) 20–42; W. Jaeger, *The Theology of the Early Greek Philosophers* (Oxford 1947).

18. Plato *Symposium* 201d–212c; the structure is (1) *elenchos* = purification, (2) instruction, including the myth of origin (203b–e), and (3) *epoptika* (210a). See Riedweg 1987, 2–21.

19. Demosthenes 18.259 (see chap. I, n. 34); Villa, Herbig 1958 no. 2 pl. 19; Farnesina house, Matz 1963 pl. 5 (a triptychon, not a book scroll); mosaic from Djemila-Cuicul, Geyer 1977, 148 pl. 14.

20. See chap. II, n. 10.

21. Pausanias 4.26.7, 27.5; *LSCG* 65.12; W. Speyer, *Bücherfunde in der Glaubenswerbung der Antike* (Göttingen 1970), 66–68. Cf. Pausanias 8.15.1f. on writings preserved and used for the mysteries at Pheneos.

22. Apuleius *Metamorphoses* 11.17.2; Le Corsu 1977, 176.

23. *CIMRM* 44; Bidez-Cumont 1938, II, 154. Cf. Pausanias 5.27.6, on Iranian fire-priests using books.

24. Cicero *Letters to Atticus* 1.9.2 asks for *Eumolpidon patria*, evidently a book, probably an *Exegetikon*, cf. Clinton 1974, 93; this is not directly connected with the mysteries. See also chap. II, n. 38. *Schol. Theocr.* 4.25c (p. 143 Wendel; *codd.* P and T, "genus Laurentianum" in Wendel's terminology) says that at the Thesmophoria noble virgins took the "customary and holy books" on their heads and thus went to Eleusis; this at any rate is confusing Thesmophoria and Mysteria, and "books" must be corrupt: *biblous* misread for *kistas* (in minuscule writing)?

25. J. G. Smyly, *Greek Papyri from Gurob* (Dublin 1921), no. 1; text also in *OF* 31, *DK* 1 F 23; W. Fauth, *PW* IX, A 2257–2262; West 1983, 170f.

26. See chap. II, n. 108.

27. Livy 25.1.12. At Ephesus, those converted by St. Paul burned their magical books, Acts 19.19. Bishop Porphyrius, fighting paganism at Gaza, had all "books full of charlatanism, which the priests called 'sacred,' from which they performed their *teletai* and the other illicit rites" collected and burned, Marcus Diaconus *Vit. Porph.* 71. See W. Speyer, "Büchervernichtung," *Jahrbuch für Antike und Christentum* 13 (1970) 123–152, esp. 130f., 141.

28. Plato *Republic* 364e. The seer with his book is ridiculed in Aristophanes *Birds* 974–989, as the mantic art had become literate.

29. Plato *Meno* 81a; see also at n. 128.

30. See chap. II at n. 99.

31. Col. XVI; see chap. II, n. 4.

32. Plutarch's formulation, *Isis* 378a. Authors and titles of books

on mysteries are collected by A. Tresp, *Die Fragmente der griechischen Kultschriftsteller* (Giessen 1914), 28; the oldest is Stesimbrotus (= *Pap. Derveni?* See chap. II, n. 4); note Melanthius *On the Mysteries of Eleusis, FGrHist* 326; add Arignote, *Bakchika* and *Teletai of Dionysus*, p. 51 Thesleff (cf. n. 15); books on Mithras by Eubulus, Porphyry *Antr.* 6, *Abst.* 4.16, and Pallas, Porphyry *Abst.* 2.56, 4.16.

33. These three levels do not coincide with the tripartite system of Bianchi (see Introduction, n. 59); levels (2) and (3) largely correspond to his section called "misteriosofico."

34. Nilsson *GGR* I, 469: "In die Demeterreligion greift der Mythos ungewöhnlich tief ein."

35. The most complete older study is R. Foerster, *Der Raub und die Rückkehr der Persephone* (Stuttgart 1874); a recent survey in Richardson 1974.

36. The most important Greek texts are Diodorus 1.21f. and Plutarch *Isis;* see J. Gwyn Griffiths, *The Origins of Osiris* (Berlin 1966) and *Plutarch De Iside et Osiride* (Aberystwyth 1970).

37. Pausanias 7.17.10–12 and Arnobius 5.5–7, printed as parallel texts in Hepding 1903, 37–41; cf. Neanthes *FGrHist* 84 F 37 (a *mystikos logos*); Alexander Polyhistor *FGrHist* 273 F 74; *S&H* 104, 110f.; for Timotheus, see chap. II, n. 43.

38. Diodorus 3.62.8; Harpocration s.v. *leuke; Schol. Pind. Isthm.* 7.3; the ritual prescription "not to roast boiled meat" and some *Telete* in Aristotle *Probl. ined.* 3.43 Bussemaker; as Plato *Phaedo* 62b (*phroura, en aporrhetois*), *Cratylus* 399e, Xenocrates *fr.* 20 Heinze = 219 Isnardi Parente seem to belong together, we get a complex of "Orpheus," secret mysteries, and Dionysus myth; for Herodotus' allusions, see *HN* 225; comprehensive treatment of the myth in West 1983, 140–175. Firmicus *Err.* 6.5 links the dismemberment myth to trieteric celebrations; *Orph. Hymn.* 44.8f. combines "mysteries" with the normal myth of Dionysus' birth; Euripides' *Bacchae* refers to mysteries (*GR* 291f.), but not to the dismemberment myth. It may not have been the sole and exclusive myth of Bacchic mysteries.

39. Porphyry *Antr.* 18; *mysta booklopies* Firmicus *Err.* 5.2 (cf. n. 70); Mithras struggling with the bull in the cave, Statius *Thebaid* 1.719f.

40. Earliest reference: Justin Martyr *Dial.* 70; see Cumont 1923, 118, 3. For the type "monster born from the rock" see Burkert, *Würzburger Jahrbücher* 5 (1979) 253–261. Normal mythological logic demands that an ejaculation onto the rock have previously taken place (cf. Hieron. *Adv. Iov.* 1.7, *PL* 23.219), perhaps by Kronos-Saturnus, who is shown sleeping in the reliefs. This would put Mithras on a par with Ullikummi, son of Kumarbi, and Typhoeus, son of Kronos (*Schol B Il.* 2.783), and make him a potential successor to Zeus, similar in this respect to Chthonian Dionysus.

41. There is a good survey of *l'imagerie mithriaque* in Turcan 1981a,

38–70, esp. 48–52; see also Cumont 1923, 118–125, who, however, is too prone to project edifying theology onto the scenes; there must have been a level of plain mythical tale. See Fig. 11 with caption.

42. See Dieterich 1923, 76–78; Schwertheim 1979, n. 77; Turcan 1981a, 51f.; Merkelbach 1984 on fig. 115.

43. For the parallel Mithras-Hermes-Heracles see Burkert, "Sacrificio-sacrilegio: Il 'Trickster' fondatore," *Studi Storici* 24 (1984) 835–845; an attempt to retrieve the Mithras myth from Armenian sources: Widengren 1980, 658f.

44. *Schol. Aristid.* p. 53,15 Dindorf: "in an abnormal way she had intercourse with Keleos"; Eubulus her son: *Orph. Hymn.* 41.8; intercourse with Dionysus-Iacchus: *Schol. Aristoph. Ran. 324;* cf. Tertullian *Ad nat.* 2.7: *cur rapitur sacerdos Cereris, si non tale Ceres passa est?* Theocritus 3.50f.: Demeter bestowed on Iasion, her lover, a kind of bliss which the uninitiated will never learn; Isocrates *Panegyricus* 28: Demeter brought to Eleusis benefits that only the initiates may know; Plato *Republic* 377e f.: myths such as the sufferings of Kronos should only be told to those who make a big sacrifice in advance, not just those who offer a pig, as at Eleusis. for the child born at Eleusis, see *HN* 289; birth of Aion: chap. II, n. 46.

45. The myth from some *telete* about Meter and Hermes which Pausanias 2.3.4 declines to relate is explicit in Clement *Protr.* 20.1.

46. Herodotus 2.171; cf. Diodorus 1.97.4 (*pathe* of the gods); Dionysius of Halicarnassus *Ant.* 2.19 (gods who disappear, abduction of Persephone, *pathe* of Dionysus); Plutarch *Isis* 25, 360d; *De E* 389a; *Def. or.* 415a. The identification of the initiate with the fate of his god has been held to be the distinguishing characteristic of ancient mysteries; see, for example, Berner 1972, 266f. (with criticism); Lohse 1974, 171–179; Colpe 1975, 381. Cf. n. 56.

47. Lactantius *Inst. epit.* 18 (23) 7; cf. *HN* 275f.

48. For the festival calendar see Wissowa 1912, 321f.; Cumont 1931, 52f.; Sfameni Gasparro 1985, 56–59; on Damascius *Vit. Is.* 131 see chap. I, n. 73.

49. Firmicus *Err.* 2.9, cf. Seneca in Augustine *City of God* 6.10, Seneca *Apocolocyntosis* 13, Vitruvius 8 *praef.*, Juvenal 6.527, Lactantius *Inst. epit.* 18 (23).

50. Firmicus *Err.* 22; the ritual has been variously identified as belonging to Osiris (Loisy 1930, 104; Nilsson *GGR* II, 612), Attis (Hepding 1903, 196f.; Cosi 1982, 489), Dionysus (Wilamowitz 1932, 381), or Eleusis (G. Thomson, *JHS* 55 (1935) 26, 34). Firmicus says the devil is imitating Christian religion (cf. Introduction, n. 11) in this case; it may have been a special case indeed; the role of anointment is unique (see at chap. IV, n. 76).

51. Cf. Colpe 1969; *S&H* 99–101.

52. See chap. IV at nn. 51–70.

53. On Adonis, see W. Atallah, *Adonis dans la littérature et l'art grec* (Paris 1966); M. Detienne, *Les jardins d' Adonis* (Paris 1972) [*The Gardens of Adonis*, Atlantic Highlands 1977]; *S&H* 105–111; S. Ribichini, *Adonis, Aspetti 'orientali' di un mito greco* (Rome 1981); *Adonis, Relazioni del colloquio in Roma (22–23 maggio 1981)* (Rome 1984).

54. There is a much-discussed Akkadian text about the sufferings of Marduk, kept prisoner in the "mountain"; see H. Zimmern, "Zum babylonischen Neujahrsfest," II, *Ber. Leipzig* 70 (1918) 2–9, cf. W. v. Soden, *Zeitschrift für Assyriologie* 17 (1955) 130–166; 18 (1957) 224–234.

55. Bianchi 1979, 12f., amply discussed in that volume, see esp. M. V. Cerutti, ibid. 385–395, Sfameni Gasparro, ibid. 397–408; Sfameni Gasparro 1985, xviif.; cf. Berner 1972, 266f. Too much has been made of the term *transitus* in monuments to Mithras (*CIMRM* 1495, 1497, 1722, 1737, 1811, 1900, 2205); a certain date or festival, cf. n. 104.

56. Romans 6.1–11, on which see Wagner 1962 with the review of C. Colpe, *Gnomon* 38 (1966) 47–51; Wedderburn 1982.

57. See chap. I, n. 49; for the reading *Gaias* in the Hipponion text, see G. Zuntz, *WSt* 89 (1976) 132f., 142f. As Titans are sons of Heaven and Earth, the myth of the Titans and Dionysus (n. 38) has often been adduced; *contra*, Zuntz 1971, 364–367. Another "son of Heaven and Earth" is Triptolemus: variant reading in Apollodorus *The Library* 1.32 = Pherecydes *FGrHist* 3 F 53; P. Cornell 55 (Pack^2 2646) line 5, cf. A. Henrichs in J. Bremmer (ed.), *Interpretations of Greek Mythology* (London 1987), 250.

58. *IC* I, xxiii 3 = *CCCA* II, 661, also in *OF* 32 IV. The rendering of the second line is controversial. The translation given here relies on the established use of *genea* and the contrast with the third verse. Alternative interpretations: "who present themselves for birth," A. Dieterich, *Mutter Erde* (Leipzig 1905; 3rd ed. 1925), 112f.; "who take the responsibility of procreation," that is, care for children, Sfameni Gasparro 1985, 86 n. 7 (after others).

59. Plato *Epistles* VII 334b7, cf. 333e *myein kai epopteuein* (see chap. II, n. 78), which makes the reference to Eleusis explicit; cf. also Plutarch *Dio* 56. The importance of the passage was seen by E. Howald, *Die Briefe Platons* (Zurich 1923), 166.

60. (Plato) *Axiochus* 371d, cf. Rohde 1898 II, 422f. See also chap. IV at nn. 57, 60. On the concept of "charter myth," which goes back to B. Malinowski, see G. S. Kirk, *Myth: Its Meaning and Functions in Ancient and Other Cultures* (Berkeley 1970), 22f., 256f.

61. Ovid *Fasti* 4.535f., 493f.

62. Clement *Protr.* 20.1.

63. *Homeric Hymn to Demeter* 192–211; Richardson 1974, 211–217; *HN* 267–274.

64. Cf. n. 49.

65. Arnobius 5.16.

66. Ovid *Fasti* 4.230f.

67. Diodorus 3.62.8 (cf. n. 38). Omophagy is made a *deigma* of the dismemberment myth in *Schol. Clem. Protr.* 119.1, p. 318 Stählin.

68. Harpocration s.v. *leuke*.

69. Clement *Protr.* 17.2 = *OF* 34; Gurob-papyrus, cf. n. 25; *OF* 208–209; see West 1983, 154–169.

70. Pausanias 8.54.2 (near Tegea); this gave the title to a paper by G. F. Rizzo, "Dionysos Mystes," *Mem. dell' Acc. Archeologica di Napoli* 1914 (I) 37–102, dealing mainly with the Villa of the Mysteries. The addressee of *mysta booklopies* in Firmicus *Err.* 5.2 (cf. n. 39) is the initiate, as *tradidit nobis* indicates, not the god.

71. Attis-figure wearing the scourge of the *galloi: CCCA* VII, 132.

72. Plutarch *Isis* 27, 361de.

73. See, in general, F. Buffière, *Les mythes d'Homère et la pensée grecque* (Paris 1956); J. Pépin, *Mythe et allégorie* (Paris 1958); cf. also K. Reinhardt, "De Graecorum theologia," diss. Berlin 1910; Ch. Schäublin, *Untersuchungen zur Methode und Herkunft der antiochenischen Exegese* (Cologne 1974). On the Derveni papyrus (Stesimbrotus?), see chap. II, n. 4.

74. Demetrius *Eloc.* 101. The treatise is variously dated between the third century B.C. (G. M. A. Grube, *A Greek Critic: Demetrius On Style*, Toronto 1961, 39–56) and the first century A.D. (G. P. Goold, *TAPA* 92, 1961, 178–189.)

75. Macrobius *S. Sc.* 1.2.17f.

76. Heraclitus B 123 = *fr.* 8 Marcovich, who records ten quotations and adaptations of this saying, five of them by Philo, but omits Strabo and Macrobius *loc. cit.* See also P. Hadot, "Zur Idee der Naturgeheimnisse," *Abh. Akad. Mainz* 1982, 8.

77. Strabo 10.3.9 p. 467 = Posidonius *fr.* 370 Theiler.

78. Cicero *De nat. deorum* 1.119.

79. Firmicus *Err.* 2.7.

80. Philo *De fuga* 179. Philo's "mystic" terminology is analyzed in Riedweg's study; see n. 6 above.

81. Philo *Cher.* 42–48, taking his start from Genesis 4.1. Reitzenstein 1927, 247f. takes this to be the "theological justification" of a "custom" by which women became wives of gods. Philo, however, is merely using rhetorical metaphors to speak about the Bible, not about mysteries. See Riedweg 1987, 71–92.

82. Mark 4.11; Matthew 13.11; Luke 8.10. Ephesians 5.31f. makes Genesis 2.24 a *mysterion* to be explained by reference to Christ and the church.

83. Plotinus 3.6.19; he is indirectly referring to Herodotus 2.51 and Samothrace, *GR* 283f.

84. Cleanthes *SVF* I no. 547 = Plutarch *Isis* 377d, cf. 367c.

85. Demetreioi: Plutarch *Fac.* 943b, *ut sinus et gremium quasi matris mortuo tribueretur*, Cicero *De legibus* 2.63; golden ears: P. Wolters in

Festschrift J. Loeb (Munich 1930), 284–301, *GGR* I, pl. 42,2; sprouting grain in a tomb on an Apulian amphora, Leningrad St. 428, *RVAp* 18/50, *GGR* I, pl. 42,3.

86. Hippolytus *Ref.* 5.8.39; *HN* 290f.

87. Varro in Augustine *City of God* 7.20: "Much is transmitted in the mysteries of Demeter which has only to do with the invention of grain." For Theophrastus in Porphyry *Abst.* 2.6 see chap. IV at n. 22; see also Graf 1974, 177–181.

88. Tertullian *Adv. Marc.* 1.13. For Meter = Earth see also Lucretius 2.589–643, Varro in Augustine *City of God* 7.24, Cosi 1976, 54, 60 n. 16.

89. Hippolytus *Ref.* 5.9.8; Th. Wolbergs, *Griechische religiöse Gedichte der ersten nachchristlichen Jahrhunderte* (Meisenheim 1971), 60–75, esp. 73f.

90. Firmicus *Err.* 3.2, referring to the "Phrygians who live at Pessinus" who "want" this interpretation. Porphyry has Attis corresponding to spring flowers that do not bear fruit; this makes him an equivalent of Adonis, Eusebius *P.E.* 3.11.12 = Porphyry *Peri agalmaton fr.* 7, p. 10* Bidez; Augustine *City of God* 7.25, cf. Ammianus Marcellinus 19.1.11, 22.9.15.

91. Attis with grain and poppy, *CCCA* III, 394; grain, cista, cock sacrifice, *CCCA* III, 395; Meter with grain and torch, *CCCA* IV, 122.

92. Diodorus 3.62.8 Columella 12.29; see, in general, Eisler 1925, esp. 265.

93. Heraclitus *Alleg.* 6. Attis is made the sun god in Macrobius *Saturnalia* 1.21.7–11, Martianus Capella 2.191; Proclus *Hymn.* 1.25.

94. Macrobius *Saturnalia* 1.17 = Apollodorus *FGrHist* 244 F 95, Macrobius *Saturnalia* 1.18.

95. Wild 1981. The procession with the water vessel is mentioned in Plutarch *Isis* 365b.

96. Plutarch *Isis* 363d.

97. Heliodorus 9.9.

98. Porphyry in Eusebius *P.E.* 3.11 = *peri agalmaton fr.* 10 p. 19* Bidez = Chairemon *fr.* 6 Schwyzer (*fragmentum dubium*) = *fr.* 17 D van der Horst.

99. Plutarch *Isis* 364a; 367a. Sallustius 4.3 attributes to the Egyptians the equations Isis = earth, Osiris = moisture, Typhon = heat.

100. Tertullian *Adv. Marc.* 1.13.

101. Athenagoras 22.9.

102. See *CIMRM* Index, I, 349f., 351; II, 425; *mihr* became the common Persian word for "sun." See also Bianchi 1979, 20.

103. For excellent photographs with detailed commentary, see Merkelbach 1984. Moon = bull: *Schol. Stat. Theb.* 1.719.

104. See Vermaseren 1971, 5; W. Lentz in Hinnells 1975, 358–377; Merkelbach 1984, 143.

105. This is not explained in any known text; see Merkelbach 1984, 131f.

106. The famous text in Origen, *Cels.* 6.22 has a sequence corresponding to the days of our week (in inverse order), that is, to the system of Hellenistic astrology (cf. Merkelbach 1984, 208–215), but the Mithraea of St. Prisca and of Felicissimus at Ostia (Merkelbach 1984, fig. 38, cf. pp. 77–80) have an ascending sequence Mercury-Venus-Mars-Jupiter-Moon-Sun-Saturn; this is basically pre-Hellenistic, using the old Iranian sequence stars-moon-sun (Burkert, *Rhein. Mus.* 106, 1963, 106–112) topped by Saturnus (cf. n. 40). The arrangement in the Mithraeum *delle sette sfere* at Ostia is difficult to interpret; see R. L. Gordon, *Journal of Mithraic Studies* 1 (1976) 119–165; R. Beck in Bianchi 1979, 515–529; in general, Bianchi 1979, 32–38.

107. Vermaseren and van Essen 1965, 118–126.

108. *Schol. Stat. Theb.* 1.719, *iuxta tenorem internae philosophiae.*

109. S. Insler, "A new interpretation of the bull-slaying motif," in *Hommages à M. J. Vermaseren* (Leiden 1978), 519–538; cf. A. Bausani in Bianchi 1979, 503–511; D. R. Small, ibid. 531–549; M. P. Speidel, *Mithras-Orion* (Leiden 1980), with the review of R. M. Ogilvie, *CR* 31 (1981) 305.

110. Plutarch *Isis* 364a (see at n. 99).

111. Plutarch ibid.; the exposition covers chaps. 32–42; for interpretation in detail, see the commentary of Griffiths (n. 36 above).

112. *phortikoi*, 377b; cf. *apaideusia* in Sallustius 4.3.

113. *Fr.* 39 Leemans = *fr.* 55 Des Places = Macrobius *S. Sc.* 1.19.

114. See Clinton 1974, 43.

115. Cf. n. 86.

116. Mesomedes *Hymn.* 5 Heitsch; he gives the sequence of a wedding in the netherworld (Persephone), the birth of a child, "unspeakable fire" (in the Telesterion), and the "harvest of Kronos" (*Kronios ametos*), that is, cutting the ear of grain (the imagery recurs in Nonnus 18.228). The reference to Eleusis becomes clear with the word *anaktora* (18). Cf. *HN*, 291n.

117. Hippolytus *Ref.* 5.7.13 cf. 5.8.39, 5.9.1–11; Julian *Or.* 5.9, 168d–169b; Sallustius 4.7–11. Proclus wrote a *Metroake biblos*, Marinus *Vit. Procl.* 33; cf. Damascius *Princ.* II, 214.5, 154.15; Sfameni Gasparro 1981. In a different way Plotinus 3.6.19.30 makes Meter, surrounded by castrated *galloi*, personify matter that is sterile (*agonon*). See also D. M. Cosi, *Casta Mater Idaea* (Venice 1986).

118. Plato *Timaeus* 35a; for interpretation, see F. M. Cornford, *Plato's Cosmology* (London 1937), 59–66; *krater*, 41d; cf. *OF* 241.

119. Plutarch *Isis* 35, 364e–365a, equating Dionysus with Osiris on account of his *pathe*, implies that the interpretation of Osiris' dismemberment (373a) must hold true for Dionysus too. In *De E* 9, 388e–389c he has another, stoicizing interpretation: Dionysus stands for the cosmos, divided up in elements; Apollo is unification of the whole in *ekpyrosis*. Plotinus 4.3.12. (= *OF* 209), cf. J. Pépin, "Plotin et le miroir de Dionysos," *Rev. intern. de Philos.* 24 (1970) 304–320.

120. Proclus *Tim.* I, 336.29, II, 80.19, 145.18 and other texts assembled in *OF* 209–210; Olympiodorus *Phaed.* 1.5 p. 45 Westerink (= *OF* 209), Damascius *Phaed.* 1.4 p. 31 Westerink, 1.129 p. 81 Westerink (= *OF* 209); cf. Macrobius *S. Sc.* 1.12.12 = *OF* 240. This text makes it clear that just the plain myth, not the Platonizing interpretation, *in . . . sacris traditur.*

121. Turcan 1975; Merkelbach 1984, 228–244; Fauth 1984.

122. Porphyry *Antr.* 6.

123. See Chap. I at nn. 84–86; on the "ladder" of seven steps in Origen *Cels.* 6.22 (n. 106 above) see also Turcan 1981a, 110–112.

124. Porphyry *Abst.* 4.16: the "general tendency" (*koine phora*) links the animal names such as raven and lion to the zodiac, that is, astrology; Eubulus and Pallas, however, take them to refer to reincarnation of souls in animals.

125. But cf. n. 59 on *psychon syngeneia.*

126. The dismemberment myth belongs to theogony, anthropogony, genealogy, cf. at n. 57; it is difficult to integrate it into a doctrine about the soul. Even in Orphic literature we find simple juxtaposition, see *OF* 224.

127. For a discussion of transmigration doctrines see *L&S* 120–165, *GR* 298f.

128. Plato *Laws* 870de; he makes the point that an individual's death is "natural punishment" for a crime committed in an earlier life; this is the "justice of Rhadamanthys" mentioned by Aristotle *Nicomachean Ethics* 1132 b 25; it gives sense to the complicated formulation in Pindar *Olympian* 2.57f.; it also goes well with the exceptional status of those killed by lightning (cf. Burkert 1975, 93f.): this cannot be retaliation, hence it means transformation to some higher status.

129. Pindar's reference to *teletai, fr.* 131a = Plutarch *Cons. ad Apoll.* 120c is linked to *fr.* 129 by Wilamowitz and Snell; there the system seems to correspond to what is stated in *Olympian* 2. The Plutarch text links *fr.* 131a to 131b, where transmigration is not expressly mentioned.

130. On the gold leaves, cf. chap. I, n. 49. The doctrine of transmigration explains the prominent role of *Mnemosyne,* "recollection," in these texts, cf. *L&S* 213, Zuntz 1971, 380f.; the Hipponion text says that the normal souls "cool themselves" at the first spring, which must be avoided by those who are to reach the lake of *Mnemosyne.* The other souls, by contrast, probably drink forgetfulness (*Lethe*) and thus return to the upper world.

131. The basic texts are Plato *Phaedo* 70c (= *OF* 7), on the *phroura,* and Plato *Cratylus* 399e (= *OF* 8), mentioning "those around Orpheus"; Xenocrates *fr.* 20 Heinze = *fr.* 219 Isnardi Parente; Aristotle *fr.* 60 = Iamblichus *Protr.* p. 48 (*hoi tas teletas legontes*); Pindar *fr.* 133 is often connected with this complex; see n. 38 and *GR* 296–301.

132. E. Rohde, "Mystik war ein fremder Blutstropfen im griechischen Blute," *Kleine Schriften* II (Tübingen 1901), 338. For possible contacts with India in the time of Pythagoras see K. v. Fritz, *Gnomon* 40 (1968) 8f.

IV. The Extraordinary Experience

1. See chap. I, n. 90 – *Orph. hymn.* 77.9. A more specific function is given to "memory" by the theory of transmigration, see chap. III, n. 130.

2. Aristotle *fr.* 15, see chap. III, n. 13. One gold plate from Thurii has the words "be glad to have suffered the suffering which you never suffered before," A 4 Zuntz, see Zuntz 1971, 328f.; *OF* 32f. It is controversial whether this refers to an initiation ritual that the deceased had experienced during his life, or just to his death (by lightning?).

3. Dio Chrysostom *Or.* 12.33. It is unclear which mysteries Dio has in mind. The *thronismos* is attested for corybantic rites by Plato *Euthydemus* 277d (see chap. I, n. 32), and it has been conjectured for Samothrace by Nock, *AJA* 45 (1941) 577–581, but see Cole 1984, 29; a form of *thronismos* also belongs to Eleusis, but hardly to the festival in the Telesterion, see n. 21 and *HN* 266f. – Cleanthes *SVF* 1 no. 538.

4. Marcus Aurelius in Fronto 3.10, p. 43,15 v.d. Hout.

5. Sopatros *Rhet. Gr.* VIII, 114f.

6. Dio Chrysostom *Or.* 36.33f.; he uses the simile to describe the situation of poetry versus "true" theology.

7. Cf. M. Oppitz in H. P. Duerr (ed.), *Der Wissenschaftler und das Irrationale* I (Frankfurt 1981), 57 on the study of shamanism: "Wird einer, der mit verbundenen Augen und mit einem zappelnden und noch warmen Widderherzen im Mund für Stunden allein auf einem Baum gesessen hat, eine Schamanengeburt nicht anders beschreiben als der, der wie die Laien nur unten gestanden hat?"

8. Craterus *FGrHist* 342 F 16 = *Schol. Aristoph. Av.* 1073, cf. Melanthius *FGrHist* 326 F 2–4; *Diagorae Melii et Theodori Cyrenaei Reliquiae*, ed. M. Winiarczyk (Leipzig 1981), T 7 A, cf. T 15–20.

9. Hippolytus *Ref.* 5.8.39f., cf. *HN* 251; 288–292.

10. See chap. III at nn. 115 and 116.

11. Plutarch *fr.* 168 Sandbach = Stobaeus 4.52.49; the attribution to Plutarch ("Themistios" Stob.) is made certain by the quotation in Clement *Ecl. proph.* 34f.; see Graf 1974, 132–138. Dunand 1973 III, 248,2, 250f. would connect the text with Isis mysteries. Eleusis is suggested by the "wanderings" (grotto of Pluto?) and the "dances in the Meadow" (*HN* 279; but see Graf 1974, 133). For Cleanthes and Dio see nn. 3–6. The ritual details become blurred through philosophical transformation. For "looking down" on people in this world, cf. Plato *Sophist* 216c, referring to "the philosophers."

12. Plato *Symposium* 209e f.; see Riedweg 1987, 5f.

13. Plato *Phaedrus* 250bc, *myoumenoi kai epopteuontes* c4, *deimata* 251 a 4.

14. Aristides *Or.* 22 (*Eleusinios*) 2, cf. 10: "The present feeling of good cheer (*euthymia*) . . . being released and free of the unpleasant events of the time before"; *Or.* 48.28 in a simile: In mysteries, "together with

terror there is at hand good hope"; *Or.* 26.6f. mentions "purifications" and "good cheer." We know nothing about the context of Aeschylus *fr.* 387 Radt, which already combines "dread" and "desire for this (?) mystical *telos.*"

——15. Artemidorus 2.39, mentioning "Demeter, Kore, and the so-called Iacchus"; in addition Artemidorus mentions Sarapis, Isis, Anubis, Harpocrates, and their "mysteries," which in a dream mean "confusion and dangers and threats and crises" and "salvation against expectations and hopes."

——16. Plutarch *De aud. poet.* 47a (in a simile; the reference is to the *elenchos* one has to suffer when studying philosophy); *De fac.* 943c (the reference is to the soul having left the body, cf. at n. 11); see also Plutarch *Prof. virt.* 81d; Proclus *Theol. Plat.* 3.18 p. 151 Portus: *ekplexis* before the "mystic sights."

17. G. L. Dirichlet, *De veterum macarismis* (Giessen 1914); see, for Eleusis, *Homeric Hymn to Demeter* 480–482; Sophocles *fr.* 837 Radt; for Dionysus, Euripides *Bacchae* 73f.; gold plate from Thurii A 4, see n. 2; parody in Demosthenes 18.260.

18. Plato *Phaedrus* 250b: *makarian opsin te kai thean;* Aristophanes *Frogs* 745: *epopteuein* as a metaphor for supreme pleasure. Kerényi 1967, 95–102 speaks of *visio beatifica.* It is difficult to be sure about the precise meaning of the preposition in *ep-optes* (cf. *HN* 265,1).

19. See Mylonas 1961. Important was the reconstruction by J. N. Travlos, *Ephem. arch.* 89/90 (1950/51) 1–16, of the throne of the hierophant next to the entrance of the small central building, the *anaktoron,* within the Telesterion; cf. O. Rubensohn, *JdI* 70 (1955) 1–49; Kerényi 1967, 86f.; *HN* 276,8.

20. Cf. chap. III, n. 35.

21. "Lovatelli urn," sarcophagus of Torre Nova, and Campana reliefs, see G. E. Rizzo, *Röm. Mitt.* 25 (1910) 89–167; Deubner 1932, 77f., pl. 7; E. Simon in W. Helbig (ed.), *Führer durch die öffentlichen Sammlungen klassischer Altertümer in Rom* ⁴III (Tübingen 1969), 73–75 no. 2164e; Kerényi 1967, 52–59; *HN* 267–269. See Figs. 2–4.

22. Clement *Protr.* 21.2 (followed by Arnobius 5.26). A decisive advance in interpretation is due to A. Delatte, *Le cycéon, breuvage rituel des mystères d'Eleusis* (Paris 1955), 5–8, who used the testimony of Theophrastus in Porphyry *Abst.* 2.6; cf. *HN* 269–273.

23. See chap. III, n. 116; cf. chap. II, n. 68 for Isis laying claim to Eleusis. Read *astea*, "cities," in line 17 (*aistea*, Horna, *astra*, Wilamowitz, Heitsch), the "charioteer" being Triptolemus who travels "through the world."

24. G. De Petra, *Not. Scav.* 1910, 139–145; A. Maiuri, *La Villa dei Misteri* (Rome 1931); Nilsson 1957, 66–76; 123–126; Herbig 1958; Simon 1961; Zuntz 1963b; Matz 1963; Brendel 1966. Le Corsu 1977, 163–171

claims the Villa pictures for mysteries of Isis, without any good argument. See Fig. 5.

25. Matz 1963, 10–16, pl. 4–11. See Fig. 6.

26. Matz 1963, 8 nos. 4–5, pl. 12–13.

27. Matz 1963, 9 nos. 12–14, pl. 22–23; Geyer 1977, 61f., pl. 2–3; F. Matz, *Die dionysischen Sarkophage*, Berlin 1968–1975, no. 210; 38; 163.

28. L. Leschi, *Mon. Piot* 35 (1935/36) 139–172, pl. 8–9; Nilsson 1957, 113–115; Matz 1963, 9 no. 16, pl. 24; Horn 1972, fig. 33; Geyer 1977, pl. 14. See Fig. 7.

29. *Liknon* with female: Villa, Campana relief (Matz 1963, pl. 13), mosaic Djemila; *liknon* with silenus: Campana relief (Matz, pl. 12), Villa Farnesina (Matz, pl. 8; destroyed and unclear: pl. 10), helmet with reliefs (Matz, pl. 14), cf. drawings of a lost painting (Matz, pl. 20–21).

30. H. Jeanmaire, "Le conte d'Amour et Psyché," *Bulletin de l'Institut Français de Sociologie* 1 (1930) 29–48 = "Die Erzählung von Amor und Psyche," in G. Binder and R. Merkelbach (eds.), *Amor und Psyche* (Darmstadt 1968), 313–333; Merkelbach 1962, 41–45.

31. Interpretation of this scene is most controversial. That drinking of wine and that a mirror effect are involved have both been contested. It remains attractive to assume that the boy sees himself changed into an old satyr, Herbig 1958, 42–44 following K. Kerényi, *Eranos Jahrbuch* 16 (1948) 183–208, cf. Kerényi 1976, 285; *contra*, Zuntz 1963b, 182–188; Simon 1961, 152–159; Matz 1963, 30–34.

32. See at nn. 90–91.

33. Simon 1961, 112; 160–169 tried to trace the composition back to Pergamon, finding links with the Telephos frieze.

34. *RVAp* 6/94; Simon 1961, 171 fig. 37; Bérard 1974 pl. 2–3.

35. For reliefs in Munich, Vienna, and Copenhagen, see Th. Schreiber, *Die hellenistischen Reliefbilder* (Leipzig 1894), pl. 80, 98, 69.

36. Demosthenes 18.259, see chap. I, n. 34. The detail about the frightening demon "Empusa" is in Idomeneus *FGrHist* 338 F 2. Frightening ghost appearances (*phasmata kai deimata*) in Bacchic *teletai* are mentioned by Origen *Cels* 4.10, in Hekate *teletai* by Dio Chrysostom *Or.* 4.90. Some scenes of "sitting down" with allusions to purification appear in Italiote vase painting: Pelike Taranto 117503, *RVAp* 10/18 (youth with thyrsus sitting on an altar, female holding a torch to the base of the altar; the scene is similar to the middle scene in the Torre Nova sarcophagus, see n. 21); scyphoid pyxis Moscow 510, *LCS* p. 604 no. 105, pl. 236,6 (veiled, sitting initiand).

37. Plato *Republic* 560de; the reference is to the change of an "oligarchic" to a "democratic" personality.

38. Apuleius *Metamorphoses* 11.23.6–8.

39. Apuleius *Metamorphoses* 11.24.1–4.

40. Machinery for ghost appearances is assumed by S. I. Dakaris for the Nekromanteion of Ephyra; see his *Altertümer von Epirus: Das To-*

desorakel von Acheron. Ephyra-Pandosia-Kassope (Athens n.d.), 15–17, cf. *Antike Kunst Beiheft* 1 (1963) 52.

41. Servius *Aen.* 6.741; Servius G. 2.389, with explicit reference to *sacra Liberi;* "purification by air" is brought in to explain the custom of hanging up *oscilla;* cf. Servius *G.* 1.166 on *mystica vannus Iacchi.* We may add purification by earth = clay, see at n. 36. See S. Eitrem, "Die vier Elemente in der Mysterienweihe," *Symb. Oslo.* 4 (1926) 39–59; 5 (1927) 39–59.

42. Cf. n. 56. On the Ravenna sarcophagus, see chap. I, n. 78.

43. See chap. I, nn. 32–33; chap. III, n. 38; cf. Dio at n. 3. Dionysus enthroned, while the Corybants dance around him, is represented on a relief from the Theater of Perge, and on an ivory pyxis at Bologna, Kerényi 1976, fig. 66.

44. Clement *Protr.* 15.3, hence *Schol. Plat. Gorg.* 497c; the alternative version in Firmicus *Err.* 18.1; cf. Dieterich 1923, 216f.; Hepding 1903, 184–195. For *pastos* cf. Posidippus (?) *Suppl. Hellenist.* 961,8; Peek *GV* 1680, 1823; Clement *Protr.* 4.54.6; Lucian *Dial. mort.* 23; Musaeus 280.

45. Prudentius *Peristeph.* 10.1006–1050; *Carmen contra paganos,* ed. Th. Mommsen, *Hermes* 4 (1870) 350–363 = *Anthologia Latina,* ed. Riese I^2 no. 4; see Hepding 1903, 61; 65f.; Duthoy 1969, 54–56; cf. Introduction, n. 24. The inscriptions from the Phrygianum at Rome, first collected *CIL* VI, 407–504, are now in *CCCA* III, 225–245. The earliest clear case is *CIL* X, 1596 = Duthoy no. 50 = *CCCA* IV, 11, repetition of a taurobolium at Puteoli in 134, that is, first taurobolium in 114 A.D.

46. See chap. I, nn. 27–28.

47. For this sense of *nymphus* see Merkelbach 1984, 88–90. In the main literary testimony for the seven grades, Jerome *Ep.* 107.2, this word had been ousted by conjecture, even in the standard edition of I. Hilberg in the *Corpus Scriptorum Ecclesiasticorum Latinorum,* 55, 1912. Cf. chap. II, n. 70.

48. The phrase is *tradere hierocoracia, leontica, persica, patrica,* see *CIMRM* 400–405 = *CIL* VI, 749–753 (epoch of Julian, 357/8 A.D.).

49. Vermaseren 1971; *CIMRM* 180–199; Merkelbach 1984 figs. 28–32 with detailed description. See Fig. 12.

50. See below at nn. 77ff. An attempt to reconstruct seven initiations: Schwertheim 1979, 69–71.

51. M. Eliade, *Birth and Rebirth* (New York 1958), based on the lectures "Patterns of Initiation" (Chicago 1956), reissued in paperback as *Rites and Symbols of Initiation* (New York 1965). See also Kern, *PW* XVI, 1331–1333; Brelich 1969, 33f.

52. Cf. chap. I at nn. 44ff.

53. Cf. chap. III at nn. 46ff.

54. Apuleius *Metamorphoses* 11.21.6, *ad instar voluntariae mortis et precariae salutis;* cf. at n. 38. D. Levi, *Antioch Mosaic Pavements* (Princeton 1947), 163–166, pl. XXXIIIa (cf. Le Corsu 1977, 238) interprets a scene in

which a person is led by Hermes toward an open door as a scene from mysteries of Isis. It may as well refer to real death, as in the scene on an Apulian lutrophoros in Basel, M. Schmidt and W. Batschelet-Massini, *AK* 27 (1984) 34–46 (with inscription).

55. Plutarch *Isis* 13,356c.

56. A statuette of Isis from Cyrene has a net-like garment that has been interpreted as mummy-bandage: P. Romanelli, *La Cirenaica Romana* (Rome 1943), fig. 27; Le Corsu 1977, 243; R. Merkelbach in *The New Encyclopaedia Britannica*[15] 24 (1985) 707. But it is Osiris rather than Isis who should become a mummy.

57. Apuleius *Metamorphoses* 11.24.5 *natalem sacrorum*, cf. *renatus* 11.16.2; 11.21.6.

58. See chap. I at n. 26.

59. Vermaseren-Essen 1965, 207–210 = *CIMRM* 498; *imaginem resurrectionis*, Tertullian *Praescr. haer.* 40.

60. Duthoy 1969 nos. 78, 79, 124, 132, pp. 106f. Duthoy rejects this interpretation; cf. Cosi 1982, 490f. Sallustius 4 mentions "nutrition by milk, as if one were reborn" (*anagennomenon*). The text of Firmicus *Err.* 18.1 says the password of Attis mysteries (see n. 44) was pronounced in the temple *ut in interioribus partibus homo moriturus possit admitti*, "in order that one who is about to die could be admitted to the interior parts"; this is so strange and isolated that textual corruption has been suspected (*oraturus*, Lobeck 1829, 24; or *moraturus*, "about to stay"?). For the Hilaria see chap. I, n. 73.

61. This suggestion was made by Nancy Evans. Plato *Republic* 620ef., cf. Burkert 1975, 98; see also chap. III at nn. 57–60.

62. A. Koerte, *ARW* 18 (1915) 16–26, using Theodoretus *Gr. aff. cur.* 7.11 (who, however, mentions the Thesmophoria at 3.84), followed by O. Kern, *PW* XVI, 1239; cf. n. 22 and *HN* 270,21.

63. See n. 9 above and chap. III, n. 44.

64. Sophocles *Oedipus Coloneus* 1050: The goddesses of Eleusis *semna tithenountai tele*, a word for child care.

65. See n. 43; chap. III, n. 38.

66. *Crepundia* Apuleius *Apologia* 56 cf. 55, *OF* 34, *Pap. Gurob* (see chap. III, n. 25); Mystis is the nurse of Dionysus in Nonnus 9.111–131.

67. Harpocration s.v. *leuke*, cf. n. 36.

68. Boyancé 1961; Bérard 1974.

69. Livy 39.13.13, cf. chap. II, n. 11.

70. See chap. III, n. 56. Spiritual rebirth (*gennasthai*) is circumstantially introduced in John 3 (speech to Nicodemus); baptism becomes the "bath of rebirth" with Titus 3.5, cf. Justin Martyr *Apol.* 1.66.1. See also J. Dey, *Palingenesia* (Münster 1937); *RAC* s.v. *Auferstehung*.

71. It is claimed for Mithras and Isis by Tertullian *Bapt.* 5.1, cf. *Praescr. haer.* 40, but see nn. 74 and 79.

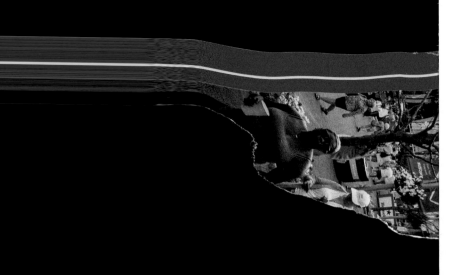

72. Eupolis *frr.* 76–98 Kassel-Austin; *GGR* I, 835.

73. Deubner 1932, pl. 6,3; *GGR* I, pl. 45,2; Kerényi 1967, fig. 14; Berner 1972, 15. The alternative explanation is by E. Simon, *AM* 69/70 (1954/5) 45–48. There may have been a ritual bath at Samothrace, Cole 1984, n. 267; a "sacred bath" of Dionysus (text restored) in an inscription from Halicarnassus, *SEG* 28 n. 841.

74. See Wild 1981.

75. J. Z. Smith 1978, 13–16 on Augustine *Serm.* 216.10 (*PL* 38,1082). Milk and honey: H. Usener *Kleine Schriften* IV (Leipzig 1913), 404–413; in general, P. Brown, *Augustine of Hippo* (Berkeley 1967), 124f.

76. Only in Firmicus *Err.* 22.1, see chap. III, n. 50.

77. Gregory of Nazianzus *Or.* 39.5 (*PG* 36,340) mentions "the punishment of Mithras, justly applied to those who undergo initiation in things like that," and *Or.* 4.70 (*PG* 35,592; ed. J. Bernardi, Paris 1983, p. 180), "the mystic tortures and burnings in the sanctuaries of Mithras, justly applied"; a third reference with the same pun of "just punishments," ibid. 89 (*PG* 35,620; ed. Bernardi, p. 225); the passages are collected in Cumont 1896, II, 15.

78. So-called Nonnus Abbas, *PG* 36,989; 1010; 1072 = Cumont 1896, II, 26–30 (with later texts dependent on "Nonnus"); reedited in S. Brock, *The Syriac Version of the Pseudo-Nonnos Mythological Scholia* (Cambridge 1971), 169f.

79. Pseudo-Augustine *Quaestiones Veteris et Novi Testamenti* CXIV, 11 (*PL* 35,2343) = Cumont 1896, II, 7f.; cf. Cumont 1923, 147f.

80. Cumont 1923, 148.

81. Himerius *Or.* 41.1 Colonna.

82. Yašt 10.122 (translation in W. W. Malandra, *An Introduction to Ancient Iranian Religion,* Minneapolis 1983, 73); cf. Merkelbach 1984, 34,25.

83. See n. 49; Merkelbach 1984, fig. 30 = *CIMRM* 188 (see Fig. 12) and Merkelbach fig. 31 = *CIMRM* 193.

84. See *CIMRM* 78–79 and 543, Merkelbach 1984, figs. 20 and 65, cf. the relief *CIMRM* 383, Merkelbach fig. 51. Santa Prisca, Vermaseren and van Essen 1965, 224–232; cf. also the graffito from Dura-Europos, *CIMRM* 68; Gordon in Hinnells 1975, 235f.; Beskow in Bianchi 1979, 496f. "Purification" by fire, then by honey: Porphyry *Antr.* 15. Tertullian *Praescr. haer.* 40 speaks of a "seal on the forehead" applied to the *miles,* cf. F. J. Dölger, *Sphragis* (Paderborn 1911), 170; this was hardly branding, cf. the discussion of Beskow 1979.

85. Schwertheim 1979, 72–74 with figs. 38f.; a different explanation by W. Lentz and W. Schlosser in *Hommages Vermaseren* (Leiden 1978), 591f.

86. *Hist. Aug. Commodus* 9.6; human skulls found in Mithraea: Socrates *Hist. eccl.* 3.2f. = Cumont 1896, II, 44f.; Turcan 1981a, 91f.

87. See at n. 11; cf. n. 36.

88. Prudentius *Peristeph.* 10.1076–1085: *sacrandus accipit sp...*
1076; on *sphragis* see n. 84. Cf. *Et.M. gallos;* the satirical express...
of scourges and branding irons," Lucian *Peregr.* 28.

89. The tattoo marks are "lilies and tympana" accordin...
De adul. et am. 56e, "ivy leaves" according to *Et.M. gallos;* b...
king himself. By contrast, 3 Maccabees 2.29 has the mar...
bodies of disobedient Jews who would not participate i...
chap. II, n. 117).

90. For literature, see n. 24, esp. Matz 1963, ...
called Dike by Nilsson 1957, 123–125, Nemesis b...
Brendel 1966, 233 (cf. n. 92), Erinys by Turcan 1969 (...
who insists on the allegorical character of the figure. Rea...
assumed, *inter alios,* by Simon 1961, Boyancé 1966.

91. Plautus *Aulularia* 408f., cf. W. Stockert, "Die Anspielungen auf die Bacchanalien in der Aulularia (406–414) und anderen Plautuskomö-dien," *Festschrift Walter Kraus* (Vienna 1972), 398–407; cf. Achilles Tatius 5.23.6: the narrator is suddenly beaten up, and "as in a mystery, I did not know anything" of what was happening. On flogging scenes on sarcophagi, see M. C. Vermaseren, "Fragments de sarcophage de Sainte-Prisque. Pan enfant corrigé par un satyre," *Latomus* 18 (1959) 742–750; Matz 1963, 68f.

92. Brendel 1966, 235 fig. 18: "Lycurgus crater," *RVAp* 16/5, cf. 16/29, 18/7, 18/297; Aeschylus *Prometheus Bound* 682; most graphic is Virgil *Aeneid* 7.376ff. (Brendel 235,51): *dant animos plagae* (383).

93. Horace *Odes* 3.26.11f.

94. Hesychius *katharthenai: mastigothenai;* cf. Theocritus 5.119; *HN* 27.

95. See Introduction, n. 43.

96. Diodorus 4.6.4.

97. *GGR* 590–594, pl. 35, 2/3; *HN* 69–71.

98. Diodorus 4.3.3, cf. Euripides *Phoenissae* 655f.; but Euripides *Bacchae* 694 (text controversial) seems to have virgins among the *bakchai.*

99. Plutarch *Cons. ad ux.* 611d.

100. Marriage: M. Bieber, *JdI* 43 (1928) 298–330; Matronalia: Brendel 1966, 258f.

101. See at nn. 24ff.

102. G. Patroni, "Questioni vascolari," *Rend. Linc.* III, 21 (1912) 545–600; H. R. W. Smith 1971.

103. Cf. chap. I at nn. 49 and 56.

104. Livy 39.15.9; *stuprum,* 39.10.7, 13.10, 8.7. Cf. chap. II, n. 11.

105. Cf. G. Bleibtreu-Ehrenberg, *Mannbarkeitsriten: Zur institutionellen Päderastie bei Papuas und Melanesiern* (Frankfurt 1980); H. Patzer, "Die griechische Knabenliebe," *Sitzungsber. Frankfurt* 19,1, 1982.

106. Clement *Protr.* 2.16.2; Arnobius 5.21; Firmicus *Err.* 10; *Pap. Gurob.* (see chap. III, n. 25) I, 24; see Dieterich 1923, 123f.

107. Plutarch *Alexander* n; on the Nektanebos story, see R. Merkelbach, *Die Quellen des griechischen Alexanderromans*² (Munich 1977), 77–83.

108. Diodorus 5.4.4.

109. For *arrheta* at Eleusis see Graf 1974, 194–199; *HN* 280–287; the evidence for a "sacred marriage" is slim, *HN* 284; for secret myths, see chap. III, n. 44. Fourth-century iconography adds Aphrodite to the circle of Eleusinian gods, and Kore is a few times represented half naked (Metzger 1965, pl. 23), cf. the sexual overtones of "seeing Kore," Cicero *De nat. deorum* 3.36 (*GR* 284,45). Psellos' account of "Eleusinian mysteries" in *De operatione daemonum* pp. 36f. Boissonade is a hodgepodge of Clement *Protr.* 15–23.

110. Pseudo-Plutarch *De fluv.* 23 (cf. Burkert, *Würzburger Jahrb.* 5, 1979, 260). On the meaning of *nymphus* see n. 47 above; for Attis mysteries see n. 44.

111. Josephus *Jewish Antiquities* 18.4 (73); see Merkelbach 1962, 16–18.

112. Tibullus 1.3.26; Propertius 3.31.2; Fehrle 1910, 135–137.

113. S. Şahin in *Hommages à M. J. Vermaseren* (Leiden 1978), 997f.; *SEG* 28, 1585; for *demnion*, cf. Callimachus *Hymn* 4.248.

114. *Telos = gamos* seems to be old, cf. Aeschylus, *Seven Against Thebes* 367; Pollux 3.38; H. Bolkestein, *"Telos ho gamos,"* *Meded. Kon. Nederl. Ak. Wet.* 76 (1933) 21–47. For playful elaboration of Eros mysteries see, for example, Xenophon of Ephesus 2.9.2–13.8; 3.9.2–4.2.10; Achilles Tatius 1.2.2; 2.19.1.

115. *Mystike syndiagoge* for homosexual relationship, Diogenes Laertius 10.6 (slander against Epicurus); "priest of mother and daughter," Andocides 1.124; *arrhetopoioi*, Lucian *Lex.* 10.

116. Petronius *Satyricon* 16–26.

117. See Introduction, n. 12.

118. See Fehrle 1910; *HN* 60f. *Schol. Nik. Alex.* 410 attests the use of *peganon* (rue), believed to repress sexuality, by "those who are initiated" *tout court*. The Eleusinian hierophant uses hemlock for temporary chemical castration, *HN* 284. Abstinence in Dionysus mysteries: Livy 39.9.4, 10.1, Ovid *Fasti* 2.313ff.; in cult of Meter, Marinus *Vit. Procl.* 19; for Isis, see n. 112.

119. Kerényi 1967, 96; 179f.; 1976, 36–38; cf. W. Schmidbauer, "Halluzinogene in Eleusis?" *Antaios* 10 (1968/69) 18–37.

120. For the origin of Vedic *soma*, the fly agaric hypothesis may be taken seriously; see R. G. Wasson, *Soma: Divine Mushroom of Immortality* (New York 1968); criticism: J. Brough, *Bull. School of Or. and Afr. Studies* 34 (1971) 331–362.

121. Wasson 1978.

122. The proof lies in the incisions, marked with paint, on the poppy capsules of the statue; P. G. Kritikos, *Bulletin on Narcotics* 19 (1967) 23; Kerényi 1976, 35–39.

124. [...] ageoigenis, CRAI 1976, 394f.; BCH [...] (1979) 881, fig. 78. Ovid Fasti 4.531–534, 547f.

125. R. A. Bowman, *Aramaic Ritual Texts from Persepolis* (Chicago 1970), found evidence for Haoma ceremonies in fifth-century stone vessels; a different interpretation of the inscriptions is given by W. Hinz, *Acta Iranica 4: Monumentum H. S. Nyberg*, 1975, 371–385.

126. C. Castaneda, *The Teachings of Don Juan* (Berkeley 1968). This is not the place to document the discussion provoked by this best-seller.

127. Wasson 1978, 17, 20–22; "sleeping bag," 21.

128. Demetrios Poliorketes, Hegesandros in Athenaeus 167f.

129. Nilsson 1950.

130. But wine and inebriation could also be seen as a revenge of the god, as a strange passage in Plato *Laws* 672b indicates. In this sense "liberation" is contrasted with "madness," Dionysos Lysios with Dionysos Bakcheios, Pausanias 2.2.6.

131. *HN* 292,85.

132. Juvenal 2.111–116, 6.511–521; Julian *Or.* 5, 173c; *S&H* 119. A stele of Mysia with a sacrificial feast, Foucart 1873, 238–240, *GGR* II, pl. 14, 4; *cubiculum, CCCA* III, 471; see also *CCCA* IV, 2; 125.

133. Cf. chap. II, n. 34.

134. *Deipna, SIRIS* 44, cf. 120; pp. 54f. CE 99; *kline*, p. 64 *CE* 20; cf. no. 111; 270; *oikos, SIRIS* 109, cf. also 149, 265, 291. H. C. Youtie, "The Kline of Sarapis," *HThR* 41 (1948) 9–29 = *Scriptiunculae* I (1973) 487–509.

135. Turcan 1981b, 346f.; 1981a, 78–80; Kane 1975; against, Cumont 1923, 150: "knieten im Gebet," cf. 153.

136. See especially the often-reproduced relief from Konjic, Dalmatia, *CIMRM* 1896; Merkelbach 1984, fig. 148.

137. Justin Martyr *Apol.* 1.66.4.

138. *Homeric Hymn to Demeter* 208–210; Eleusinian *synthema*, see at n. 22; Kerényi 1967, 177–185; Richardson 1974, 244–248.

139. Harpocration *neelata*, referring to Demosthenes 18.259, cf. n. 36. Even in more spiritualized religion paradise is often represented as a feast, see F. Cumont, *After Life in Roman Paganism* (New Haven 1922), 204–206; A. D. Nock, *Early Gentile Christianity and Its Hellenistic Background* (London 1964), 72–76; cf. also Plato *Phaedrus* 247a.

140. Herondas 4.94f.; Athenaeus 115a; Hesychius s.v. *hygieia; Anecd. Bekk.* 313.13; R. Wünsch, *ARW* 7 (1904) 115f.

141. The idea was spread especially by J. G. Frazer, *The Golden Bough* VIII³ (London 1966), 48–108, partly following W. Robertson Smith's theory of sacrifice, *Lectures on the Religion of the Semites*² (Cambridge 1884).

142. See at chap. III, n. 38.

143. *Schol. Clem. Protr.* p. 318, 5 Stählin; for the distinction between maenadism and the dismemberment myth, see W. F. Otto, *Dionysos*⁴ (Frankfurt 1980; 1st ed. 1933), 120 (*Dionysos: Myth and Cult,* Bloomington

1965, pp. 131f.). See also M. Detienne, *Dionysos mis à mort* (Paris 1977; Eng. trans. *Dionysus Slain*, Baltimore 1979).

144. *HN* 218–226.

145. Cf. n. 86; Ma Bellona: Dio Cassius 42.26.2.

146. Henrichs 1972, esp. 28–36; cf. A. Henrichs, "Pagan Ritual and the Alleged Crimes of the Early Christians," *Kyriakon, Festschrift, J. Quasten* (Münster 1970), 18–35.

147. See *HN passim.*

148. Vermaseren and van Essen 1965, 217f.; H. D. Betz, *Novum Testamentum* 19 (1968) 7f.; Hinnells 1975, 304–312, Kane 1975, 314–321; for the present state of the inscription see E. Paparatti in Bianchi 1979, 911–913 with Appendix II, pl. 23, and figs. 12–13 ibid. before p. 127.

149. Since Pindar *fr.* 70b = *Dith.* 2, cf. Euripides *Bacchae* 118ff.

150. See S. G. Cole, *GRBS* 21 (1980) 226–231; *GR* 292.

151. See chap. I at nn. 32–33.

152. Plato *Phaedo* 69c; *OF* 235.

153. This expression is in Herodotus 4.79.4.

154. Philo *Vit. cont.* 12; cf. 85: "In bacchic ecstasy they imbibe love of the gods, unmixed . . . "

155. Plutarch *Def. or.* 417a, c.

156. Aretaeus 3.6.11, cf. Caelius Aurel. 152; *apomainesthai* in the context means the end of enthusiasm, *pace LSJ*, cf. R. Renehan, *Greek Lexicographical Notes* (Göttingen 1975), 37.

157. Aristides Quintilianus 3.25, p. 129, 12–15 Winnington-Ingram; for *ptoiesis* cf. Euripides *Bacchae* 214, Plato *Phaedo* 108b, Plutarch *De fac.* 943c. For *katharsis* see chap. I at n. 32, for the social prejudice chap. II at n. 7.

158. Livy 39.15.9 (cf. 8.8, 10.7): *vigiliis vino strepitibus clamoribusque nocturnis attoniti.*

159. But see Graf 1974, 136.

160. See Clinton 1974, 43.

161. *In Remp.* II 108,17–30 Kroll: αἱ τελεταὶ . . . συμπαθείας εἰσὶν αἴτιαι ταῖς ψυχαῖς περὶ τὰ δρώμενα τρόπον ἄγνωστον ἡμῖν καὶ θεῖον· ὡς τοὺς μὲν τῶν τελουμένων καταπλήττεσθαι δειμάτων θείων πλήρεις γιγνομένους, τοὺς δὲ συνδιατίθεσθαι τοῖς ἱεροῖς συμβόλοις καὶ ἑαυτῶν ἐκστάντας ὅλους ἐνιδρῦσθαι τοῖς θεοῖς καὶ ἐνθεάζειν. Cf. I 75, 5–16.

162. Euripides *Bacchae* 75.

Index of Greek Terms

General Index